BRASSEY'S ARTILLERY OF THE WORLD

Guns, howitzers, mortars, guided weapons, rockets and ancillary equipment in service with the regular and reserve forces of all nations

Editor: Brigadier Shelford Bidwell

Co-authors, Compilers and Consultants: Brian Blunt
Tolley Taylor

BONANZA BOOKS · NEW YORK

Acknowledgements

The task of compiling this inventory of artillery weapons in service and of collecting illustrations was only made possible by the generous cooperation and assistance we have received from various official sources, from firms and from individuals. It must be stressed that the information on which it is based is from open sources available to the public: where officials and firms manufacturing defence equipment have given invaluable help is in guidance and indicating where to look. The use we have made of the information and the responsibility for errors or omissions is ours alone.

We would like to record our gratitude to the many firms consulted, and to the representatives of Defence Ministries of the Federal Republic of Germany, France, Israel, Sweden, Switzerland, the United Kingdom and the United States. We have had particular help from the United States Field Artillery School, Fort Sill, the Royal School of Artillery, Larkhill; the Royal Artillery Institution, the Imperial War Museum; The International Institute for Strategic Studies, and owe special thanks to Major Robert Elliot of that Institute; Brigadier Michael Calvert; Mr. Jac Weller; Herr J. F. Lehmanns Verlag; Major C. J. Davidson, of Forenade Fabriksverken, and Captain B. L. Grawe.

Drawings: Pierre-Andre Tilley of Blitz Publications

First published in Great Britain by
Brassey's Publishers Ltd.,
15 Cavendish Square,
London W1M 0HT
England

© MCMLXXVII by Brassey's Publishers Ltd.

This edition is published by Bonanza Books,
a division of Crown Publishers, Inc.,
by arrangement with Brassey's Publishers Ltd.
a b c d e f g h
BONANZA 1979 PRINTING
Manufactured in the United States of America

Library of Congress Cataloging in Publication Data
Blunt, Brian.
   Brassey's artillery of the world.
   Includes index.
   1. Artillery.   2. Ordnance.   I. Taylor,
Tolley, joint author.   II. Bidwell, Shelford.
III. Title.   IV. Title: Artillery of the world.
UF560.B53   623.4   76-3797
ISBN 0-517-27718-2

Foreword

By Field Marshal Sir GEOFFREY BAKER GCB CMG CBE MC
Master Gunner, St James's Park

It gives me great pleasure to write the foreword to this book, not least because it is the work of four members of the Royal Regiment of Artillery. Richard Cox, the managing director of Brassey's Limited, the publisher, a well-known commentator on defence questions is a Territorial Gunner. Brigadier Shelford Bidwell, the editor, until recently Deputy Director of the Royal United Services Institute for Defence Studies and editor of its Journal, was once Chief Instructor, Tactical Employment at the Royal School of Artillery. The co-authors, Lieutenant Colonel B. E. Blunt and Major M. T. Taylor are both active, regular officers of the Royal Artillery.

This book covers a very wide spectrum of weapons from the famous French soixante-quinze—still in service, I am interested to note—to the most modern guided missiles, but what strikes me forcibly as one who was commissioned into the Royal Artillery forty-four years ago is the abiding value of what is sometimes called 'tube' artillery: guns, howitzers and mortars. 'Artillery', said Stalin, meaning cannon, 'is the God of War', and certainly it formed the backbone of British as well as Russian tactics in World War II. It was used on a large scale in Korea, it played a decisive part at Dien-Bien Phu, and in the long struggle of the Vietnam war both sides made effective use of heavy artillery. The mortar is part of the basic equipment of the modern guerrilla. The Israelis, as a result of their experience in the Yom Kippur War, are improving and increasing their artillery arm. As for the Soviet Army, its artillery, preserving the Russian military tradition, is probably the strongest in the world. It can be said that the strength and efficiency of the artillery arm is a measure of the effectiveness of any modern army, however powerful its tanks and supporting aircraft. It must not be forgotten that weapons complement each other. The complex surface-to-air guided missile and the simple gun are still a formidable combination against aircraft, and the field gun, which itself can still kill a tank, can also support tanks against their deadly enemy the anti-tank guided weapon. Artillery must be seen as as whole.

It is, unfortunately, a part of the science of war which is little understood except by specialists, because gun and guided weapon-systems are highly technical, both in design and in their tactical employment. Here I think that this book can help. While it is primarily a descriptive catalogue of equipment of all kinds, it includes simple but adequate explanations of how the various weapon systems function, problems of design, the technical application of fire and the basic philosophy of their tactical employment. It will, I am sure, prove valuable both to the professional soldier, the military commentator and journalist and all those concerned with the study of warfare, from whatever standpoint, but especially those interested in the vital subject of national defence.

GEOFFREY BAKER

Contents

Introduction

The aim of this book is twofold. It provides in a convenient form a catalogue of all artillery systems likely to be found in service with the field armies in the world today as complete in detail as possible when relying only on overt sources and published information. It also explains in non-technical terms the role of the various categories of gun and rocket, and their method of employment in the major armies of the world.

Artillery weapon-systems are technologically complex, and properly operate from outside the actual combat zone. Accordingly, they tend to be overlooked or ignored in defence studies, where the 'guns' are overshadowed by the far more dramatic tanks in the ground battle, by strike aircraft and, more recently, anti-tank and guided missiles. It is often forgotten that successful ground operations in conventional war are the result of close coordination between infantry, armour and artillery. At least half the ground-based fire power on the battlefield is provided by artillery, and the gunner's vital contribution is unaffected by climate, weather or time of day: it is also less vulnerable to enemy interference. The weapon inventories of the Soviet and Warsaw Pact armies reflect a much greater understanding of this fact than is apparent in the NATO order of battle. It is hoped therefore that this book provides information essential for the military man, the defence orientated general reader, the military commentator and the defence correspondent.

The term 'artillery' is a wide one which can be applied to a whole spectrum of weapons ranging from the simplest cannon designed for use at short ranges over open sights, i.e. with the target in full view of the gun's crew, to rocket-propelled guided missiles with computerised fire-control systems. The difficulty is to decide on boundaries between categories. Strictly speaking, artillerymen regard all 'cannon' as lying within their province, provided that they satisfy the criteria of employing sophisticated delivery systems, e.g. either indirect fire or guidance, are crew-served and have range and lethality exceeding those weapons found normally in the tables of equipment of infantry or armoured units. This leads us to include all tactical weapons fired from stationary land platforms and to exclude some hand-held, man-portable weapons, the weapons in armed helicopters and the cannon in armoured fighting vehicles, including tanks, although these may well be in some cases larger and heavier than some systems which are by our definition 'artillery'. A wide range of indirect fire artillery still in service, however, has a secondary anti-tank direct fire capability, and some armies still retain classic type towed field guns designed specifically for anti-tank defence; these are included as they fall into the general category of cannon. The family of air defence weapons includes both surface to air guided missiles and guns. Guns proved to be as valuable as ever in the Arab–Israeli war of October, 1973.

The term 'indirect fire' crops up so regularly and is so frequently misunderstood by the non-artilleryman that it must be explained here: else much of what follows will not be clear. *Direct fire* is extremely efficient and effective, using as it does the best target acquisition system over short ranges yet designed—the human eye, and the cheapest computer—the human brain. It is simple to operate; a vital consideration for hastily trained conscript armies or part-time national armies such as Israel's. It also permits the cannon to be used at its optimum accuracy, say 1,000–2,500 metres, where the chance of a first round hit is very high. But all direct fire guns are exposed to equally effective counter-fire: therefore the crew must be protected and we end up with the tank. As the range is short, the area dominated by a single tank is very small and so large numbers of tanks are required for a given mission. A gun with a range of 15/20 kilometres dominates an enormous area by comparison.

Indirect fire arose from the need to conceal long-range artillery systems from counter-fire. The weapon therefore became a *weapon-system*, made up of the gun itself, a means of acquiring targets on the now distant battlefield, a network of communications and a technical and tactical fire control system.

Immutable laws of physics dictate that the accuracy of a ballistic projectile decreases with range. To reduce the limitations imposed by an inherent spread in the fall of shot, or 'zone', the concentration of as many guns as possible on to the target is an unchanging artillery maxim: thus the battery and not the individual gun is the basic fire unit.

By correcting the fall of shot, an observer overcomes, or 'shoots out', all the inaccuracies in the weapon-system except the zone of the gun. This arrangement seems ideal except that it is slow because of the time taken for each round to fly from gun to target. Furthermore, the system of observed indirect fire depends on having a competent observer in the right place, and his seeing the target.

The basic data needed to set the gun sights for indirect fire is calculated from the known coordinates of gun and target positions. The processes of determining these coordinates are similar to those used in land survey, except that they have to be done with great rapidity. The meteorological data must be continuously measured, the muzzle velocity of each gun known, and so on. Calculations to assess the effect of all these and provide correct data have to be made for every gun and every mission, manually in most systems but by computer in technologically advanced armies.

The only way to reduce delivery error is to use guidance. Delivery error can never be eliminated completely, but for practical purposes the operator and not the mechanism of guidance is the source of guidance error. There are a wide variety of guidance systems, some of which rely on monitoring the trajectory and transmitting correctional data while others use inertial guidance, by which the missile carries its own self-sufficient navigational system, and is therefore invulnerable to electronic counter measures (ECM) or 'jamming'. The latest and most refined technique is terminal guidance, by which a free ballistic trajectory is corrected in the last seconds of flight by homing devices based on lasers or electro-optical systems. These have already been used in aircraft bombs, but the system is adaptable for artillery shells or surface-to-surface missiles. Compared with ordinary free flight shell or shot guidance is immensely expensive in terms of research and development as well as cost per round fired. Conventional artillery is labour intensive, using elementary techniques, and a large number of relatively cheap missiles for suppressive and harassing fire. Guided missiles are not only capital intensive, but highly cost effective, achieving ideally an exchange rate of one missile per mission on target.

Whatever system is used it must be emphasised that the actual vehicle for carrying the lethal agent, whether this is ordinary chemical reaction high explosive or nuclear, is only one element of the weapon system. All artillery systems have an inherent error which we minimise by various means, but the total accuracy also depends on the accuracy of target location. The mathematical relationship is such that one can say without over simplification that money spent on target acquisition and surveillance equipment doubles or even redoubles the effectiveness of the artillery system as a whole. As we shall see when we come to the field artillery section the crude, mass-fire blanketing techniques developed in the period 1917–1945 are being replaced by far more sophisticated methods aimed at maximum effect for minimum shell use.

Before going on to a detailed study of the various categories of artillery there is one basic question which must be answered and kept in mind throughout by military students when considering the subject. What is 'artillery' for? In other words, how does it differ from the other arms, considering that each of them in their own way are producers of fire power?

Indirect fire field artillery and anti-aircraft are essentially deterrents. To be sure, they are designed to have the best probability within the constraints of the system to inflict lethal damage, but they can achieve their object indirectly by forcing the enemy to adopt some other mode of attack or to desist from attacking for fear of an unacceptable casualty rate. For instance, well sited air defence weapons can deter strike aircraft from using the optimum height and angle of approach; medium artillery of 152 mm or 155 mm calibre can take the sting out of a tank attack by damaging the tanks themselves or by causing casualties among the accompanying motorised infantry and SP artillery; artillery covering fire can suppress the fire of troops in defensive positions by direct attack, or by blotting out their observation with smoke screens. Unguided rocket systems are used to obtain the same effect, saturating the target with large numbers of ripple fired missiles which arrive in the target area within a few seconds. Guided weapons are essentially different, in that an expensive system is used to carry a large or at any rate, a highly lethal warhead to a high-value target and the aim is not to 'neutralise', to use the British tactical term, or render temporarily ineffective, but to destroy.

The same is true of the out-dated but still effective categories of anti-tank and anti-ship guns. A near-miss may inflict superficial damage, but is still a miss; to be effective, the target must be actually struck and set on fire or sunk. Anti-tank guns rely on the simplest and most primitive methods. Coast defence artillery, now virtually obsolete, is as sophisticated as anti-aircraft artillery, requiring radar and computerised fire control.

To summarise, we therefore consider in this book six categories of artillery equipment, each prefaced by a note on tactical employment and the main features of design and operation and two on ancillary equipment:

(a) Field artillery—guns and howitzers;
(b) Mortars;
(c) Battlefield surface to surface missiles carrying either nuclear or conventional warheads;
(d) Ancillary equipment essential to surface-to-surface systems—fire-control, surveillance, target acquisition, survey and for providing ballistic data.
(e) Anti-tank guns and long range anti-tank guided missiles;
(f) Air Defence artillery;
(g) Ancillary equipment essential to air defence systems: surveillance and tracking radars, and fire control computers;
(h) Coast artillery, or 'anti-ship' artillery.

Figure I: Anatomy of the Gun.

Figure I(a): Elevation.

I. Characteristics of Guns and Howitzers

The following remarks on gun design and characteristics apply equally to field artillery, and the guns covered by the other sections in the book. The general comments will not be repeated in the introduction of each section, except where they are of singular importance.

The basic layout of a gun is determined by its primary role and any constraints imposed by the user. The requirement for a field gun will state the desired range and the target effect. Special constraints may include a weight limit or the desire to take advantage of existing ammunition types. The user will also dictate the priorities between the inevitable design compromises: thus the barrel of the Italian Pack Howitzer is kept light enough for pack transports, accepts an existing ammunition (American M 1) but has too short a range for modern tactical needs.

Such diverse requirements make a statistical comparison between the efficiency of different weapons difficult. A quick assessment of performance is given by the equation:

$$\frac{\text{Shell Weight} \times \text{Range}}{\text{Equipment Weight}}$$

This equation shows that the Russian 152 mm D 1 is 30 per cent more efficient than the older 152 mm ML 20, which is fair comment on ten years of development.

A gun consists of a number of components as figure 1 demonstrates. For convenience these components are divided into two 'sub-assemblies': the recoiling parts, and the mounting. The recoiling parts consist of the barrel (sometimes referred to as the piece) muzzle brake, jacket, breech ring, breech block and moving parts of the recoil system. The mounting consists of the rest of the equipment, and may be a wheeled carriage, a complete vehicle, or a fixed emplacement. The term ordnance is often used to describe a weapon, but is properly the recoiling parts less any part of the recoil system.

The gun barrel must absorb many stresses. There are three main types: the great pressures of the explosive propellant gas presses outwards against the walls and is greatest in the area of the chamber: the shell being twisted by the grooves in the rifling, tends to stretch the barrel lengthways: the barrel must be strong enough to support it's own weight without drooping at the muzzle. The size and weight of the barrel structure, its wall thickness and jacket (if fitted) will be dictated by the strength of the steel used. If the barrel can be pre-stressed it will be stronger for a given size and quality of steel.

One method of construction is to build-up the barrel from a number of concentric tubes, which are shrunk onto each other and are thus pre-stressed. Most modern barrels are of monobloc construction, that is to say that the barrel is made from a single forging. In the 1930s the French developed a system of pre-stressing a barrel made in this way by subjecting it to hydraulic pressure. The process is known as autofrettaging and allows the use of relatively low grade steel while retaining the manufacturing simplicity of a single forging.

Central to the gun's design is the detail of chamber and breech. The options revolve around the choice of ammunition type. It is clearly an advantage if the gun accepts the ammunition of existing equipments and that used by allies. This desirable bonus does not preclude the production of a new (and improv·d), ammunition, but it should be noted that the new ammunition may not fit other guıs. For instance, FH 70 is chambered to accept existing NATO 155 mm shells and bag charges, so is the French GCT, but the ammunition designed specifically for these guns is peculiar to them.

Figure II: Breech Mechanisms.

The choice of breech block design is related to the ammunition type, and will affect the rate of fire. The strongest, and oldest of present systems is the interrupted screw type. It was developed by the French at the end of the nineteenth century. Unlike earlier attempts, the threads are not continuous so that the block does not have to be literally 'unscrewed': they run in arcs of 45° with a clear machined space between: a quarter turn of the block disengaged the threads and allows the block to be pulled or swung clear. The threads and machined surface of the block are tapered, so is the corresponding opening in the breech ring: the quarter turn of the closing movement forces the breech inwards to mate the tapering machined surfaces. The design lends itself to good obturation, and is commonly, but not exclusively associated with bag charge ammunition. Its strength leads to its exclusive use with heavy guns.

This interrupted screw thread breech is designed for use with a cased charge. The firing pin passes through the hole in the face of the block.

Example of QF horizontally sliding breech block.

The alternative is a sliding, or sliding wedge block, moving horizontally or vertically. Its strength depends entirely on the open ended claw in which it moves. The actuating lever moves in one direction only to operate this type of block, and this allows varying degrees of automation. On closing, the block moves in a plane off-set from the block face so that it closes into the face, to ensure the correct seating of the cartridge (and with fixed ammunition the shell) and forces home an obturator pad or ring if bag charges are used.

Between a fully automated breech and a manual one lies the semi-automatic action: a vertically sliding block which moves up to open can be arranged to close automatically by the loading of a cartridge: a downward opening block can be allowed to open on recoil and the momentum of its fall used to eject the spent case. These effects can be achieved by spring loading a horizontal block. A semi-automatic breech will either open or close automatically—not both.

The rate of fire is dictated by a number of factors including the weight of shell, size of detachment, access to the breech, breech design and the ammunition type. Few towed guns run to the luxury of automatic loading, because of the bulk of machinery involved: however, the paramount need for a high rate of fire from air defence guns makes the penalty of a large carriage worthwhile.

Easiest to load is fixed ammunition since only one action is needed. This advantage can be combined with a variable charge by the semi-fixed round: the shell and cartridge case are mated (or re-mated) for loading after the charge has been adjusted. The popular American 105 mm M 1 range is of this type. Separate ammunition is a slower option requiring the loading and ramming of the shell, then the loading of the propellant. Power ramming is very desirable, especially for heavier shells: it saves effort and leads to a consistent ram which is vital to the gun's accuracy. Bag charges (which have economic

Figure III: Muzzle Brake.

and logistic advantages) require a third action, which can be concurrent with the other two, in loading the primer cartridge. A minor inconvenience with bag charges is the need to check that there are no smouldering remnants from the previous charge before a new one is loaded.

An important recognition feature of a gun is the muzzle brake. Amongst the few guns not to have one are the two most widely used American equipments M 114 and M 101. A muzzle brake provides rearward facing baffles or flaps against which the propellant gases react as they move forward out of the bore behind the shell. The effect is partly to counter recoil, and partly to stabilize the gun at the moment of departure of the shell.

The recoil system must absorb the shock of firing—which is the reaction to the enormous acceleration of the shell in the bore—leaving the carriage stable. There are two components to the recoil system—the buffer which stops the recoil, and the recuperator which returns the recoiling parts to the firing position. The buffer is almost invariably hydraulic because this allows for the progressive deceleration of the recoiling mass. An arrangement of mechanical limbs and adjustable valves can be included in the design to shorten the recoil as the elevation increases. This avoids the need for a recoil pit beneath the breech, and the greater stress passed to the carriage as a result is acceptable because it has a greater vertical component and does not therefore, tend to cartwheel the gun. The recuperator is either hydro-pneumatic or a mechanical spring.

Recoil
System

Plan Section

Buffer

Recuperator

Full
Recoil

Running Out

Figure IV: Recoil System of 25 pounder.

Note complexity of outwardly simple weapon. Recoil is checked by flow of oil in buffer (dark stipple) through ports in buffer piston. At same time oil in recuperator (black) acting on free piston (white) compresses air (light stipple) which re-expands to cause run out to firing position (below).

Carriage design is influenced by the use to which the weapon will be put. The earliest, pole trail arrangement has now been totally eclipsed because of its limitation on the arc of fire in both azimuth and elevation. The box trail is an improvement, but still limits the traverse available without moving the trail. This arrangement has found favour in the specialist application to the German 90 mm anti-tank gun, but here the need is for ultra-rapid deployment, which this layout permits.

The most common layout is the split trail—two trail legs which are brought together for travelling and spread in action. Traverse of the barrel is limited by the need for horizontal recoil stresses to pass within the arc of the legs. This is an operational limitation which is more apparent than real. Properly handled, batteries can be deployed and redeployed to cover the battle within quite narrow primary arcs of fire. An equipment with a traverse of less than 45° will generally impose an operation limitation or problem. If the gun has to be traversed complete, the difficulty increases with the size and weight of the equipment. The effort of freeing bedded in spades must not be underestimated. A useful expedient is the provision of castor wheels on the trail legs.

Some split-trail carriages are provided with a firing jack attached below the saddle whose purpose is to raise the forward part of the equipment and wheels off the ground and absorb the vertical component of the recoil force, so making for steadiness.

The ability to fire in a 360° arc from a static platform has its attractions. In practice, good gun positions which enable the exploitation of such a potential are few and far between. However, this capability is often seen as worthwhile, although its achievement can lead to other limitations, such as a weight penalty. One solution is to mount the saddle directly on to the centre of a three or four spoked arrangement of trail legs. Another is to use a platform on which the road wheels rest. The American M 102 combines the box trail and platform configuration used by the old British 25 pounder. Because the platform absorbs horizontal recoil forces, the trail can be carried on a longitudinal roller on which it rotates.

The Auxiliary Propulsion Unit (APU) is not a new idea, but one in which interest has recently been re-awakened. Guns like the Swedish FH 77 and tri-national FH 70 have been designed to provide limited self propulsion. The system is popular on the small Soviet equipments. The APU provides power for loading and laying as well as assisting deployment. With APU towed guns can occupy platforms inaccessible to heavy tractors and also, if detected by hostile surveillance, redeploy locally without bringing the tractors up from the rear.

The alternative to the classical wheels-plus-trail design is the 'self-propelled' (SP) gun mounted on armoured, tracked chassis for indirect fire. It is an artillery weapon and not to be confused with the tank it so closely resembles externally and which is a direct-fire close-combat vehicle. Developed originally in the 1920s by the British for the close support of tanks, one school of artillery thought considers that now, when all formations are mixed infantry/armour and protection is required against nuclear as well as kinetic weapons, the SP is the only viable equipment for full scale war. There are, however, conflicts of cost, mobility, simplicity and flexibility.

Clearly the development of a simple split trail carriage is quicker and easier than of an SP chassis (or even the conversion of an existing tank design). The production cost per unit is also much smaller. Often, a new barrel can be fitted into an existing carriage, or the same carriage used for different equipments: the Russian M 1938/M 1943 122 mm and 152 mm guns are an example of carriage sharing.

It would be an over-simplification to say that any vehicle will tow a gun, but in extremis when battle damage or mechanical failure has immobilised the specialist artillery tractor, this is the case. The towed gun, man handled or hitched to any passing vehicle as an expedient, can still be redeployed. Other aspects of the towed gun's flexibility of movement may depend on its size, but transport options for this type of equipment can include animal packing, portee (i.e. carried in a vehicle), air movement by aircraft or helicopter and parachute delivery. Examples of guns expressly designed to exploit these options will be found in this section.

Simplicity is not just a function of design and construction. It also makes for a more robust equipment, and one which is easier to maintain. It is also important as a function of training. There are real difficulties in teaching and up-dating operating drills in the confines of an SP turret. These are most apparent in a conscript army.

To set against these formidable arguments, there are virtues in the SP gun which find favour in Western armies: it is highly mobile, easier to deploy, can be re-deployed fast and has a greater chance of survival.

The SP has an excellent cross country performance. It enables the gun to travel over damaged roads, round traffic blocks and point-to-point across country. It can be made to swim. This is all highly important in getting the gun to its firing position because a gun on the move is useless. On the battery position, the SP can drive into the best platform (a virtue shared by towed guns with APU) and dispenses with the need for concealed tractor positions. Track planning is easier.

The SP is quicker to bring *into* action than the towed gun because the limiting factor in this drill is the time taken to establish orientation. The SP does score in the immediate availability of ammunition, and the avoidance of double-handling first line holdings off the tractor. The SP is also much faster at coming *out* of action, thus reducing overall travelling time.

Automatic loading is very difficult to achieve with a towed gun, and magazine loading unheard of. The SP has the power supply necessary for either or both these functions, with consequent benefits in a high rate of fire and in consistency of loading and target accuracy. The ultimate in present service is the Swedish VK 155 L/50. This is a bulky equipment but achieves a rate of fire of fifteen 155 mm rounds per minute.

Survivability is not an inherent quality of the SP. Indeed, it is vulnerable to loss through mechanical failure. Open designs such as the American M 110 and French Mk III are no better protected than their towed equivalents. However, enclosed types, which make up the majority, offer splinter protection to the crew and delicate components such as sights. In nuclear war, the enclosed SP offers flash protection, and air filtration which also serves to protect the detachment from chemical attack.

In most cases the SP is built on an existing chassis often with modification to lock the suspension for greater stability during firing. However, the SP is not always a hybrid weapon and the Americans are notable for producing 'one-off' chases: e.g., the M 109 and M 110/107. One disadvantage of the use of a tank chassis is the unnecessary weight of hull armour, the removal of which can negate the cost and development benefits of using an existing design. When a tank chassis is used, it usually travels 'backwards' because whereas the tank engine is behind the turret, access to the breech area of the gun for ammunition supply makes a front engine essential.

Finally a word about sighting and laying. In general, direct laying is only used against moving targets such as tanks and aircraft. The aim has to be offset in azimuth to compensate for the movement of the target while the projectile is in flight: this offset is known as lead and can be set by using graticules in the sight, or by offsetting the whole sight so that the point of aim remains at its centre. The latter system (centre laying) is easier to operate.

Adjustments to elevation to compensate for range can be made in the same two ways using graticule or centre laying. A system using a fixed fore-sight and an adjustable back-sight is known as a tangent sight: the size of the rear sight needed to accommodate large angles of elevation is such that the tangent sight is only suitable for direct laying. The alternative is a rocking bar sight which incorporates both fore- and back-sights in one mounting and is offset by the amount of elevation required and the gun and sight elevated until the sight is realigned.

It will be an advantage if the direct fire sight magnifies the target, but care must be taken in choosing the degree of magnification so that the field of view is not so small as to make it difficult to pick up the target.

Indirect laying in azimuth is achieved by using a 'dial sight', which is a periscopic device free to rotate about a vertical axis. It has a suitably graduated scale. On coming into action the gun is accurately laid in a known bearing, and the dial sight turned to align with a reference object. To lay on a target the sight is turned by an amount equal to the difference between the known bearing of the gun and that of the target, and the gun is traversed until the sight is realigned with the reference object.

The elevating sight is of the rocking bar type but the lay of the gun is determined by a spirit level as opposed to the alignment of the fore and back-sight, as is the case with direct laying. The sight must compensate for any difference in level of the trunnions, and one which does this automatically is called a 'reciprocating' sight.

Reference is made to 'split-function' laying in some of the equipment descriptions: this is an arrangement whereby laying for azimuth and elevation is separated into two functions employing two crew members who usually work one on each side of the barrel.

II. Ammunition

The number of shell and warhead types available to the artilleryman is increasing, and the efficiency of familiar types is improving. Design and development is influenced by the nature of the expected target and by the desired target effect.

The most useful type of shell with the greatest variety of applications and a multiple target effect is High Explosive (HE). It consists of a hollow shell of cast steel fitted with one of a number of chemical explosives.

Figure V(a): Basic shape   High Explosive (HE).

A high explosive is a substance which, when subjected to a shock wave of a suitable size and shape, will, in rapid and exothermic reaction, decompose mainly into a gas with a violent rise in pressure and temperature. It must be insensitive so that it can stand the shock of discharge from a weapon, and also (APHE) impact on the target. It should be cheap to make and be safe to manufacture and store. An ideal filling will give the highest possible density, freedom from cavitation, and good internal strength. One of the best methods of filling from the economical aspects is casting at a temperature of about 80°C: higher temperatures are dangerous and lower temperatures give problems in storage and handling in the tropics. Trinitrotoluol (TNT) can be handled in this way and is widely used either on its own or mixed with other explosives. When mixed with ammonium nitrate it is called 'Amatol', and with PETN as 'Pentalite'.

A higher energy explosive was designed by the UK Explosive Research Department in the 1930s and given the name 'Research Department X' or 'RDX'. RDX/TNT mixtures are known as Hexogen. RDX has a high melting point and is sometimes used with a small proportion of inert wax such as paraffin wax and press filled into shells and rockets to achieve a very high density and energy content. A derivative of RDX is HMX which has a greater energy content per cubic centimetre and is now being used in a number of shell fillings, rocket heads, and in HEAT projectiles which require a high performance in a small-calibre, hollow-charge warheads. To increase the blast effects of explosives, aluminium can be added. Aluminium and magnesium can also be used to increase the incendiary effects.

The explosive effect of HE damages both man and material, and the heat generated has an incendiary effect, but the radius of damage of the shell is greatly increased by the flying fragments of the casing. The composition and manufacture of the shell case must enable it to withstand the shock of firing and on detonation, shatter into fragments of a regular size. The optimum size of fragment is large enough to possess sufficient kinetic energy to inflict damage, yet small enough to yield the maximum number of fragments from each shell.

In recent years development has concentrated on pre-fragmented shells: by casting a pattern into the internal surface of the shell case, the size and regularity of the fragments is assumed. Care must be taken not to weaken the shell so that it fails under the stress of firing.

The external shape of the shell with its ogival nose is designed to give the best performance in flight. Given the calibre the weight of the shell is determined by the length of the shell (a function of good ballistic shape and the size of the chamber) and the proportion of explosive filling to metal case content.

Figure V(b): Carrier shell—Base ejection smoke, illuminating, minelet, chemical, leaflet.

In the conventional indirect fire role, the most common artillery shell after HE is smoke. White phosphorus is one sort of smoke agent whose chief virtue is an instant effusion of dense smoke. Its burning action gives a valuable bonus effect against both men and material. Alternatively hexa-chloro-ethane can be used to produce smoke: it burns slowly to give a slower build-up than white phosphorus but a longer lasting effect. Hexa-chloro-ethane is usually delivered in cannisters in a carrier shell whose base is blown off over the target area using a time fuze and small explosive charge. The cannisters are ejected and fall in a random pattern and yield a good spread of obscuration. The two types are known as WP and BE (base ejection). They are not competitive but complement each other: WP's instant effectiveness is offset by its tendency to 'pillar' in vertical columns on still days: BE smoke is less prone to this effect. BE smoke can be coloured in manufacture and used to indicate targets to ground attack aircraft.

Chemical, propaganda (or leaflet) and illuminating shells are all variations on the basic carrier shell. In order to allow for the ejection of cannisters of the optimum diameter, carrier shells do not taper at their base and as a result, have different ballistic characterisitics from the 'standard' HE shell.

Conventional direct fire anti-tank weapons, both guns and guided missiles use specialised armour defeating ammunition. Many field artillery equipments have an anti-armour projectile, useful for the defence of the gun position, but also offering a secondary anti-tank role. This philosophy of increasing the weapon's flexibility is actively followed by the Russians, as shown by their 76 mm family of guns, and also the 122 mm towed howitzer.

There are two basic types of attack against armour using kinetic energy or specially adapted HE projectiles. Only guns with very high muzzle velocities can generate the energy needed for the former, but both guns and missiles can use the specialised explosives. Altogether, six types of anti-tank projectile are used by the weapons described in this book and are known as: AP, HVAP, APDS, HEAT, HESH and APHE.

AP (Armour Piercing) and HVAP (High Velocity Armour Piercing) are solid shot which penetrate armour by their kinetic energy and thrash round inside the tank.

| Figure V(c) Hollow charge HE anti-tank (HEAT) | HE Squash head (HESH) | Armour piercing HE (APHE) | Rocket assisted projectile (RAP) |

AP is an elderly and very limited value projectile that is no longer produced. HVAP is associated with small calibre weapons and implies the use of a special and powerful propellant charge to raise the muzzle velocity of the gun: like AP it is out-dated. An associated type of projectile is APDS (Armour Piercing Discarding Sabot) a specialist projectile fired by a few tank guns. (The only anti-tank gun to use APDS is the obsolete British 17 pounder.) The projectile is a small diameter pointed shot or dart of super-hard tungsten carbide which offers little air resistance and therefore sustains a high velocity during its flight. To fill the bore of the gun a light alloy collar, or sabot, is fitted around it and is automatically discarded on leaving the barrel. Used against light armour a solid shot may pass through a vehicle leaving it and its crew unscathed: the ideal is for the round to dissipate sufficient energy on entry to ricochet about inside.

HEAT (High Explosive Anti-Tank) consists of a shaped charge which concentrates its energy into a narrow beam and burns a small diameter hole through armour. Its effect is to introduce a small quantity of high energy particles into the vehicle, but the attack is chiefly on the crew by blinding, deafening, concussing and burning. Its efficiency depends on a good impact angle which leads to some degradation of performance as range (and fall off in the trajectory) increases. The depth of penetration is a function of the diameter of the shaped charge, hence the continued use of HVAP with small calibre weapons. The efficiency of HEAT is reduced if spin stabilization is used. It is the usual warhead for anti-tank missiles. Some new HEAT shells fired from a rifled gun avoid spin by using a freely rotating collar in place of the usual driving band.

HESH (High Explosive Squash Head) is also known as HE/P (High Explosive/Plastic). It is a shaped plastic charge which flattens against the target before the base fuze initiates explosion. The effect is to set up shock waves in the armour which release a large scab

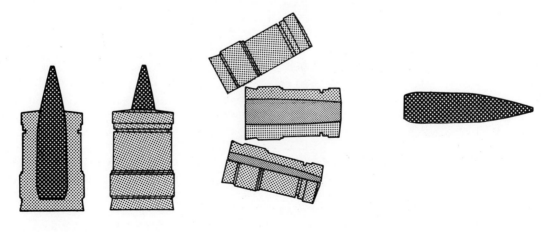

| Figure V(d): Armour piercing discarding sabot (APDS) | Figure V(e): APDS after discharge—shot flying free. |

from inside of the armour plate itself which ricochets inside the vehicle, causing crew casualties and damage to fittings. This type of shell is effective over a wide angle of impact and is therefore less subject to range limitations than HEAT. Performance is directly related to the size of the explosive and therefore the bulk of the shell. Unlike HEAT, HESH has some value as an anti-personnel weapon in an emergency as its explosive effect and the fragmentation of the shell case are lethal.

APHE (Armour Piercing High Explosive) has a similar anti-personnel effect to HESH. It is a combination of kinetic energy and explosive types of shell. Its nose is a solid cone designed to penetrate armour plate like an AP round, within which is a small high explosive charge, and behind that a base fuze. The object is to penetrate the vehicle and explode the charge inside. In practice, this is easier said than done, because of the difficulty in providing a sufficient delay in the operation fuse, and the tendency of the nose-cone to shatter, and waste the HE filling in a harmless explosion outside the tank.

Because each type of anti-armour shell has its own limitations, the various options tend to be complementary. A gun will often have more than one type of anti-armour round in its ammunition inventory.

As a result of infantry and artillery adopting armoured SP vehicles, the array of hard targets on the battlefield has increased. Faced with a predominantly armoured enemy, it is not sufficient to rely on only direct fire anti-armour weapons. Attrition must begin as far forward as possible, and the most efficient and readily available weapon delivery system is the gun. The concept of using the field gun in an indirect fire anti-armour role has produced a difficult problem. It is not sufficient to deliver an anti-armour projectile *near* a tank: a direct hit is necessary, but the zone of a field gun is too large to guarantee a hit. Furthermore, the time needed to adjust fire to the best accuracy possible against a moving target negates the whole process.

One solution lies in the development of multiple warheads which actually benefit from the inherent spread of artillery fire. The attack is against the weakest parts of an armoured vehicle—its roof or belly. A shell of suitable calibre contains either a number of 'minelets' or 'bomblets'.

A free flight rocket tends to be less accurate than a gun, but presents a formidable system for the delivery of multiple warhead weapons. It is less restricted by calibre, imposes lower firing stresses, and requires a relatively inexpensive launcher. A multiple launcher can deliver a great weight of fire very quickly, so that its delivery error is compensated for by the saturation of a large area. Speed of delivery and good delivery dispersion are important virtues against moving targets. The inter-relation of warhead and weapon design are illustrated by the design of the new West German rocket system LARS, which can deliver anti-tank minelets as well as anti-personnel warheads.

The successful use of the so called 'Smart' bomb by the Americans in Vietnam presages the development of a new long range anti-armour weapon for the artillery. Terminal guidance of a conventionally fired shell, homing on to a target illuminated by a laser beam, could soon be in service. The Americans have successfully test fired a 155 mm cannon-launched guided projectile (CLGP). At ranges of more than 10,000 m, and despite deliberate aiming errors of several hundred metres, direct hits have been achieved. The cost of each round and the associated target markers will be high, but still cost-effective against a tank especially since the delivery weapon enjoys immunity from direct retaliation.

Most shell types are designed to operate with a particular fuze, but the familiar high explosive shell can be fitted with a variety of fuzes, an examination of which illustrates the options open to both the designer and tactician. Most common is the impact or point-detonating: it provides for a combination of damage from explosion and fragments. To optimise the explosive effect on prepared defensive positions and other 'solid' targets a delay fuze can be used. It is common for one design to cater for both options by a small adjustment before loading.

HE shells can be used to cause casualties by blast, by the kinetic energy of the fragments, or by internal explosion. The type of fuze fitted determines which effect will be achieved by the shell. The cheapest and most common type is the impact fuze. Fitted with a delay device this simple fuze will allow the shell to penetrate the target before exploding: this increases the shell's effectiveness against earth-works and concrete.

Impact bursting is inefficient because a large percentage of the fragments are driven harmlessly into the ground. A better lethal effect is obtained by bursting the shell above the target. To achieve this a time-fuze which is adjustable to the time of flight is used. The older time-fuzes were of the powder-burning or clockwork types neither of which produced the accuracy or consistency needed to give the optimum height of burst. The most advanced method of obtaining an air burst is the Variable Time (VT) fuze which consists of a small radio transceiver set to initiate the explosion at the correct height when its signals are echoed back from the ground. The anti-aircraft 'proximity' fuze works on exactly the same principle, giving the warhead a large lethal radius and obviating the need for a direct hit.

Fuzes are technically described as 'point detonation' (PD), 'point impact delay' (PID), 'proximity' (P) and 'time' (T).

Field artillery shells are normally appropriately fuzed on the gun-position to suit the fire mission, but the future concept is the PPD fuze which will combine all these capabilities in a single complete round unchanged between factory and gun position.

The discussion of ammunition types must include the nuclear shell. The rocket has long been a prime delivery vehicle for atomic weapons. The development of a nuclear device able to withstand the shock of firing, and contained in a shell has not displaced the rocket, but complements it. The yield of gun-delivered nuclear weapons is small— a desirable quality when troop safety is critical or when the damage radius must be limited. In turn the sub-kiloton yield requires precise delivery, and the suitability of the gun with its inherent accuracy illustrates again the interdependence of warhead and weapon design.

The foregoing has dealt with the types of shell, projectile and warhead to be found in use today. The other aspect of ammunition is the propellant, i.e. the explosive substance used to propel the projectile up the bore of the gun.

A propelling explosive can be defined as a substance which, when ignited, decomposes at a controllable rate under confinement, producing high pressure gases. It is designed to leave no appreciable residue of solids after combustion. It should be insensitive to shock.

Figure V(f): Types of charge.

| Fixed. | Semi-fixed. | Cartridge-sealed. | Bagged. |

The rate of burning should remain fairly constant under all conditions of storage and use in service and should not be affected by age, or variation in ambient temperature. When a propelling explosive in a gun chamber or rocket motor is suitably ignited by means of a primary explosive, assisted where necessary by a booster in the form of an igniter, the gas pressure will rise until the projectile commences to move. Pressures will then continue to rise until it reaches a maximum when it will decrease as the shot accelerates and so increases the volume for the chamber gases.

It is clear that the control of the burning rate affects the gas pressure, the velocity of the projectile and in turn the safety of the gun or rocket motor walls. It is possible with solid propelling explosives to control the rate of burning not only by varying the chemical composition of the propelling explosive but also by controlling the surface area. The larger the surface area the greater is the volume of gas produced in a given time. To meet the different requirements for individual weapons, propellant explosives are made in many forms such as flake, rods, pellets, balls, and small and large tubes: multi-hole tubes can be designed to increase progressively the volume of gases as the burning proceeds to correspond with the increase in area of the chamber as the shot accelerates.

The most common types of propellant can be grouped under four headings: gunpowder, single base, double and triple base and solventless (in plastic).

Liquid propellants such as alcohol/liquid oxygen or high-test peroxide/nitric-acid mixtures have been tried in guns but have not been satisfactory from the handling and safety aspects. They are used in large rockets.

Gun and ammunition designers are constantly striving to achieve increased range, so that their artillery can not only reach out to targets far behind the enemy's front lines, but also have the flexibility to fire diagonally across its own front, when required, to augment the fire support available to neighbouring formations. As much as a 30 per cent improvement in range can be achieved by two types of ammunition. First, a rocket assisted projectile (RAP) (see fig Vc) has a longer trajectory, boosted by a rocket propellant in the shell body behind the warhead. This is the most effective method in service at present, but a RAP is not so accurate, and its HE content, and hence its lethality, is less than a conventionally designed shell. Secondly, there are special streamlined extended range projectiles (ERP), which fly further because they are less affected by drag than other shells. These achieve greater accuracy than RAP, but they are less popular because they are expensive to produce and because their long, non-standard shape leads to logistic problems.

Figure V(g): Example of a long, thin, sub-calibre fin stabilised ERP projectile. Compare length and calibre with standard HE type shell for the same gun.

III. Field Guns and Howitzers

The term 'field artillery' covers a group of weapons used to support ground troops. Rockets and mortars (discussed separately) fulfil a similar role and are often embraced by the term to distinguish them from air defence, coast or anti-tank artillery.

The word gun is used loosely to cover two types of equipment: the *gun* is a high velocity, flat trajectory weapon noted for its range: the *howitzer* fires a generally heavier projectile in a high and variable trajectory. In practice, the qualities of the two types are merged and some equipments—the British 25 pounder—were even called 'gun-howitzers'. In all modern equipments a set of graded propellant charges is provided with each complete round which enables the trajectory to be varied and also no more energy used, and so no more than the required shell velocity to reach the target, which reduces wear in the bore. Gun characteristics confer a secondary direct fire anti-tank capability: howitzers are easier to site to clear intervening crests (in forests or mountainous country) and can search into deep valleys.

Any heavy weapon has an anti-armour potential. This can be developed as a self defence quality, or exploited to add flexibility to the weapon's deployment. A good example is the Italian type 56 pack howitzer: an alternative mounting for the wheel axles presents either a low silhouette anti-tank gun or a field howitzer capable of high angle fire. The Russians are particularly adept at investing guns with a dual anti-tank/field artillery role. Perhaps this is in response to the fluid battle to be expected on the featureless Russian plains—in any event their artillery is deployed well forward. This and their techniques of fire control, which place the responsibility for the production of gun sight data on the observer and not the gun position command post, facilitates changes between the two roles. The result is a number of Soviet equipments which do not fall readily into a simple classification. The names by which they are known differ, and different user nations have their own deployment plans. The 85 mm M 1945 (D 44) is known as a field gun, yet its elevation is limited to 35°, its silhouette is low, and it is mounted directly on the ASU-85 as a self propelled tank destroyer. For the purposes of this section, a recognised and usual employment in the field role is the criteria for inclusion.

The essential feature of the field gun is its indirect fire capability. This, and its range potential, allows its removal from the line of contact to a position where it can exploit its all weather, 24 hour capabilities in relative immunity from direct attack. Its range can be exploited forward of the immediate battle, or laterally to assist flank units, making it a thoroughly flexible weapon system.

There are two systems for controlling indirect shooting—'observed' and 'predicted' fire. They are not mutually exclusive, because both methods are combined in modern systems so as to ensure speed and accuracy.

In the simplest form of observed fire the observer using his map gives a rough indication of the target locality and the battery immediately responds with a single round from which corrections are ordered based on observation of the fall of shot: the process is repeated until there is evidence that the mean point of impact coincides with the target and the necessary fire for effect of so many rounds from the whole battery is ordered. With good drill at the gun position and a skilled observer it is a fast and effective method, but eye-

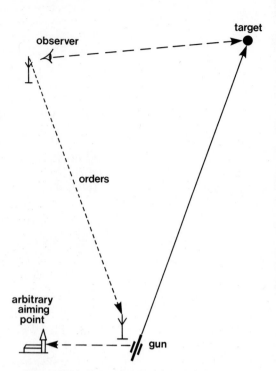

Figure VI(a): Indirect laying, the gun, with appropriate angle set on the dial sight is laid on the Aiming Point A and so points at the invisible target T.

Figure VI(b): Remotely sited forward observer controls fire by radio from gun on to distant target.

shooting is a knack rather than a skill and some never acquire it. It is still used for short range weapons, especially infantry mortars, and for air observation from helicopters. Its disadvantages are that the ranging, or adjusting rounds may alert the target; if, as is now often the case, the target is armoured and mobile it will be gone before adjustment is complete. At the long ranges at which modern guns are used the time of flight is long and this slows the process down.

This basic technique is retained because it is always effective in the stress of battle and proof against all system failures except the death of the observer or the failure of his communications.

The laser range finder and gyro-compass can now produce highly accurate bearing and distance information of the target for the observer, and can be used in conjunction with night observation devices. They depend for their effectiveness on the precise survey of the observer's own position. Each can be pressed into service as survey instruments for this purpose, but the practical problems of conducting a survey scheme at the forefront of the battle cannot be underestimated. One answer being developed in Great Britain is the Position and Azimuth Determining System (PADS), designed to carry survey forward using the movement of a vehicle on the inertia guidance principle which is well tried in the aerospace industry.

It has been observed from operational analysis of target engagements that target damage is nearly all inflicted in the first few seconds of fire for effect, so that the aim with 'observed-predicted' fire is to achieve three or four on-target salvos without preliminary adjustment; thus obtaining maximum effect with maximum economy of ammunition and also freeing the battery for the next mission in the shortest possible time.

Indirect fire, whether predicted or observed, requires that two pieces of information are given to the gun sight: an angle in azimuth (a bearing), and an angle of elevation. (Some equipments such as the British 25 pounder, have sights which accepted range in terms of distance which is mechanically translated into an angle of elevation: this method is not suited to the inclusion of calculated adjustments for range necessitated by predicted shooting.)

The components of the equation to produce predicted gun sight data are three-fold: those relating to the relative locations of gun and target; the gun's performance; and the variables influencing the shell in flight. All three types lend themselves to computer solution. The first group is:

1. The distance between gun and target, i.e. map range.

2. The direction of the target from the gun, i.e. map bearing.
3. The difference in elevation between gun and target, i.e. angle of sight. This difference leads to an adjustment of range.
4. The displacement of individual guns from the battery centre.
5. The rotation of the Earth beneath the shell in flight.
6. Jump, or the small adjustment in the barrel's elevation as the projectile travels up the bore.

The gun performance factors are:
7. Variation in muzzle velocity from firing table data caused by wear.
8. Variation in shell weight. This can be an individual variation in manufacture, or the difference between types of projectile.
9. Charge temperature.
10. The accuracy of the gun sights.

Influences on the shell in flight vary with the time of flight, and in the case of meteorological factors, with the height of the trajectory. They are:

11. Wind.
12. Air density varying with temperature and barometric pressure.
13. The difference in the ballistic performance of different types of shell.
14. Drift, which is a displacement in azimuth arising from the yaw angle developed by the spinning shell.

The data necessary to determine the effect of these factors is available from three sources: the target and gun fixation data: calculations based on experimental firings; and continual monitoring of the meteorological environment, and gun performance. The last of these is the most difficult because of the speed with which the weather can change, and the time taken to make observations. It is not practicable to establish the atmospheric conditions throughout the shell's trajectory much of which will be over enemy territory. The sampling technique is to release a balloon equipped to measure and transmit temperature information. By observing the speed of ascent and lateral movement, the necessary data can be calculated. This time-consuming task requires highly specialised equipment, and clearly can only be done behind the fighting line. The optimum compromise is to make observations as near to the probable trajectory as possible, sighting the equipment to serve the maximum number of batteries. Up-dating must be frequent. There must be a minimum delay in the production of results, for even in the most stable climatic conditions there are times of rapid change at dawn and dusk.

One solution to the problem is the British AMETS. Its significance lies not so much in the detailed technology of the equipment and its handling, as in the computerisation of the results. These are produced as data intelligible to the gun position computer, making automatic data transfer possible.

The other variable factor which requires monitoring is the gun's muzzle velocity. In the past an assessment has been made based on the observed performance of the piece during experimental firings, or calculated from carefully conducted calibration shoots. The job is now done at the gun position, in action, electronically. The equipment works on the doppler principle. There are several systems in use.

Fourteen factors which affect the accuracy of predicted fire have been noted. The accumulation of small errors in the observation or calculation of each one can be disastrous. A one mil error in only four factors affecting bearing (gun orientation, wind speed, observed target location and data computation) can result in a 60 m delivery error at a range of 15,000 m.

It has been made apparent that the handling of the many calculations needed to predict the fall of shot can now be computerised. The increase in the speed of reaction and the high degree of accuracy brought about by computers improves the quality of artillery support, and, by reducing the time taken for each minion, increases the availability of the guns to engage more targets. An important by-product is a simplicity of operation which reduces training time and removes the fatigue of long mathematical calculations. However, command post staffs still need to understand the principles of gunnery in the event of system failure or damage in action.

The first computers handled the basic calculations. A second generation incorporated memory banks, and the latest equipment forms a complete fire control system. The American FADAC, components of which are in service, goes beyond the calculation of predicted fire data, and solves the problems of weapon and ammunition availability.

The basic premise of prediction is that the location of the target is precisely known, and that its nature is sufficiently understood to select the optimum target effect projectile. Equipment to produce this information is in service. It does not replace, but complements the observer: no one technique of target acquisition being exclusive to all others.

Of the systems which dispense with the human observer, the oldest is sound ranging. It is accurate to 100 m up to a range of one and a half times the length of the microphone base. The system has been updated by the development of radio link data transmission, but the microphones are slow to deploy. It requires more expert analysis of results than radar, but is free from enemy deception and interference except in the radio link.

Two types of radar are available: battlefield surveillance and weapon locating. The weapon locating radar is only effective in placing mortars which it does by reference to the path of the bombs in flight. The problems of locating guns by reference to the trajectory are insoluble at the present time. Battlefield surveillance radar has been reduced in size in recent years, and gives details of any enemy movement which could lead to the presentation of a worthwhile target.

Sound ranging and radar have the benefit of being active simultaneously with the engagement of the target. A judicious adjustment to the operating procedures allows 'observation' of the fall of shot—a useful back-up facility to the prediction process.

New sources of target data are the 'drone' and the Remotely Piloted Vehicle (RPV). The existing systems, such as the Canadian USD 501, require recovery, processing and interpretation of film record after each sortie. Infra-red linescan adds to the versatility of the equipment, but the system does not produce details of target damage without flying a second sortie. In-flight film processing is a logical and time saving development, but one which may be overtaken by the introduction of television cameras. The next generation of RPVs is likely to be an automated aerial observation platform, able to hover and direct fire on the target it 'finds'.

It can be appreciated that the successful prediction of artillery fire is a highly complex matter, and subject to error at many stages. Ultimately, the result depends on the designed accuracy of the gun, and the size of its zone of dispersion. Development is now concentrating on the elimination of these errors as far as possible. In the meantime the continuing importance of the human observer cannot be over-stressed.

75 mm field gun M 1897

France

Calibre	75 mm
Barrel length	36 calibres
Muzzle brake	Nil
Trail type	Pole
Weight	1,139 kg
Ammunition type	Fixed
Charges	One
Ammunition options	HE (7·24 kg)
	Shrapnel
Rate of fire	12 rds/min
Muzzle velocity	529 m/sec
Range	8,550 m
Elevation limits	−11° + 18°
Traverse limits	6°
Detachment	6

This gun is best known as the 'French 75' and was, at its introduction in 1897 a great novelty. It was the first gun to be fitted with a recoil system: the resulting increase in the rate of fire over previous weapons was dramatic— nearly three times better than its contempories'. Not only did the stability of the carriage speed the relaying of the piece, but the detachment could remain close to the gun when it was fired to be ready to reload. Fixed ammunition was not new, but was used to further exploit the quick fire potential.

The French 75 is a true gun having a long barrel, high muzzle velocity (for its day), and flat trajectory. The breech is a quick action 'Nordenfelt' eccentric screw type. The hydraulic recoil system is fitted below the barrel.

The pole trail severely limits both traverse and elevation. A version known as the M 97/33 was produced for Mexico using a simple split trail. The original wooden spoked wheels were replaced by modern pneumatic tyre types when towing was mechanized between the two world wars. Because the detachment remained close to the gun a shield was fitted to offer the gunners some protection.

Over 17,000 were made including those manufactured under licence in Mexico and the United States of America. The gun remained in active service in Europe until the fall of France in 1940.

Employment	Cameroons	Morocco
	Cambodia	Mexico
	Laos	Upper Volta

The famous *soixante-quinze*. The gunners *au repos*, post 1918. This equipment is still in service with six armies. Note ammunition limber on right.

75 mm mountain gun—Type 94

Japan

Calibre	75 mm
Barrel length	20·8 calibres
Muzzle brake	Nil
Trail type	Split
Weight	544 kg
Ammunition type	Semi-fixed
Charges	One
Ammunition options	HE (5·7 kg)
	Smoke WP
	APHE
	HEAT
	Shrapnel
	Incendiary
	Illuminating
Rate of fire	10–12 rds/min
Muzzle velocity	385 m/sec
Range	8,320 m
Elevation limits	−9° + 45°
Traverse limits	6°
Detachment	4

Mountainous country requires a gun to be rugged as well as light. This pre-war (1934) Japanese equipment is just that, as its survival in active service proves.

Performance is limited by modern standards, especially because of the design compromise needed to keep the weight down to 544 kilogrammes. The barrel is longer than the average for this type of gun, but the charge is small: the complete round weighs only 7·2 kilogrammes. The result is a modest muzzle velocity and range. The recoil system, mounted below the barrel, is hydropneumatic.

A large selection of shell types are available, of which the HEAT round penetrates 85 mm of armour.

The simple box section trail legs accept vertical anchor spades in action. Old fashioned wooden spoked wheels of large diameter are used. While the whole equipment can be horse or vehicle drawn, it is also designed for pack transporting, and breaks down into six pack animal loads.

Employment China
Vietnam

Japanese 75 mm mountain gun Type 94—note split trails.

75 mm pack howitzer M 116

United States of America

Calibre	75 mm
Barrel length	15·93 calibres
Muzzle brake	Nil
Trail type	Split
Weight	653 kg
Ammunition type	Semi-fixed
Charges	4
Ammunition options	HE (6·25 kg)
	HEAT
	Smoke
	Chemical
Rate of fire	22 rds/min
Muzzle velocity	381 m/sec
Range	8,500 m
Elevation limits	−5° + 45°
Traverse limits	6°
Detachment	4

The 75 mm pack howitzer M 116 (also known as the M-1A1) was conceived before World War II. Early versions had a box trail and broke down into six loads. Later the M 8 carriage with pneumatic tyres was developed: it is this version of the weapon which breaks down into eight parts which can be re-assembled in three minutes. The M 116 was widely used with parachute troops, and for this role it could be dismantled into nine components and packed in a 'paracrate', and re-assembled in seven minutes.

There is no muzzle brake, and the barrel is scarcely longer than the recoil system beneath it. The steeply tapered jacket and lifting handle built-in over the muzzle are recognition features. The breech block is a horizontal sliding wedge. A single equilibrator on the right of the barrel is mounted on the front of the trail.

Vertical recoil forces are absorbed by a firing jack. The box trail is extensively drilled to save weight. The spade is fixed. There is no shield, and the weapon is only 940 mm high at zero elevation. Split function laying is used.

Employment	Bolivia	Honduras	Oman
	Brazil	India	Pakistan
	Congo	Iran	Taiwan
	China	Japan	Thailand
	Ethiopia	Laos	Turkey
	Haiti	Nepal	Vietnam

The compact little 75 mm M 116 pack howitzer.

76 mm divisional gun M 1942 (ZIS 3)
Union of Soviet Socialist Republics

Calibre	76·2 mm
Barrel length	42·6 calibres
Muzzle brake	Double baffle
Trail type	Split
Weight	1,116 kg
Ammunition type	Fixed
Charges	One
Ammunition options	HVAP (3·1 kg)
	APHE (6·5 kg)
	HEAT (4 kg)
	HE (6·2 kg)
Rate of fire	20 rds/min
Muzzle velocity	965 m/sec (HVAP)
	680 m/sec (HE)
	655 m/sec (APHE)
	325 m/sec (HEAT)
Range	13,300 m
Elevation limits	−5° + 37°
Traverse limits	54°
Detachment	6

The basic design of this gun dates from 1936: the ZIS 3 was the final development for field artillery use; it was also used as a tank gun, and had a naval application. Progressive development increased range, and reduced weight from 1,620 kg in 1936 to 1,116 kg for this model. The anti-tank performance of the HEAT round, which penetrates 120 mm of armour, is good for a weapon of its age and calibre.

The long barrel is fitted with a vertical sliding breech. The ammunition is fixed, and there are marked variations in the charge, shell weight, and therefore performance of each option.

The carriage—a split trail of tubular members—is from the M 1941 (ZIS 2) 57 mm anti-tank gun. The two equipments look almost identical. An important modification to the cradle increases elevation for the field gun, but not to a full 45°. The increased weight of the ammunition is reflected in a slightly lower rate of fire.

This is a light weight gun, and it is thought that a pack version was made for use with mountain troops. A version was made in China, and designated the Type 54 field gun. Both models were widely exported so that the age, performance and lasting popularity suggest a comparison with the British 25 pounder. Like the British gun, the ZIS 3 is no longer in service in its homeland.

Employment:

Albania	Ghana	Rumania
Bulgaria	Hungary	Somalia
Cambodia	Indonesia	Tanzania
China	Nigeria	Vietnam
Cuba	North Korea	North Yemen
Czechoslovakia	Morocco	Yugoslavia
Egypt	Poland	

76·2 mm divisional gun M 42 (ZIS 3).

76·2 mm mountain gun M 48 B1

Yugoslavia

Calibre	76·2 mm
Barrel length	15·5 calibres
Muzzle brake	Multi-baffle
Trail type	Split
Weight	705 kg
Ammunition type	Semi-fixed
Charges	—
Ammunition options	HE (6·2 kg)
	HEAT
	Smoke
Rate of fire	6–7 rds/min
Muzzle velocity	398 m/sec
Range	8,600 m
Elevation limits	−15° + 45°
Traverse limits	50°
Detachment	6

This equipment is sometimes referred to as the M 48 howitzer. It is a light-weight weapon, similar in concept to the Italian pack howitzer (Model 56). Both are designed for use in difficult terrain, breakdown into pack loads, and are towed with trail legs folded. The Yugoslav gun is regularly horsedrawn.

The barrel is short, even with its multi-baffle muzzle-brake fitted, a fact which must contribute to its modest performance. The breech block is a horizontal sliding

76 mm (Yugoslav) Mountain Gun.

wedge type. The recoil system is mounted beneath the barrel.

The trail legs are of tubular section and are each fitted with a vertical anchor type spade. They fold to shorten the carriage when being towed.

Several versions have been produced, with minor modifications to the basic design. One such version is used as a heavy support weapon by the infantry.

The high shield with straight top and wings is a recognition feature.

Employment Burma
Sri Lanka
Yugoslavia

85 mm field gun M 52

Czechoslovakia

Calibre	85 mm
Barrel length	56 calibres
Muzzle brake	Double baffle
Trail type	Split
Weight	2,095 kg
Ammunition type	Fixed
Charges	One
Ammunition options	HE (9·5 kg)
	HVAP (5·0 kg)
	APHE (9·3 kg)
Rate of fire	15 rds/min
Muzzle velocity	805 m/sec (HE)
	820 m/sec (APHE)
	1,070 m/sec (HVAP)
Range	16,160 m
Elevation limits	−6° + 38°
Traverse limits	60°
Detachment	6

The Russian 85 mm M 1945 has been classified as an anti-tank weapon, this being its primary role. The Czech M 52 is the equivalent of that gun, and is designed to fire the same ammunition. However, it carries the clear title 'field gun', is well suited to that role and is

therefore classified as such. It is manufactured at the Skoda Works in Pilsen.

The barrel is marginally longer than the Russian guns, and performance is improved accordingly. Elevation is also increased, and, although it still falls short of the optimum 45°, contributes to a better maximum range. The vertical sliding breech is retained. The recoil system, mounted below the barrel, projects forward of the shield.

The HVAP round with its larger charge, gives a muzzle velocity of 1,070 metres/second and penetrates 107 mm of armour at 1,000 m. The APHE shell penetrates 123 mm of armour at 1000 m.

The M 52 shares the distinctive wavy topped shield with its Russian equivalent. The trail is similar, with fixed spades, but a stowage box is carried across the legs when travelling.

Employment Algeria
Austria
China*
Czechoslovakia
Egypt

* as Type 56

25 pounder gun/howitzer
United Kingdom

Calibre	88 mm
Barrel length	28·3 calibres
Muzzle brake	Double-baffle
Trail type	Box
Weight	1,741 kg
Ammunition type	Separate
Charge	4
Ammunition options	HE (11·34 kg)
	Smoke BE
	Illuminating
Rate of fire	5 rds/min
Muzzle velocity	520 m/sec
Range	12,250 m
Elevation limits	−5° + 45°
Traverse limits	8° (360° on platform)
Detachment	6

25 pounder gun/howitzer.

The 25 pounder 'gun-howitzer' was designed in 1935 to replace the then standard 18 pounder field gun and the 4·5 QF field howitzer. The final stages of development were hastened by the outbreak of war in 1939. After trials with a split trail, a box trail was adopted with a turntable/platform under the wheels. This design proved highly successful, giving 360° traverse; the latest British gun, the 105 mm light gun has the same arrangement. In both cases, the platform travels on the trail and is lowered for firing. The platform digs in to give stability to the equipment, and a trail spade is not needed.

The whole gun is extremely rugged in its design, and in 34 years' service had only one major modification—the fitting of a double baffle muzzle brake in 1943. The barrel is autofrettaged and carries a vertically sliding breech block. The variable length recoil is controlled by a three cylinder hydro-pneumatic system mounted beneath the barrel. Rocking-bar type sights are used, incorporating a calibrating range drum.

The ammunition is separate. A high rate of fire can be achieved by a well trained detachment—well above the official rapid rate of five rounds/minute. Three basic charges were provided, each represented by a coloured bag in the brass cartridge case. Incremental charges were developed, but never widely used. 'Charge Super' is a special sealed cartridge. During the desert campaigns of 1942/3 an increment to the super charge increased the muzzle velocity of the solid shot anti-tank round to 600 metres/second. The only modification needed to cope with the extra stresses was the muzzle brake already mentioned.

A large number of ammunition options were available at the height of development; HE, smoke, coloured smoke, solid shot, cannister, HEAT and illuminating. The smoke rounds are of the base ejection type, and with HE illuminating are the only type currently in use. Several fuses were developed and used: percussion, mechanical and variable time, and powder burning.

The gun's main disadvantage was its weight—1,741 kilogrammes. For many years a two-wheel limber/trailer between the gun and tractor enabled a relatively light towing vehicle to be used. The limber also carried first line ammunition: deployment of the gun and limber together gave instant access to this. The alternative (adopted towards the end of the gun's useful life) was a 3-ton vehicle. In both cases cross-country mobility was limited.

For weight reasons an airborne version was never adopted. A special, narrow axle and shortened barrel was developed for use in the jungles of South-East Asia.

More than twelve thousand 25 pounders were produced and used throughout the world. It is still active in some parts today, but in the British Army it is now used only for training purposes. Perhaps its last major campaign was the Indo-Pakistan war of 1971. Despite its long history of service, the 25 pounder is best remembered for its part in the campaigns in the Western Desert—especially for its anti-tank performance. In fact, it was the basic close support artillery weapon of the Commonwealth for 30 years.

Several self-propelled versions were produced. Only the Bishop (Valentine chassis) and Sexton (Canadian Ram chassis) saw service. South Africa has reputedly produced its own version of the 25 pounder, locally manufactured and referred to as the 90 mm field gun.

Employment:

Abu Dhabi	Indonesia	Pakistan
Australia	Israel	Qatar
Bangla Desh	Jordan	Rhodesia
Burma	Kuwait	Singapore
Egypt	Mozambique	South Africa
Eire	New Zealand	Sudan
Ghana	Malaysia	UK (practice only)
Greece	Nigeria	United Arab Emirates
India	Oman	

105 mm light field howitzer M 61/37

Finland

Calibre	105 mm
Barrel length	—
Muzzle brake	Single baffle
Trail type	Split
Weight	1,800 kg
Ammunition type	Separate
Charges	—
Ammunition options	HE (14·9 kg)
Rate of fire	7 rds/min
Muzzle velocity	600 m/sec
Range	13,400 m
Elevation limits	−6° + 45°
Traverse limits	53°
Detachment	6

This gun is also known as the M 61. It is basically the Russian 76 mm M 36 fitted with a Finnish designed barrel and cradle. The M 36 was originally German, but large numbers were captured by the Russians and taken into their service. An earlier Finnish adaptation of this design was the LFH 37/10, a weapon now relegated to static defence posts. The weapon described here is used by the artillery battalions of infantry brigades.

The single baffle muzzle brake appears to be crude in design. The recoil system is carried beneath the barrel.

The trail legs are straight, of box section, and each has a fixed spade and lifting handle. A small seat is fitted to the left trail leg for the layer. Large disc-type wheels are a recognition feature and a small shield is fitted.

Employment Finland

---

105 mm light gun

France

Calibre	105 mm
Barrel length	30 calibres
Muzzle brake	Double baffle
Trail type	Split
Weight	1,200 kg
Ammunition type	Separate
Charges	8
Ammunition options	HE (Mk 63) (16·16 kg)
	HE (M 1) (14·9 kg)
	HEAT (Occ-105-F1)
	Smoke WP
	Chemical
	Illuminating
	Carrier
	Blank
Rate of fire	—
Muzzle velocity	—
Range	15,000 m
Elevation limits	−5° + 70°
Traverse limits	45°
Detachment	—

This new gun, first seen in public in 1971, has yet to be accepted for service, but trials have reached an advanced stage. It has been designed as a high mobility dual role (anti-tank or field) weapon with the support of airborne forces in mind. It is classified with field equipment because of its similarity to the British light gun.

The long barrel with its vertical sliding breech block and high efficiency muzzle brake is mounted over the recoil system. A variable length recoil allows full use to be made of the upper register potential of the mounting: a recoil pit is not needed.

The chamber accepts American M 1 type ammunition which increases the shell option and gives logistic flexibility. The range is limited to 11,600 m using this ammunition. The gun is primarily designed to use the French Mk 63 hollow base shell and its associated charge system. The anti-armour round is the non-rotating hollow charge OCC-105-F1. It is effective to 850 m.

The trail legs are simple box section members, whose attachment to the carriage is ingenious. The legs are hinged so that the action of opening them from their travelling position lowers the carriage on to the ground. As the whole carriage rests on the ground it is completely stable. Extreme lightness confers high mobility: the gun is heli-portable, air-droppable and can be towed at speeds up to 90 km/hour. For the tow to be stable at high speed, the barrel must be traversed to the rear and clamped over the trail legs, but for short tactical moves it can travel in the firing position. It shares this dual configuration with the British light gun.

A shield has been designed, but is not always fitted.

Employment Trials only.

105 mm light field howitzer M 18

Germany

	M 18	M 18M	M 18/39	M 18/40	M 18/49
Calibre (mm)	105	105	105	105	105
Barrel length (calibres)	28	28	28	28	28
Muzzle brake	Nil	Double baffle			Double baffle
Trail type	Split	Split	Split	Split	Split
Weight (kg)	1,985	2,040	1,915	1,800	1,750
Ammunition type	Separate	Separate	Separate	Separate	Separate
Charges	—	—	—	—	—
Ammunition options (kg)	HE (14·8)	HE (14·8)	HE (14·8)	HE (14·8)	HE (14·8)
Rate of fire (rds/min)	6–8	6–8	6–8	6–8	6–8
Muzzle velocity (m/sec)	470	540	470	540	540
Maximum range (m)	10,675	12,320	10,675	12,325	12,320
Elevation limits	−5° + 42°	−5° + 42°	−5° + 42°	−5° + 45°	−5° + 42°
Traverse limits	56°	56°	56°	60°	60°
Detachment	6	10	8	8	8

In 1928/29 Germany developed the 105 mm M 18 light field howitzer. It entered service in 1935. It became the standard divisional artillery weapon and 4,845 were built.

The M 18M was a heavier development, based on the M 18 and firing the same shell to 12,325 m, an increase of 1,650 m.

In common with other German equipments of that era, a hydraulic buffer and hydro-pneumatic recuperator are fitted under and over the barrel. The breech is a horizontal sliding wedge. A brass cartridge case carried the variable charge and is separately loaded. Split function laying is used.

Both these weapons, which were fitted to a number of carriages, are obsolete, except in Yugoslavia, but several derivatives are still in service. These have been grouped together for ease of reference and their specifications tabulated. The Swedish guns are known as the Haub M 39.

M 18/39: The M 39 piece was made by Krupp for export. The outbreak of war prevented delivery and the guns were pressed into German service on the M 18 carriage. A few remain in service with the Norwegian Reserve.

M 18/40: This is the M 18M piece mounted on a tubular section split trail anti-tank carriage from the PAK 40. The large spoked wheels were of light alloy. The weapon is issued to the Austrian reserve forces.

M 18/49: This derivative of the M 18/40 was made in Czechoslovakia. The original spoked solid wheel types have been replaced. A double baffle muzzle brake is fitted.

The M 18M is the heaviest version of the M 18 family of German 105 mm howitzers. Note the split trail and large spades, hinged for ease of deployment.

Employment:

M 18	Yugoslavia	M 18/40	Austria
M 18M	Yugoslavia		Argentina
M 18/39	Norway		Chile
	Sweden		Portugal
		M 18/49	Czechoslovakia

105 mm field howitzer (L)

Federal Republic of Germany

Calibre	105 mm
Barrel length	35·5 calibres
Muzzle brake	Single baffle
Trail type	Split
Weight	2,500 kg
Ammunition type	Semi-fixed
Charges	7
Ammunition options	HE (14·9)
	HEAT
	Smoke WP
	Chemical
	Illuminating
	Carrier
	Blank
Rate of fire	8 rds/min
Muzzle velocity	640 m/sec
Maximum range	14,500 m
Elevation limits	−5° + 65°
Traverse limits	45·5°
Detachment	8

This is a much modified American M 101 A1 produced by Rheinmetall Gmbh for the Bundeswehr.

The barrel is new and longer by 13½ calibres. A simple single baffle muzzle brake is fitted. The effect, using the same M 1 ammunition, is to increase muzzle velocity to 640 m/sec and range to 14,500 m.

The carriage and general arrangement are unchanged although weight is increased by 280 kg. There are minor modifications to the lighting for peace-time road use, which are to meet local regulations. The split trail is of conventional design. The over and under recoil system is retained.

The disadvantage arising from these modifications is that the gun is unbalanced when travelling. It can be towed for short distances only, and even so care must be taken to avoid grounding the muzzle in undulating terrain. The gun is therefore normally carried in the Faun GT 8 truck. The vehicle is modified by the addition of a simple hydraulic hoist, consisting of two booms mounted either side of the cargo space.

The weapon is used in the general artillery reserve of a corps, but is soon to be phased out of service.

Employment   West Germany

105 mm field howitzer (L). The German adaptation of the American M 101 A1.

105 mm field howitzer

India

A new 105 mm field howitzer is being produced by an Indian ordnance factory. It is described as an interim design and little technical data is available.

It has a light box section split trail. A massive muzzle brake is fitted, and the variable length recoil system is mounted below the barrel. A steeply raked shield is fitted, with provision for direct fire sights. The carriage is remarkably similar to that of the Italian 105 mm pack howitzer.

This picture shows the massive muzzlebrake. The recoiling parts seem new.

Pack howitzer 105/14 model 56

Italy

Calibre	105 mm
Barrel length	14 calibres
Muzzle brake	Multi-baffle
Trail type	Split
Weight	1,290 kg
Ammunition type	Semi-fixed
Charges	7
Ammunition options	HE (14·9 kg)
	HEAT
	Smoke WP
	Chemical
	Illuminating
	Carrier
	Blank
Rate of fire	8 rds/min
Muzzle velocity	416 m/sec
Maximum range	10,575 m
Elevation limits	−5° + 65°
Traverse limits	36°
Detachment	6

This outstandingly successful howitzer has been exported to 23 countries since coming into service in 1957. Its chief virtues are its versatility, lightness and cost effectiveness. The design is a short barrel, split trail howitzer which breaks down to 12 pack loads.

The need to minimize the weight of each component part for pack transport demanded a short barrel of 14 calibres; even so it weighs 122 kg. Although the gun was designed to fire the universally available American M 1 105 mm howitzer ammunition, the length of barrel is insufficient to make full use of its potential range.

The box section trail legs are each made in three lengths which are folded for travelling. The wheel stations have high and low mountings for normal firing or a low silhouette anti-tank configuration. The weapon fires in both high and low angle without preparation. A second elevating hand wheel provides a split function laying facility, normally used for anti-tank shooting.

The pack loads are animal- or man- and air-portable. All these methods (except pack animal) tend to be uneconomical in effort, but provide almost limitless flexibility in deployment over every sort of terrain. Dismantling and reassembling the weapon is quick and simple: the only tool required is a lifting yoke which clamps to the shields for travelling. More usual is deployment of the assembled gun. It flies well beneath a Wessex class helicopter, is air-droppable, air-portable and can be towed conventionally by a Land-Rover type vehicle. For long road journeys it is normally carried portee in a 3-ton truck. Skis can be fitted to the wheels for towing over snow.

A special German version features a redesigned single-baffle muzzle brake to replace the multi-baffle type, and the Spanish use a version which looks similar but is reputedly built under licence in Spain.

Employment:

Argentina	France	Pakistan
Australia	Ghana	Rhodesia
Austria	West Germany	Saudi-Arabia
Bangla Desh	India	Spain
Belgium	Italy	Sri Lanka
Canada	Malaysia	Sudan
Chile	Nigeria	UK
Eire	New Zealand	Zambia

The howitzer, in action after helicopter delivery with the lifting harness still fitted. Note the yoke used in dismantling and reassembling fixed to the shield.

The same—at maximum elevation for high-angle fire.

Light howitzer 105/26

Spain

Calibre	105 mm
Barrel length	26 calibres
Muzzle brake	Double baffle
Trail type	Split
Weight	1,978 kg
Ammunition type	Semi-fixed
Charges	—
Ammunition options	HE (15·27 kg)
	HE (14·9 kg)
	HEAT
	Smoke WP
	Chemical
	Illuminating
	Carrier
	Blank
Rate of fire	4 rds/min (see text)
Muzzle velocity	504 m/sec
Maximum range	11,450 m
Elevation limits	−5° + 45°
Traverse limits	50°
Detachment	6

Note the simplicity of the trails with folding traversing levers.

The 105/26 is a Spanish weapon of post-war design (1950) which fires American M 1 ammunition as well as its own type of shells. The American round weighs 0·3 kilogrammes less, has a lower muzzle velocity and therefore produces less range.

The monobloc barrel is fitted with a double baffle muzzle brake which is very similar in design to the British 25 pounder. The breech has a horizontal sliding block. The hydropneumatic recoil system is mounted below the barrel. Sighting is conventional, to the left of the barrel; a second elevating hand wheel is fitted to allow split function laying.

The carriage is a conventional split box section trail running on large section tyres. A hand spike is built in to each trail leg. It has no shield.

The sustained rate of fire is quoted as 4 rounds/minute, but this can be doubled for short periods to give a burst of fire effect.

Employment Spain

---

105 mm light field howitzer M/40

Sweden

Calibre	105 mm
Barrel length	22 calibres
Muzzle brake	Nil
Trail type	Split
Weight	1,850 kg
Ammunition type	Separate
Charges	8
Ammunition options	HE M/60 (14·5 kg)
	HE M/34 (15·5 kg)
Rate of fire	10 rds/min
Muzzle velocity	620 m/sec
Maximum range	14,300 m (M/60)
Elevation limits	−5° + 45°
Traverse limits	50°
Detachment	6

105 mm M 40 howitzer.

The M/40 is a very elderly equipment dating from before World War II. It boasts a good rate of fire (10 rounds/minute), and an equally good range for its age (14,300 m).

The barrel is short and without a muzzle brake. The breech is a horizontal sliding wedge type. Two types of projectile are available, the M 34 being heavier is not to be used with Charge 8; its range is therefore shorter by 1,300 m. The recoil system is mounted below the barrel.

The sighting gear is very simple, and probably detracts from the accuracy of the gun by modern standards.

The carriage is a rivetted box section split trail type with large spades, and built-in hand spikes. The large diameter spoked wheels have iron rims. A shield is fitted.

The M/40 has been replaced by the 4140 and is now used only in reserve.

Employment Sweden

105 mm light field howitzer 4140
Sweden

Calibre	105 mm
Barrel length	28 calibres
Muzzle brake	Single baffle
Trail type	Cruciform
Weight	2,800 kg
Ammunition type	Semi-fixed
Charges	8
Ammunition options	HE (15·5 kg)
Rate of fire	8 rds/min (see text)
Muzzle velocity	607 m/sec
Maximum range	14,600 m
Elevation limits	−5° + 65°
Traverse limits	360°
Detachment	6

Something of the Bofors' expertise with the design of air defence guns has been incorporated into the design of this gun. The carriage is designed for all round traverse, and features four legs in a 'quadruple span'.

The barrel tapers to a stubby single baffle muzzle brake. The recoil system, mounted below it extends nearly to the muzzle. The weight of the recoil system being well forward and the rearward position of the trunnions makes it necessary to fit equilibrators which run forward from a rear mounting over the saddle.

A very high burst-rate of fire of 25 rounds/minute is possible, partly because semi-fixed ammunition needs only a single action to load, and partly because of the excellent access to the breech. The sustained rate of fire is eight rounds/minute.

In action, the road wheels remain fixed to the carriage, but are raised to clear the trail legs: the arrangement is similar to the Russian 122 mm D 30. High angle fire up to 65° is possible; the height of the trunnions, which are well to the rear of the barrel, prevents any loss of elevation when the barrel is in line with a leg. Each leg is flattened into a small pad at its end, and accepts a vertical ground spike, which acts as a spade. Vertical firing loads are passed to a firing jack beneath the centre of the cruciform. As might be expected, this arrangement makes it a heavy gun for its calibre. A shaped shield is fitted behind the wheels.

The Swiss refer to this weapon as the 105 mm gun 35; it is also known as the Bofors L/28.

Employment   Sweden
Switzerland

Swedish 105 mm 4140 on the move.

105 mm gun M 35

Switzerland

Calibre	105 mm
Barrel length	42 calibres
Muzzle brake	Single baffle
Trail type	Split
Weight	3,840 kg
Ammunition type	—
Charges	—
Ammunition options	HE (15·3 kg)
Rate of fire	5 rds/min
Muzzle velocity	800 m/sec
Maximum range	21,000 m
Elevation limits	−3° + 45°
Traverse limits	60°
Detachment	6

Like the M 46 howitzer, the M 35 is a Bofors design made under licence in Switzerland. It is very elderly and still has the original metal spoke, solid tyre wheels.

The long tapered barrel is mounted over the recoil system. There is a square, upright shield which overlaps the wheels. A semi-cylindrical counter weight merges into the breech ring, which is fitted with a horizontal sliding block. The straight trail legs end in angled hand spikes with spades fitted beneath them.

Performance has been improved by the introduction of a new ammunition. Muzzle velocity is raised to 800 metres/second from 785 metres/second by a bigger charge, and range is improved from 17,500 m to 21,000 m. Stocks of the older ammunition are still being used.

Employment Switzerland

The 105 mm M35 gun in action.

The M 35 in the travelling position—fitted here with solid tyred wheels.

105 mm field howitzer M 46

Switzerland

Calibre	105 mm
Barrel length	22 calibres
Muzzle brake	Multi-baffle
Trail type	Split
Weight	1,850 kg
Ammuntion type	—
Charges	—
Ammunition options	HE (15·15 kg)
Rate of fire	—
Muzzle velocity	490 m/sec
Maximum range	10,000 m
Elevation limits	0° + 65°
Traverse limits	60°
Detachment	6

This gun is of Swedish Bofors design, made under licence in Switzerland up to 1953. It is distinguished by its five baffle muzzle brake and the recoil gear mounted under the barrel—the cradle containing it reaches nearly to

105 mm howitzer M 46.

the muzzle. The straight box section legs are fitted with seats for the layer and the loader. Laying arrangements are to the left of the barrel, behind the curved-top shield.

It was replaced in mechanized divisions by the M 109U, but remains in service with infantry formations.

Employment Switzerland

105 mm light gun

United Kingdom

Calibre	105 mm
Barrel length	317 cm
Muzzle brake	Double baffle
Trail type	Box
Weight	1,768 kg
Ammunition type	Separate
Charges	7
Ammunition options	HE (15 kg)
	Smoke BE and WP (15 kg)
	Coloured smoke (15 kg)
	Illuminating (15 kg)
	HESH
Rate of fire	6 rds/min
Muzzle velocity	708 m/sec
Maximum range	17,500 m
Elevation limits	−5° + 70°
Traverse limits	360° (top traverse 10°)
Detachment	6

The 105 mm light gun is designed to replace the Italian pack howitzer Model 56 with a modern more robust but light air-portable weapon. The requirement for improved range has been met by using Abbot Mk II ammunition. The weapon has been accepted for service, and is now in full production.

The autofrettaged barrel is probably in the order of 30 calibres in length. The vertical sliding block is fitted with an electric firing mechanism. A special barrel which fires American M 1 ammunition is available; it can be installed in two hours, but having a limited range performance will be used for training only. The trunnions

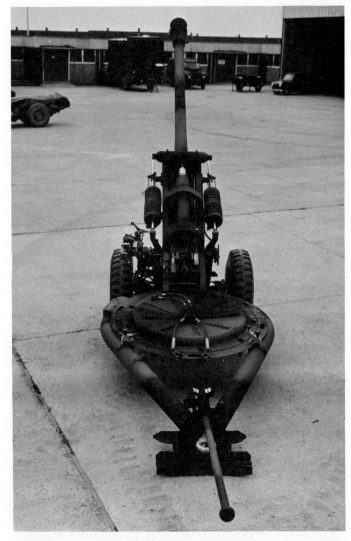

Note the bowed trails and detail of sights and breech.

The 105 mm light gun in its battlefield towing configuration, with the barrel in the firing position. For long-distance travel the piece is rotated and clamped to the trail. The towing vehicle is a 1 tonne Landrover 4 × 4.

105 mm light gun in action.

are set well to the rear of the barrel. Although the centre of gravity of the breech and recoil system is close to them equilibrators are necessary. They are simple exposed coil spring types, and are mounted almost horizontally beside the recoil system. The recoil system is hydro-pneumatic and incorporates a cut-off gear which halves recoil length at full elevation. (1·05 m at 0° elevation, 0·5 m at 70° elevation.) It is mounted under and over the barrel.

The Abbot Mk II ammunition has a 25 per cent more lethality than the American M 1 type. The HE round can be fitted with the L32 percussion fuse, the L27 proximity fuse or the L33 fuse which combines mechanical time and impact detonation. The cannister round is effective from 250 to 500 m. The carrier-type shells are ballistically matched to the HE round. While the special barrel is needed to use M 1 ammunition complete, the M 1 shell only can be fired with a special charge system in the normal barrel.

Both the direct and indirect fire sights are illuminated by 'Trilux' nuclear light sources and the laying system is fully compatible with present and projected British fire control systems.

The box trail of hollow tubular members, and circular platforms are reminiscent of the 25 pounder. In plan view, the trail members have a curved shape. The arrangement of the carriage saves 150 kilogrammes over a split trail design, and allows speedy 360° traverse. Important features of the design are the advanced material used (a new high quality steel), and the construction methods; welds have been placed only in low stress areas and explosive forming is used to shape complex sheet steel members.

Stability is provided by the platform, but a four spade system is available, viz:

1. A large flat sole plate, used with the platform, to allow easy traverse of the trail.
2. A field spade (the sole plate rotated) for use without the platform.
3. A shallow, rock spade.
4. Digger attachment to the rock spade to improve stability in soft ground.

The gun is normally towed with the barrel rotated to the rear to clamp over the towing eye. This compact folded configuration adds to towing stability and is used for air movement, and for air dropping on a medium stress platform. Rotation requires the removal of a road wheel and adds one minute to the into/out-of action time. For battlefield movement an unfolded towing configuration is possible. The complete gun can be lifted by Puma class helicopters: to fly beneath the Wessex, the carriage and piece are separated and reassembled in the field in ten minutes, with the help of one simple tool.

A trailing arm suspension with laminated torsion bars and shock absorbers is used to reduce the stress of cross-country movement. It stays in operation during firing and is used to assist stability. Brakes are of the hydraulic over-run type with a hand brake which can operate on each wheel independently. Light-weight wooden or alluminium skis are under development for over snow travel.

The British light gun is heavier than some of its rivals, but is now a proven and robust design, offering a remarkable performance for its size and weight. The ratio muzzle energy/weight is 640, compared to the Russian D 30 (537), American experimental XM 164 (370) and 25 pounder (280).

Employment   Entering service in United Kingdom

105 mm howitzer M 101 A1

United States of America

Calibre	105 mm
Barrel length	22·5 calibres
Muzzel brake	Nil
Trail type	Split
Weight	2,220 kg
Ammunition type	Semi-fixed
Charges	7
Ammunition options	HE (14·9 kg)
	HEAT
	Smoke WP
	Chemical
	Illuminating
	Carrier
	Blank
Rate of fire	8 rds/min
Muzzle velocity	473 m/sec
Maximum range	11,200 m
Elevation limits	−5° + 66°
Traverse limits	45°
Detachment	8

The M 101 A1 is one of the most successful guns ever produced. Between 1940 and 1953, 10,202 were built and supplied to 46 armies. Development of a weapon known as the M 1 started as early as 1928, but by 1940 only 14 had been made. It is a contemporary of, and rival to, the British 25 pounder, which is lighter by 500 kg, outranges it by 2,000 m, but fires a lighter shell of only 11·34 kg.

The barrel is short, a fact which contributes to the modest range. It has a life of 20,000 EFCs. A horizontal sliding breech block is used with percussion firing mechanism. The hydro-pneumatic recoil system, mounted over and under the barrel, is a constant recoil length type.

The M 1 ammunition system was designed for this gun and has become a standard NATO ammunition usable by a number of more recent equipments, including the Abbot, French light gun, and Italian pack howitzer, model 56. Several HE shells are available (M 1, M 3, M 413 and M 444). The HESH round penetrates 102 mm of armour at a range of 1,500 m. Among experimental shells are a CS gas round (XM 629): Beehive (XM 546), and a new HEAT projectile (XM 622). Two rocket assisted projectiles have been designed (XM 482, XM 548). Various fuses, timed and percussion, were developed. The semi-fixed ammunition design speeds loading and leads to a high rate of sustained fire. The quoted rate can be doubled for short periods.

The layout of the carriage is conventional and simple. The box-section, split-trail legs are straight and carry recoil stresses to built-in spades. The gun fires off its road wheels, above which the elevating mass is mounted at its centre of gravity: there is no balancing gear.

A number of experimental and modified weapons have been produced from the basic design. These are listed below. The M 101 A1 has now been replaced in the United States' Army by the M 102.

M3: A war-time expedient for use in the jungles of South-East Asia. Barrel length was reduced to 15½

105 mm howitzer M 101 A1.

105 mm HM 2. The French adaptation of the American M 101 A1. Note the new muzzle brake.

The 105 mm M 101 A1 howitzer in action on a hill-top fort in Vietnam—barrel at maximum depression.

calibres and the 75 mm field howitzer carriage used. Weight was reduced to 1,134 kg and range to 6,400 m.

M7 (Priest): An SP mounting developed during World War II on the M 3 Grant chassis. It is no longer in service.

XM 124: An SP version featuring 'Major/Minor' wheels: three balloon-tyred wheels are mounted radially around the axle. On level surfaces two wheels in contact with the ground rotate about their own axles; to cross obstacles the whole wheel assembly rotates in a 'walking' motion. Power is provided by a pack mounted, with a driver, on the trail. The trail and motor unit are supported on a dolly wheel. Lockhead Aircraft Service Company carried out the work on an M 101 A1 less shield. Performance of the gun is unchanged.

HM 2: The French used the M 101 A1 fitted with the barrel of the AMX 105/50 SP howitzer. Later, the weapon was modernised by the fitting of the 30 calibre barrel used in the AMX 105-B SP howitzer. Performance for both versions is the same as the SP weapons. A further adaptation of the HM 2 was produced during the development of the French light gun.

105 mm C 1: This is the Canadian version fitted with a new barrel and breech ring. The barrel is of auto-frettaged monobloc construction and made by Sorel Industries of Quebec. Deliveries started in 1955.

105 mm field howitzer (L): This German modification is described in a separate entry.

Employment:

Australia	Greece	Morocco
Austria	West Germany	Netherlands
Argentina	Guatemala	Norway
Bangladesh	Haiti	Pakistan
Belgium	Italy	Pathet Lao
Bolivia	Indonesia	Peru
Brazil	Iran	Phillipines
Cambodia	Israel	Portugal
Canada	Japan	Spain
Chile	Jordan	Taiwan
Columbia	South Korea	Thailand
Denmark	Laos	Turkey
Ethiopia	Liberia	USA
Dominican Republic	Libya	Venezuela
France	Mexico	Vietnam

105 mm howitzer M 102
United States of America

Calibre	105 mm
Barrel length	333 cms
Muzzle brake	Nil
Trail type	Box
Weight	1,470 kg
Ammunition type	Semi-fixed
Charges	7
Ammunition options	HE M 1 (14·9 kg)
	HE XM 482 (12·7 kg)
	HEAT
	Smoke WP
	Chemical
	Illuminating
	Flechettes
Rate of fire	3 rds/min (see text)
Muzzle velocity	—
Maximum range	14,000 m
Elevation limits	−5° + 75°
Traverse limits	360°
Detachment	8

This weapon was conceived to replace the highly successful M 101, and primarily designed for air-transportability. The result is a weapon which is air-portable and airdroppable and weighs only 1,470 kilogrammes: this is at least 1,000 kilogrammes lighter than any previous American guns of the same calibre. Since its introduction to United States Airborne formations in 1965 both French and British light guns have been announced. The former is even lighter, the other outranges it by 3,500 m but at a cost of 300 kilogrammes. Many other 105 mm guns and howitzers (including the Italian Model 56) appear to rival the lightness of these new generation weapons, but none approach their range.

The barrel is 12 per cent longer than that of the M 101 A1, which increases range by 500 m using the same ammunition. A muzzle brake was fitted to early development guns, but it is not used for the production model. A screw-type breech is fitted. The barrel is mounted at its extreme rear and two exposed spring equilibrators are mounted on the base of the saddle.

The hydro-pneumatic recoil system is fitted over and under the barrel. To make best use of the high-angle fire potential, avoiding the need for a recoil pit, the maximum recoil of 1,275 mm is reduced by half at full elevation.

Two ammunition types are used: the M 1 system and a new XM 482 long-range (rocket assisted) round. In addition to the wide variety of M 1 shells, a flechette projectile has been developed. Burst fire of 30 rounds in three minutes is possible.

The M 102 has a deep section aluminium box trail. A circular base plate travels beneath the trail and is lowered to raise the wheels clear of the ground for firing. At the rear of the trail a longitudinal roller fitted with a 'Terra-Tire' replaces the usual spade. The roller allows rapid one-man traverse through 360°. The weapon is only 1·37 m high in action at zero elevation.

Employment   Cambodia
Saudi-Arabia
United States of America
Vietnam

The firing platform cannot be seen in this picture, but the raised road wheel is clear, as is the deep section of the trail members.

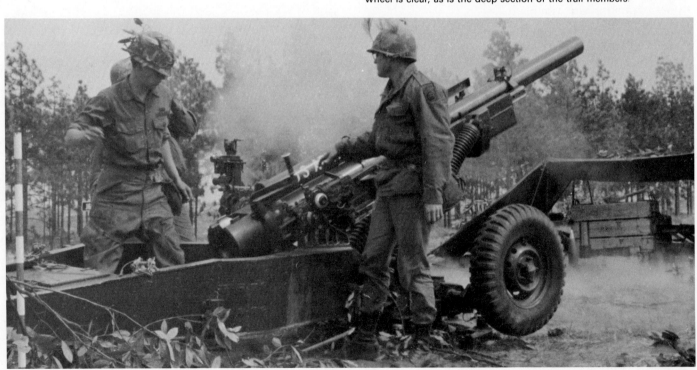

105 mm field howitzer XM 204

United States of America

Calibre	105 mm
Barrel length	—
Muzzle brake	Nil
Trail type	Nil
Weight	1,814 kg
Ammunition type	Separate
Charges	—
Ammunition options	HE
Rate of fire	10 + rds/min
Muzzle velocity	—
Maximum range	14,000 m
Elevation limits	−5° + 75°
Traverse limits	360°
Detachment	—

The experimental 'soft-recoil' 105 mm howitzer. Note radically re-designed carriage.

The XM 204 is an experimental weapon. It is designed to be light yet stable by dispensing with the conventional recoil system for absorbing the shock of recoil, and needs no trail to pass firing stresses into the ground. Design work started in 1962, and the first prototype was produced in 1970.

It embodies the 'soft recoil' system, which works as follows: At the beginning of the firing cycle the recoiling parts of barrel and breech, with a control cylinder, are held by a catch in the extreme recoil position against the pressure of the hydro-pneumatic recuperator. To fire the gun the whole recoiling mass is released, and begins to run forward accelerating as it goes. The run-out velocity is monitored by a sensor, and at a predetermined speed the charge is initiated. The recoil forces are dissipated in checking the forward momentum of the barrel, and repositioning it in its rearward, prefiring position.

Recoil stresses transmitted to the carriage are reduced by 70 per cent. As a result no trail is needed, the gun being mounted on a turntable platform. Up to 30 three-inch spikes secure the gun in all but the softest ground; provision is made for more substantial anchor pins to be used in extreme conditions.

One practical problem is that the triggering of the charge must be very accurately controlled. A consistent fall of shot requires the charge to be initiated at exactly the prescribed barrel velocity: the velocity sensor must be both precise and robust. A variation of only 40 microseconds between the sensor reaction and charge ignition leads to unacceptable inaccuracy at the target.

The velocity sensor is adjusted according to the charge being fired. A buffer is incorporated to prevent damage in the event of a misfire.

The experimental carriage is extended forward from the firing platform to wide roller wheels which assist in traverse. The equipment is towed by its muzzle.

The weight saving brought about by having no trail is small but significant, while the main benefit is in handling the weapon. Access to the breech is excellent and recoil time is half that of conventional guns. A very high rate of fire is therefore possible. The XM 204 uses separate ammunition: logically a production version would use a fixed or semi-fixed type to give the maximum possible rate of fire.

Employment Experimental

Figure VII: Soft-recoil system—
Above: cocked ready for action.
Centre: firing. *Below:* recoiling and recocking.

105 mm howitzer M 56
Yugoslavia

Calibre	105 mm
Barrel length	27·9 calibres
Muzzle brake	Multi-baffle
Trail type	Split
Weight	2,180 kg
Ammunition type	Semi-fixed
Charges	—
Ammunition options	HE (15 kg)
	HEAT
	Smoke
	Illuminating
Rate of fire	6–7 rds/min
Muzzle velocity	570 m/sec
Maximum range	13,000 m
Elevation limits	−12° + 68°
Traverse limits	52°
Detachment	6

This weapon consists of a modified American M 101 A1 barrel made under licence and mounted on a locally designed carriage. The horizontal sliding breech is retained, but range performance is considerably improved to a claimed 13,000 m. Since no other weapon using M 1 ammunition achieves such a range, it can be assumed that a new ammunition type has been developed. The over and under recoil system is retained, but otherwise the appearance is quite unlike the original equipment. A multi-baffle muzzle brake is fitted together with a shaped and sloping shield. The spades are mounted to the trail legs at their centre—not below the legs as is more common. The M 52 is just lighter than the M 101 A1.

Employment   Yugoslavia

122 mm Tampella field gun M 60
Finland

Calibre	122 mm
Barrel length	50 calibres
Muzzle brake	Single baffle
Trail type	Split
Weight	9,500 kg
Ammunition type	—
Charges	—
Ammunition options	HE (25 kg)
Rates of fire	—
Muzzle velocity	950 m/sec
Maximum range	25,000 m
Elevation limits	−5° + 50°
Traverse limits	90°
Detachment	8

This is a very heavy equipment for its calibre, but it does have an excellent range. Principal employment is with armoured brigades, but it is also deployed in the coast defence role. Its general layout is similar to the French 155 mm M 50 howitzer.

The barrel is long, probably in the order of 50 calibres. It has a horizontal sliding breech block and a simple muzzle brake. The trunnions are at the rear of the barrel, which is balanced by equilibrators that are mounted onto a vertically extended saddle. The buffer recuperator is fitted over and under the barrel.

Split function laying is used.

The most unusual feature of this gun is the arrangement of the carriage. The split trail is of very sturdy construction with massive box section legs. At the rear of each leg is a pad, slotted to receive three anchor pins. These are hammered into the ground vertically—a time consuming task which must be very difficult in rocky or frozen terrain. Vertical firing stresses are passed into a firing jack beneath the cradle: The tandem road wheels are lifted clear of the ground in action. The wheels run on axles fixed directly to the trail legs: thus they only come parallel when the legs are clamped together. The legs are hinged well forward, which allows them to open wide enough to permit a top traverse of 90°. Reputedly 360° traverse is possible with 'additional equipment', although the nature of this equipment is not specified. The barrel rotates to clamp over the trail for travelling.

Employment   Finland

122 mm field gun 122/46
Spain

Calibre	122 mm		*Trail type*	Split
Barrel length	—		*Weight*	7,800 kg
Muzzle brake	Double baffle		*Ammunition type*	—

Charges	—
Ammunition options	HE (22·1 kg)
Rate of fire	—
Muzzle velocity	830 m/sec
Maximum range	19,900 m
Elevation limits	−4° + 65°
Traverse limits	57°
Detachment	8

Nothing is known about this equipment except the data in the table above. It does not seem to be related to any other weapon of this calibre, but the choice of calibre may well have been influenced by the availability of ammunition.

Employment   Spain (Reserve Army only)

122 mm field gun M 1937 (A 19)

Union of Soviet Socialist Republics

Calibre	122 mm
Barrel length	46 calibres
Muzzle brake	Nil
Trail type	Split
Weight	7,117 kg
Ammunition type	Separate
Charges	—
Ammunition options	HE (25·5 kg)
	APHE (25 kg)
	Smoke (25·7 kg)
Rate of fire	5–6 rds/min
Muzzle velocity	800 m/sec
Maximum range	20,800 m
Elevation limits	−2° + 65°
Traverse limits	58°
Detachment	9

The weapon was developed in time for World War II and is a contemporary of the M 1937 152 mm gun. The carriage and general layout are the same for both equipments. It has been replaced in Russian service. In Yugoslavia it is deployed only as a coastal gun.

No muzzle brake is fitted to the very long (46 calibre) barrel, which retracts for travelling. The breech is screw type. The hydraulic buffer and hydro-pneumatic recuperator are mounted below the barrel.

The APHE round is 0·5 kilogrammes lighter than the HE shell, but achieves the same muzzle velocity. It is effective to 900 m and penetrates 190 mm of armour.

The split trail is made up of box section legs of rivetted construction. Each leg carries a pad through which two anchor pins are hammered into the ground to act as spades. Two equilibrators are mounted vertically in front of the shield, and give a distinctive appearance similar to the British 5·5 inch gun.

Double wheels are fitted. These were originally spoked and have been replaced by modern disc-tyred wheels. Two wheels of smaller diameter are used for the limber, which is fitted beneath the trail for towing.

There is also an armoured tracked variant—the JSU-122 assault gun.

Employment:

Albania	Guinea	Spain
Algeria	Hungary	Syria
Bulgaria	Indonesia	Tanzania
Cambodia	North Korea	Vietnam
China	Poland	North Yemen
Cuba	Rumania	South Yemen
Egypt	Somalia	Zaire

122 mm field gun M 1937.

122 mm field howitzer M 1938 (M 30)

Union of Soviet Socialist Republics

Calibre	122 mm
Barrel length	22·7 calibres
Muzzle brake	Nil
Trail type	Split
Weight	2,500 kg
Ammunition type	separate
Charges	9
Ammunition options	HE (21·8 kg)
	HEAT (14·1 kg)
	Smoke (22·4 kg)
	Illuminating (21 kg)
	Chemical
Rate of fire	5–6 rds/min
Muzzle velocity	515 m/sec
Maximum range	11,800 m
Elevation limits	$-3° + 63\frac{1}{2}°$
Traverse limits	49°
Detachment	8

This equipment dates from World War II and is still in service in the Soviet Army, despite the appearance of the new D 30 and D 74 122 mm weapons. It was built in great numbers and widely exported. It was the standard organic 122 mm weapon of the Russian Divisional and Army Group Artillery.

No muzzle brake is fitted to the short barrel. The unusual combination of screw type breech and cased charge is used. The recoil system is mounted over and under the barrel. Firing is by a mechanical lock activated by a lanyard.

The HEAT round penetrates 200 mm of armour, but anti-tank range is limited to 630 m. This round weighs only 14·1 kilogrammes against 21·8 kilogrammes for the HE shell.

The split trail is also used for the 152 mm M 43. The box section legs are of rivetted construction. This particular design limits top traverse more than later types. The spades fold for travelling as do the permanently fitted hand spikes. The gun can be fired with the trail legs closed in their travelling position, but only 1½° of traverse is possible. The large disc wheels with narrow tyres are replaced by smaller wheels in the East German Army, and by spoked wheels in Bulgaria. The steeply arched shield has a folding centre section.

A recent development is the use of the new M 1970 APC as a towing vehicle. This comes at a time when the Soviet Army is producing its first SP guns and reflects a growing awareness of the need for troop protection.

There is a Chinese built version—'Type 54'.

Employment:

Albania	Finland	North Korea
Algeria	German Peoples'	Poland
Bulgaria	Republic	Rumania
China	Hungary	USSR
Cuba	Iraq	Vietnam
Czechoslovakia	Lebanon	Yugoslavia
Egypt	Libya	

122 mm field howitzer M 1938 (M 30).

122 mm field howitzer M 1955 (D 74)

Union of Soviet Socialist Republics

Calibre	122 mm
Barrel length	47 calibres
Muzzle brake	Double baffle
Trail type	Split
Weight	5,500 kg
Ammunition type	Separate
Charges	—
Ammunition options	HE (25·5 kg)
	APHE (25 kg)
Rate of fire	6–7 rds/min
Muzzle velocity	900 m/sec (HE)
	950 m/sec (APHE)
Maximum range	23,900 m
Elevation limits	−2° + 50°
Traverse limits	60°
Detachment	9

The D 74 replaced the 122 mm A 19 in the Soviet Army, but is in turn older than the D 30. It is used for the general support of infantry and in mechanised divisions.

The long barrel is mounted low on its carriage. The vertical sliding wedge type breech is semi-automatic. The buffer/recuperator is mounted above the barrel, well to the rear so that it hardly projects beyond the shield: the effect must be to balance the barrel, which is long and mounted well to the rear.

The variable charge is fired from a cartridge case which is separately loaded. The shell seems to be that used for the A 19: the usual shell options for Soviet 122 mm equipments are available. The APHE round is effective to 1,200 m: it weighs less than the HE round and gives a muzzle velocity of 950 m/sec. It penetrates 230 mm of armour at a range of 1,000 m.

The split trail with fixed spades is of conventional design, and is very similar to that of the 152 mm D 20. Each trail leg is fitted with a castor wheel to assist in deployment and man handling. Built-in handles run forward from these wheel mounts. In action a firing jack lets down between the wheels forward of the shield and absorbs vertical firing stresses. It is a heavy gun, and the handling provisions and 9 man detachment suggest it may be difficult to deploy and operate.

The wavy-topped shield is a recognition feature. The low silhouette and effective APHE round give the weapon a useful secondary role as an anti-tank gun.

Several tractors are used, notably the AT-S, AT-L and URAL 375 (6 × 6).

Employment:

Bulgaria	German Peoples'	Poland
China	Republic	Rumania
Cuba	Hungary	USSR
Egypt	Nigeria	Vietnam

122 mm field howitzer M 1955 (D 74).

122 mm howitzer D 30

Union of Soviet Socialist Republics

Calibre	122 mm
Barrel length	35·5 calibres
Muzzle brake	Multi-baffle
Trail type	Tri-legged
Weight	3,150 kg
Ammunition type	Separate
Charges	2
Ammunition options	HE (21·8 kg)
	HEAT (14·1 kg)
	Smoke
	Illuminating
Rate of fire	7–8 rds/min
Muzzle velocity	690 m/sec (HE)
	740 m/sec (HEAT)
Maximum range	15,300 m
Elevation limits	−7° + 70°
Traverse limits	360°
Detachment	8

The D 30 first entered service in 1967.

The barrel is longer than previous models, a fact which is partly responsible for the improved performance. The breech block is a semi-automatic vertically sliding type. The recoil system is mounted under a bulky cover over the barrel.

Only two charges are used: they are contained in large cartridge cases, and their size is reflected in the high muzzle velocity. While the shell weights and options suggest that they derive from the M 30 the HEAT round is certainly new. It is non-rotating, fin stabilized and penetrates 460 mm of armour at 1,000 m. Muzzle velocity for this round is 740 m/sec. The gun was used extensively in the anti-tank role during the Yom Kippur War—and to good effect.

The most interesting feature of the design is its three legged trail which gives 360° traverse. For travelling, the trail legs fold beneath the barrel (by which the gun is towed). For firing, the legs deploy at 120° intervals and the wheels are jacked up high enough to clear the legs when the barrel rotates about its centre pivot. It is doubtful if full elevation is possible when the breech is immediately over a trail-leg. Pads at the end of each leg accept perforated anchor pins which act as spades. A tiny shield is fitted between the wheels.

Employment

Cuba	German Peoples'	Poland
Czechoslovakia	Republic	Syria
Egypt	Hungary	USSR
Finland	Nigeria	

A battery of 122 mm D 30s deployed for direct fire. Note Y-form trail permitting all-round traverse.

130 mm field gun M 1946

Union of Soviet Socialist Republics

Calibre	130 mm
Barrel length	55 calibres
Muzzle brake	Pepper-pot
Trail type	Split
Weight	8,450 kg
Ammunition type	Separate
Charges	—
Ammunition options	HE (33·4 kg)
	APHE (33·4 kg)
Rate of fire	6–7 rds/min
Muzzle velocity	930 m/sec
Maximum range	27,000 m
Elevation limits	$-2\frac{1}{2}° + 45°$
Traverse limits	50°
Detachment	9

The M 1946 is a versatile equipment with a naval background and formidable anti-tank capability. It was developed from the M 1936 naval gun and replaced the 122 mm A 19 in the Soviet Army.

The barrel is over 7 m long (7·6 m including the pepper-pot muzzle brake). Muzzle velocity is 930 m/sec and results in the remarkable range of 27,000 m. Great claims are made for the accuracy of the gun at long ranges. The breech is of the horizontal sliding wedge-type.

The recoil system is mounted over and under the barrel. There is a distinctive collar support for the fixed end of the recuperator at the front of the cradle, well in front of the shield.

Ammunition is of the separate type, the variable charge being fitted in a conventional cartridge case. The APHE round penetrates 250 mm of armour at 1,000 m.

The sturdy deep box section split trail is mounted on two road wheels. The removable spades travel on top of the trail legs. A limber with two small disc wheels supports the trail for travelling. The barrel is retracted for travelling, and the breech sits between the trail legs not over them. A chain and pulley system is mounted on the trail, to retract the barrel. The small shield is not always fitted.

The range and shell size make this an ideal counter-battery weapon. During the Yom Kippur War it was used extensively in this role by the Egyptian Army. An automated command post with computer fire control equipment was linked to a ground radar system. This system, developed by the Russians, uses SNAR-2 X-Band fire control radar which has a range of 9,000 m. Small Yawn and Porktrough radars are also used.

The gun is built 'under licence' in China and it is this version which has been supplied to Pakistan, and India. There is also a later, 1954 model.

Employment:

Bulgaria	North Korea	Pakistan
China	India	Poland
Cuba	Iran	Syria
Egypt	Iraq	USSR
Finland	Israel	Vietnam
German Peoples'	Mongolia	Yugoslavia
Republic	Nigeria	

130 mm field gun M 1946.

Same gun, note split trail.

5·5 inch gun

United Kingdom

Calibre	140 mm
Barrel length	417 cm
Muzzle brake	Nil
Trail type	Split
Weight	5,850 kg
Ammunition type	Separate
Charges	4
Ammunition options	HE (36·3 kg)
	Smoke
	Illuminating
Rate of fire	3 rds/min
Muzzle velocity	510 m/sec
Maximum range	16,400 m
Elevation	−5° + 45°
Traverse limits	60°
Detachment	10

The 5·5 inch and 4·5 inch guns came into service in the British Army in 1942 using a common carriage to provide 'medium' artillery support. They were the backbone of the corps and army group artillery. The 4·5 inch has long been obsolete but the 5·5 inch is only now being phased out of service; its unusual calibre militated against its survival, even in a once planned SP form, as no other type of ammunition fitted it. By modern standards it is very heavy, although this did not prevent its successful deployment in unfavourable terrain in South-East Asia.

It can be recognised by its long tapered barrel without a muzzle brake, the locking ring securing the barrel into its jacket (usually polished in the British service) and the two vertical equilibrators which stand up like horns to give the equipment a height of 2·6 m. The breech mechanism is a modified interrupted thread Welin-Asbury screw; it is self-sealing and hinges to the right. Percussion firing is by lanyard tripping a trigger which fires a ballistic tube venting through the mushroom head of the breech block into the chamber.

The hydro-pneumatic recoil system is carried below the barrel. The cradle extends behind the breech to permit a loading tray being placed on it from which the shell is rammed home manually.

A quick release to bring the gun to the loading position is provided, but need only be used for extreme angles of elevation. It operates by disengaging the elevating arc and allowing the barrel to move against the action of the equilibrators.

Laying arrangements are manual and are to the left of the carriage.

Like all British systems of that period, the sight was a rocking bar with a fully calibrating elevation scale mounted on the left of the piece. Direct laying for anti-tank work was through the optical azimuth ('dial') sight set at zero.

Originally two sizes of shell were available—80 pound and 100 pound: the latter is no longer used.

The carriage consists of a heavy box section split trail with removable spades. It has two large diameter wheels with balloon tyres.

The equipment can be towed by a variety of heavy artillery tractors, the latest being the Leyland 6 × 6 FV 1103.

Employment:

Australia	Malaysia	Portugal
Burma	New Zealand	South Africa
India	Oman	United Kingdom
Iraq	Pakistan	

The 5·5 inch gun (originally 'gun-how') in action. Note vertical 'horns', in fact balancing springs for long barrel, quadrant shaped calibrating sight, loading tray with shell and bagged charges, and rammer resting on trail.

152 mm howitzer M 18/46

Czechoslovakia

Calibre	152 mm
Barrel length	487·5 cm
Muzzle brake	Double baffle
Trail type	Split
Weight	5,512 kg
Ammunition type	Separate
Charges	—
Ammunition options	HE (40 kg)
	APHE (51·1 kg)
Rate of fire	4 rds/min
Muzzle velocity	508 m/sec (HE)
	432 m/sec (APHE)
Maximum range	12,400 m
Elevation limits	0° + 45°
Traverse limits	60°
Detachment	7

This is a rebuilt German gun—the FH 18 Medium Howitzer. At the end of World War II, large numbers of these 150 mm guns were captured in Czechoslovakia, and were rebored to accept standard Russian 152 mm ammunition. The muzzle brake was also modified and a new shield fitted. The original horizontal sliding breech

Note shield, unusual in so big a gun.

block, and hydro-pneumatic recoil system (mounted over and under the barrel) are retained.

The AP round is considerably heavier than the standard HE shell, weighing 51·1 kilogrammes. It has a muzzle velocity of 432 metres/second and penetrates 82 mm of armour at 1,000 m.

The split trail is conventional, but the solid-tyre wheels give it an elderly appearance. It is now relegated to reserve formations.

Employment   Czechoslovakia

---

152 mm howitzer M 1937 (ML 20)

Union of Soviet Socialist Republics

Calibre	152 mm
Barrel length	32 calibres
Muzzle brake	Multi-baffle
Trail type	Split
Weight	7,930 kg
Ammunition type	Separate
Charges	—
Ammunition options	HE (43·6 kg)
	APHE (48·8 kg)
Rate of fire	4 rds/min
Muzzle velocity	655 m/sec
Maximum range	17,300 m
Elevation limits	−2° + 65°
Traverse limits	58°
Detachment	10

The ML 20 has been superseded in Russian service by the D 20 and has been relegated to the reserve army. It is still widely used outside Russia, and played a prominent part in the Yom Kippur War.

The long barrel gives this elderly equipment the best range of all the Soviet 152 mm weapons. The barrel is made to look longer still by the long multi-baffle muzzle brake. The square breech ring is fitted with a screw type

block. The buffer and recuperator are mounted below the barrel.

The ML 20 has the high muzzle velocity of a gun, but fires the characteristic heavy shell of a howitzer. The HE round is heavier than other Soviet 152 mm shells. The APHE round weighs more (48·8 kilogrammes) and penetrates 124 mm of armour at 1,000 m: this round is common to the D 20. The variable charge is fired from a brass cartridge case.

The 152 mm barrel is mounted on the M 1937 (A 19) split trail carriage. Twin road wheels of large diameter on a single axle are supplemented by a limber with smaller wheels beneath the trail. The rivetted box section trail legs are slotted to accept anchor pins which are hammered into the ground. The large vertical equilibrators are mounted in front of the shield, and recall the British 5·5 inch gun. The barrel retracts for towing.

Employment	Albania	Czechoslovakia	Poland
	Algeria	Egypt	Syria
	Bulgaria	Hungary	USSR
	China	North Korea	Vietnam
	Cuba	Mongolia	Yugoslavia

152 mm howitzer M 1943 (D 1)

Union of Soviet Socialist Republics

Calibre	152 mm
Barrel length	25 calibres
Muzzle brake	Double baffle
Trail type	Split
Weight	3,600 kg
Ammunition type	Separate
Charges	—
Ammunition options	HE (39·9 kg)
	Semi-AP (51·1 kg)
Rate of fire	3–4 rds/min
Muzzle velocity	508 m/sec (HE)
	432 m/sec (Semi-AP)
Maximum range	12,400 m
Elevation limits	−3° + 63·5°
Traverse limits	35°
Detachment	7

152 mm field howitzer M 1943 (D 1)

This elderly weapon shares a carriage with the 122 mm M 30 howitzer.

The barrel, fitted with a muzzle brake, is from the M 10, and the screw type breech in its square section breech ring is retained: it is cartridge obturated. The hydraulic buffer and hydro-pneumatic recuperator are mounted under the barrel.

The semi-AP round is more than eleven kilogrammes heavier than the HE shell, and has a much lower muzzle velocity: armour penetration is 82 mm at 1,000 m.

The slim box section trail legs have folding spades and lifting handles. It is not clear if this weapon can be fired without splitting the trail like the M 30 (which uses the same carriage). The road wheels are large diameter metal discs. The shield is steeply raked to the rear. Like other Soviet howitzers the D 1 fires at high angle without preparation.

The equipment is noticeably lighter than other guns of similar calibre—a fact reflected in its modest range. It has been phased out of service with the Soviet Army.

Employment	Albania	East Germany	Syria
	China	Hungary	Vietnam
	Egypt	Poland	

152 mm howitzer M 1955 (D 20)

Union of Soviet Socialist Republics

Calibre	152 mm
Barrel length	37 calibres
Muzzle brake	Double baffle
Trail type	Split
Weight	5,650 kg
Ammunition type	Separate
Charges	—
Ammunition options	HE (43·6 kg)
	APHE (48·8 kg)
	Chemical
Rate of fire	4 rds/min
Muzzle velocity	655 m/sec (HE)
	600 m/sec (APHE)
Maximum range	17,300 m
Elevation limits	−5° + 63°
Traverse limits	90°
Detachment	8

The D 20 152 mm howitzer is mounted on the same carriage as the D 74 122 mm gun. The D 20 barrel is shorter and thicker than the D 74 but is fitted with a similar muzzle brake. The breech block is of the semi-automatic vertical sliding wedge type. The breech is cartridge obturated. The recoil system is mounted above the barrel and projects beyond the shield.

The APHE round is 5·2 kilogrammes heavier than the HE shell and gives a muzzle velocity of 600 m/sec. It penetrates 124 mm of armour at 1,000 m.

The carriage is of box section split trail design with two road wheels. Two castor wheels, which fold over the legs for travelling, are used to help split the trail, and in conjunction with a firing jack beneath the saddle give easy 360° traverse. The jack folds forward to travel clamped beneath the barrel and has an integral lifting device. A spade is permanently fitted to each trail leg, folding up for travelling. In common with other Soviet guns the shield has an irregularly shaped top, is mounted over the wheel axles and overlaps the wheels. A sliding centre section accommodates elevation of the barrel.

A variety of tractors are used including the AT-L, AT-S and URAL 365.

A battalion of three four-gun batteries is organic to Soviet motor rifle divisions.

Employment:

Czechoslovakia	India	USSR
East Germany	Poland	Vietnam
Hungary	Rumania	

152 mm field howitzer M 1955 (D 20)

152 mm howitzer M 1938 (M 10)

Union of Soviet Socialist Republics

Calibre	152 mm
Barrel length	25 calibres
Muzzle brake	Nil
Trail type	Split
Weight	4,150 kg
Ammunition type	Separate
Charges	—
Ammunition options	HE (39·9 kg)
	Semi-AP (51·1 kg)
Rate of fire	4 rds/min
Muzzle velocity	508 m/sec (HE)
	432 m/sec (Semi-AP)
Maximum range	12,400 m
Elevation limits	−1° + 68°
Traverse limits	50°
Detachment	7

This is the oldest Russian 152 mm weapon still in service—but only with Warsaw Pact country reserve formations. Like the D 1 and D 10, it shares a carriage with a smaller weapon, in this case the obsolete M 1940 (M 60) 107 mm gun. The equipment was developed before World War II and the barrel, with a new muzzle brake was fitted to the M 1938 (M 30) carriage to become the M 1943 (D 1).

It has screw breech mechanism, cartridge obturated. The hydraulic buffer and hydro-pneumatic recuperator are fitted below the barrel. Spades are permanently fitted to the box section trail legs, but fold up for travelling. Double wheels are fitted to a single axle and a limber is provided. The barrel retracts for travelling.

Ammunition and performance are the same as the D 1.

Employment Warsaw Pact (Reserve Formations)
Finland

152 mm howitzer M 1938 (M 10) in travelling position.

155 mm howitzer

Finland

Calibre	155 mm
Barrel length	33 calibres
Muzzle brake	Single baffle
Trail type	Split
Weight	9,500 kg
Ammunition type	Separate
Charges	—
Ammunition options	HE (43·7 kg)
Rate of fire	—
Muzzle velocity	725 m/sec
Range	20,000 m
Elevation limits	−3° + 52°
Traverse limits	90°
Detachment	10

In action.

This weapon looks very like the Tampella 122 mm M 60. It is made under licence in Israel by SOLTAM, and is known as the M 68. The ordnance is fitted to the Israeli L 33 SP weapon. Tampella have perfected the technique of chrome plating the interior of the barrel in order to resist wear (both mechanical and chemical). When wear does occur, the barrel can be re-plated to restore its original performance

Employment Finland
Israel

In travelling position.

155 mm howitzer M 50

France

Calibre	155 mm
Barrel length	23 calibres
Muzzle brake	Multi-baffle
Trail type	Split
Weight	8,200 kg
Ammunition	Separate
Charges	8
Ammunition options	HE (43·75 kg)
	Smoke WP and BE
	Illuminating
Rate of fire	4 rds/min
Muzzle velocity	647 m/sec
Maximum range	17,750 m
Elevation limits	−4° + 69°
Traverse limits	80°
Detachment	11

This equipment is also made under licence in Sweden where it is known as the 'F' field howitzer.

The barrel carries a screw type breech block with self sealing obturation for the bag charges. The multi-baffle muzzle brake is very slim and appears at first to be part of the barrel. The cradle extends rear-wards to form a rest for the loading tray. Nearly horizontal equilibrators run from a massive collar over the trunnions to the forward end of the cradle. The variable length of the recoil system is mounted in the cradle below the barrel.

The gun fires the full range of French 155 mm ammunition (type 56 and TA 68), and other NATO types. The illuminating round is American. A rocket assisted projectile is under development and will increase the range to 35,300 m. Two types of propellant are used in the charge system: charges one to six are fast burning and charges five to eight slow burning.

Provision is made for split function laying, but normally one layer to the left of the barrel forms all the laying functions.

The split trail carriage is an interesting design. It has spades in the form of plates through which anchor pins are hammered into the ground: this arrangement is doubtless secure but must depend on the terrain for ease of deployment. The plates are removed to the top of the trail for travelling. The tandem road wheels are fixed directly to the trail legs so that they only come parallel for travelling when the trail legs are closed. This layout allows a wide spread of the trail to give a good top traverse—in this case 80°. Elevation is 60° is equally generous, and high angle fire is made possible without preparation by a recoil cut off and a firing jack beneath the cradle to absorb vertical firing stresses.

This equipment is employed in the organic artillery regiments of French mechanised brigades and is to be replaced in the fullness of time by the GCT 155 mm SP.

The weapon has been made under licence in Sweden. Local modifications were made to the trail to speed deployment and increase top traverse to 82°. The only noticeable difference to the appearance of the Swedish gun is the fitting of castor wheels to the trail legs.

Employment	France
	Israel
	Sweden

155 mm M 50 howitzer showing clearly how the wheels swing with the trail legs.

155 mm howitzer Model 'F'

Sweden

Calibre	155 mm
Barrel length	23 calibres
Muzzle brake	Multi baffle
Trail type	Split
Weight	9,000 kg
Ammunition type	Separate
Charges	8
Ammunition options	HE (43 kg)
Rate of fire	4 rds/min
MV	650 m/sec
Range	17,600 m
Elevation limits	−4° +69°
Traverse limits	80°
Detachment	9

155 mm howitzer Model 'F'.

Sweden makes this version of the French 155 mm M 1950 under licence. It is a heavy gun for its calibre and has a complicated system of hydraulics. The heavy spades on the split trails cause it to be slow into and out of action. Israel makes the same gun on a Sherman chassis.

Employment   Sweden

---

155 mm howitzer FH 70

Tri-national (Federal Republic of Germany, Italy, United Kingdom)

Calibre	155 mm
Barrel length	39 calibres
Muzzle brake	Double baffle
Trail type	Split
Weight	8,800 kg
Ammunition type	Separate
Charges	8
Ammunition options	HE (43·5 kg)
	Smoke BE
	Illuminating
Rate of fire	6 rds/min
Muzzle velocity	827 m/sec
Maximum range	24,000 m
Elevation limits	−5° + 70°
Traverse limits	56°
Detachment	10

FH 70 is a joint Italian-German-United Kingdom project. British requirements to replace the 5·5 inch gun, and a German plan to replace its American M 114A1s were reinforced by NATO Basic Military Requirement 39, written in 1963. This stated the need for a close support weapon to be available in towed and SP versions. Germany and Britain carried out joint design studies, and found increasingly similar requirements for a weapon of this kind. By 1970 a towed prototype had

F 470 ready for firing. Note the forward extension of the carriage to carry the APU and the dolly wheels folded into the crook of the trail legs.

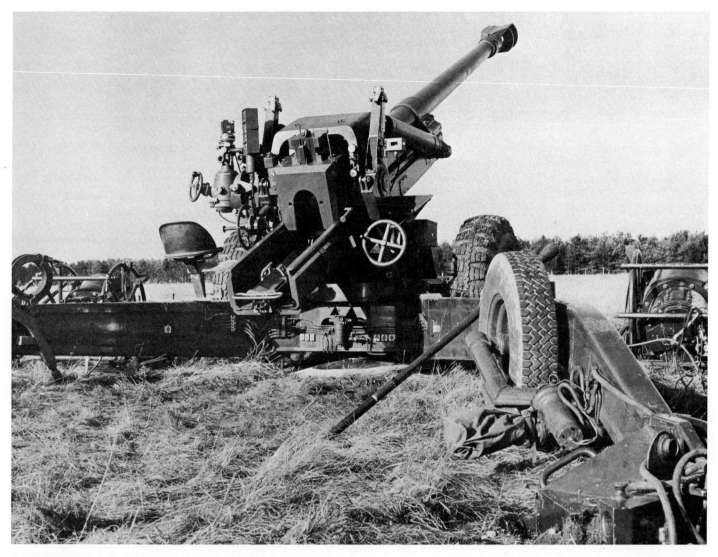

Note digital display unit to right of dial sight and loading tray
positioned below the breech.

started firing trials and Italy joined the project as the
third partner. The weapon is scheduled to enter service
in 1979.

The breakdown of national responsibilities is:

Germany: The elevating mass
Auxiliary Propulsion Unit (APU)
Sights
Projectiles (less HE)

United Kingdom: Coordinating authority
The carriage
HE projectile
Propellant system

Italy: Buffer recuperator and cradle
Elevating gear
Production assistance for HE shells
and some charges

The barrel, of monobloc construction from high yield
steel, is autofrettaged at the chamber end. The vertical
sliding breech block opens upwards and is closely
related to the one fitted to the M 109 G SP howitzer. A
ring obturator seals the breech. An automatic ignition
tube loader is fitted in the breech block and holds 12

tubes. The muzzle brake is claimed to be 32 per cent
efficient.

The recoil system is conventionally under the
barrel. Maximum recoil is 1,500 mm: a cut-off gear
reduces it at high angles of elevation. The cradle is
extended upwards to form the rear mountings for the
equilibrators.

Chamber and breech design allow the gun to fire all
NATO standard ammunitions, but the barrel was
designed around its own high performance ammunition.

The thin wall HE shell is claimed to have a better
lethality than the American M 107 projectile. Its fuze
(P/PD) has been developed to work with a wide range
of calibres. A carrier shell provides base ejection smoke
and illuminating rounds. Initially a conventional (but
new) shell will range to 24,000 m, but rocket assisted
(American M 549) projectiles are being developed to
increase the range to 30,000 m. The eight charges are
divided into three cartridges: one and two, three to
seven, and eight.

Three rates of fire are quoted: a burst rate of three
rounds in 15 seconds, an initial engagement rate of six
rounds/minute, sustained fire at two rounds/minute.

FH 70 being moved by APU. The driver controls the gun with conventional foot pedals, and steering is by tiller.

Loading is not automatic but 'assisted': during run-out a shell is presented to the breech ready for manual ramming.

The sighting system, which is mounted on the left hand side of the equipment, consists of a dial sight and an anti-tank direct fire telescope. The sight uses the coded disc system of measuring horizontal and vertical angles and this data is transmitted electronically to a data display unit mounted on the equipment. The scales of the sight will be illuminated by nuclear light sources.

The weapon has a split trail, and fires off a turntable sole plate with the wheels raised clear off the ground. A detachable APU provides limited SP mobility. The carriage is extended forward off the wheels to carry a 1,700 cc Volkswagen engine which drives the main wheels. The mechanical couplings are disengaged for conventional towing. Steering is by the trail leg dolly

wheels, which are also used to open and close the trail legs on deployment. All other deployment handling is power-assisted. When the APU is detached, power is provided by a hand pump. The main wheels have trailing arm suspension. The suspension's hydro-pneumatic dampers are also used to raise the wheels and thus lower the gun onto its sole plate for firing. The barrel is turned to the rear and clamped over the trail legs for travelling, both when towed and self propelled.

Each country is to produce its own tractor—in all cases a 6 × 6 vehicle.

wheels. The mechanical couplings are disengaged for conventional towing. Steering is by the trail leg dolly

Employment

User trials for—Italy

Federal Republic of Germany

United Kingdom

FH 77 howitzer

Sweden

Calibre	155 mm
Barrel length	—
Muzzle brake	Pepper pot
Trail type	Split
Weight	11,000 kg
Ammunition type	Fixed
Charges	—
Ammunition options	HE (43 kg)
	Smoke
	Illuminating
	Practice
Rate of fire	15 rds/min
Muzzle velocity	—
Maximum range	22,000 m
Elevation limits	−3° + 50°
Traverse limits	60°
Detachment	9

The Swedish terrain and climate demand a high cross-country performance from all equipments. The cost of developing an SP successor to the Bofors L/50 was found to be excessive and the FH 77, towed by with an auxiliary power unit (APU), has been designed by AB Bofors.

The barrel of this howitzer is comparable in length to that of the FH 70, but the range is 2,000 m less.

An extremely high rate of burst fire—equivalent to 18 rounds/minute is achieved by an automated loading system. It is unusual for a towed weapon to be equipped in this way; automation is made possible by the Auxiliary Propulsion Unit (APU). The advantages of a high rate of fire must be set against the great weight of the gun. The loading system consists of an hydraulic hoist which presents the shell to the breech, and power ramming.

The effectiveness of this weight of fire is increased by the target effect of the ammunition: the HE round is filled with Hexotol, which is more powerful than TNT or Amatol, and a special steel is used for optimum fragmentation. A new 'plastic' training round has been developed. It is believed that experiments have been carried out with liquid propellants.

During trials in 1974, three sighting systems were tested: two are mechanical and one 'automated electronic'. It is not known which has been accepted for service.

The split trail is conventional in layout. The APU is used to provide hydraulic power. The unit is the Volvo B20B, and is built into the carriage between the wheels. It has four basic functions:

(a) to propel the weapon on the battlefield. The main wheels are driven through a hydraulic transmission. The driver sits high over the left-hand wheel and the gun moves barrel first, being skid steered by braking either wheel. The dolly wheels at the rear of the trail legs, turn freely on their mountings. Top speed in this configuration is 8 kilometres/hour.

(b) To assist in cross-country mobility when being towed: a special 'coordinator' allows the tractor driver to control the tractive effort at the gun wheels. Maximum towed speed is 70 kilometres/hour.

(c) To provide power for handling functions on deployment and coming out of action. When towed, both coupling and uncoupling from the tractor are power assisted. The trail legs are spread and the spades replaced hydraulically. These deployment functions can also be used to traverse the gun beyond the 60° arc of traverse permitted by the carriage.

(d) To provide power in action for loading, and laying.

Employment Trials only, in Sweden

155 mm field howitzer 77 with Scania LBAT 110 cross country truck.

155 mm gun M 2

United States of America

Calibre	155 mm
Barrel length	45 calibres
Muzzle brake	Nil
Trail type	Split
Weight	13,880 kg
Ammunition type	Separate
Charges	—
Ammunition options	HE (57·6 kg)
	AP (59·6 kg)
	Smoke WP
	Chemical
Rate of fire	1 rd/min
Muzzle velocity	835 m/sec
Maximum range	23,500 m
Elevation limits	−2° + 63°
Traverse limits	60°
Detachment	14

This weapon was developed from a French design and entered service in 1938, as the M 1A1, and was nicknamed 'Long Tom', because of its 45 calibre length barrel. Its long range made it an effective counter bombardment weapon in World War II and remains one of its valuable characteristics. An interrupted screw pattern breech block is used with percussion firing by lanyard. The propellant is bagged. The arrangement of the variable length hydro-pneumatic recoil system, mounted below the barrel, is the same as the 8 inch M 115:

so too in the equilibrator layout.

A burst rate of fire of four rounds/minute can be achieved, and one round/minute is the sustained rate. The ammunition which includes an anti-armour round, is not inter-changeable with other equipments.

The trail is a split type made up of box-section girders which hinge behind the road wheels. From pairs of double wheels carry the main weight of the gun, and a two wheel limber supports the trail legs. The weapon can be towed without the limber.

For firing the carriage is jacked down off its wheels so that it is flush with the ground. The spades which fit under the trail legs are best dug in before deployment. Four spades are provided, one at the end of each trail leg and a pair behind the wheels. This equipment stands 2·1 m high in action.

The size of the weapon makes it difficult to manoeuvre. The piece retracts for travelling, and coming into action takes 20 minutes.

An SP version (M 40) was produced, and also an emplacement mounting for coast defence.

Employment	Argentina	Italy	Pakistan
	Austria	Japan	Spain
	Denmark	Jordan	Turkey
	Ethiopia	South Korea	Yugoslavia
	Greece	Netherlands	

The gun in action with jacks lowered.

Side view showing wheels raised.

155 mm howitzer M 114 A1

United States of America

Calibre	155 mm
Barrel length	20 calibres
Muzzle brake	Nil
Trail type	Split
Weight	5,800 kg
Ammunition type	Separate
Charges	7
Ammunition options	HE (43·2 kg)
	Smoke WP and BE
	Illuminating
	Chemical/gas
Rate of fire	2 rds/min
Muzzle velocity	564 m/sec
Maximum range	14,600 m
Elevation limits	−2° + 65°
Traverse limits	53°
Detachment	11

The M 114 entered service in 1942. It shared the same carriage as a 4·5 inch gun and these two equipments, which complemented each other tactically, were the American medium artillery equivalents of the British 5·5 inch and 4·5 inch guns. Over 6,000 M 114s were produced, and although the range is short for a weapon of this calibre, it is a robust equipment which is still widely used. It has been phased out of service in the US Army.

The barrel has no muzzle brake and is fitted with an interrupted screw type breech, which is cartridge sealed.

A variable length hydro-pneumatic recoil system is mounted under and over the barrel. An 'O' ring at the front of the recoil system is also used as the forward mounting for two horizontal spring equilibrators.

The ammunition is widely used in other 155 mm weapons and is a NATO standard type. An initial or burst rate of fire of four rounds/minute is possible: the sustained rate is two rounds/minute.

The split trail legs are girder-type welded box sections. Removable spades are carried on the legs for travelling. Vertical firing stresses are passed on a firing jack which folds forward when not in use. On the M 1 A1 carriage the jack is rack and pinion operated: on the later M 1 A2 it is of the screw type. A small shield is fitted either side of the barrel: its left hand top section folds to enable the dial sight to be used for direct laying.

The weapon is not as heavy as its massive appearance suggests: it can be lifted by a CH 47 class helicopter.

Two variants have been produced:

M 123 A1: This is an SP version using an auxiliary propulsion unit, which is the Continental Motors Corporation four cylinder 20 bhp petrol type motor. It propels the gun at 6–7 kilometres/hour. Drive is to the existing carriage wheels by hydraulic motors mounted out-board. A small dolly wheel assembly supports the trail legs. The modification does not prevent conventional towing, and the firing configuration of the carriage is unaltered. The shield is not fitted. Weight is increased to 6,350 kilogrammes. The performance of the gun is unchanged.

Field howitzer FH 155 (L): This variant is being studied by West Germany. The modifications to the weapon by Rheinmetall are still experimental. The carriage is retained, but a new, angled shield changes the weapons appearance. So does the double baffle muzzle brake. It is believed that the barrel and breech ring are new.

Employment

Argentina	Jordan	Spain
Austria	Lebanon	Taiwan
Belgium	Laos	Thailand
Brazil	South Korea	Tunisia
Denmark	Libya	Turkey
Greece	Netherlands	USA
Iran	Pakistan	Vietnam
Israel	Peru	West Germany
Italy	Philippines	Yugoslavia
Japan	Portugal	

155 mm US M 114 A1 howitzer.

Light howitzer XM 198

United States of America

Calibre	155 mm
Barrel length	—
Muzzle brake	Single baffle
Trail type	Split
Weight	6,622 kg
Ammunition type	—
Charges	—
Ammunition options	Nuclear
	HE
Rate of fire	—
Muzzle velocity	—
Maximum range	30,000 + m
Elevation limits	—
Traverse limits	—
Detachment	11

This weapon is designed to meet the requirement for a highly mobile, air delivered weapon with greater fire power than the 105 mm calibre weapons usually associated with air mobile operations. It is still in its development phase, but is scheduled to enter service with airborne and air mobile formations this year. It will also be issued to infantry divisions to replace the M 114 A1.

Although, it weighs 6,622 kilogrammes it is considerably lighter than M 2 and more robust than the M 114. It can be air lifted by the CH 47C helicopter. Aluminium is used extensively in its construction. The monobloc barrel is autofrettaged to give it strength with lightness. It is mounted at its extreme rear, behind the sliding-wedge breech block. Equilibrators run up from the base of the saddle, but are angled sufficiently to prevent their projection above the recoiling mass. A second pair of equilibrators run forward from a position above the breech. The variable length recoil system is mounted above and either side of the barrel which carried a wedge shaped single baffle muzzle brake. Elevation is by a ball and screw type mechanism.

A new ammunition system is being developed to include nuclear and conventional projectiles. Rocket assisted are to be included, and maximum range is about 30,000 m.

The trail is of deep box section members. A two position suspension setting is employed, the gun being lowered onto a firing platform in action. The platform is carried on the trial legs. Spades are fitted beneath the rear of the trial legs. The weapon can be towed with the barrel deployed, or rotated over the trail legs. The latter position is used for long journeys, and air dropping. No shield is fitted.

Employment   Trials only, in United States

Note the extreme rear mounting of the trunions, and balancing springs.

8 inch howitzer M 115

United States of America

Calibre	203 mm
Barrel length	25 calibres
Muzzle brake	Nil
Trail type	Split
Weight	13,471 kg
Ammunition type	Separate
Charges	7
Ammunition options	Nuclear
	HE (90·7 kg)
	HE spotting
	Chemical
Rate of fire	$\frac{1}{2}$rd/min
Muzzle velocity	594 m/sec
Maximum range	16,800 m
Elevation limits	$-2° + 65°$
Traverse limits	60°
Detachment	14

This is the largest artillery piece in service in the western world. It was developed during World War II. The original barrel has been superseded and of two types currently in use, the M 2 A1 is stronger. This weapon has a nuclear capability and is noted for its extreme accuracy throughout its range.

The barrel is short, and without a muzzle brake. It is supported by trunnions placed well to the rear: equilibrators run forward from angled extensions to the saddle. The breech block is of the interrupted screw type. The hydro-pneumatic recoil system (giving variable recoil length) is mounted below the barrel in a massive square section cradle.

Details of the nuclear round are classified. In addition to the shell-types listed, a rocket assisted projectile has been developed. Details of the range achieved and the type of warhead have not been published. Two charge systems are used: charges one to five green bag and five to seven white bag.

The carriage is that of the M 2 155 mm gun. The trail is a split type made up of box-section girders which hinge behind the road wheels. Four pairs of double wheels carry the main weight of the gun, and a two wheel limber supports the trail legs. The weapon can be towed without the limber.

For firing the carriage is jacked down off its wheels so that it is flush with the ground. The spades which fit under the trail legs are best dug in before deployment. Four spades are provided, one at the end of each trail leg and a pair behind the wheels. In action this equipment stands 2·1 m high.

The weapon has been replaced by the SP version M 110 in the armies of many previous users, including the United States.

Employment:

Belgium	Japan	South Korea
Denmark	Jordan	Spain
Greece	Italy	Turkey
India	Netherlands	USA (Reserve Army)

The 8 inch M 115 howitzer in action. Travelling bogie (or 'limber') is at the rear.

203 mm howitzer M 1955

Union of Soviet Socialist Republics

Calibre	203 mm
Barrel length	40 calibres
Muzzle brake	Pepper pot
Trail type	Split
Weight	20,400 kg
Ammunition type	Separate
Charges	—
Ammunition options	Nuclear
	HE (102 kg)
Rate of fire	1 rd/min
Muzzle velocity	790 m/sec
Maximum range	29,250 m
Elevation limits	−2° + 50°
Traverse limits	44°
Detachment	16

The M 1955 is remarkable in that it is the largest conventional Soviet cannon and has a common calibre with the US M 115 and M 110 (the largest Western conventional cannon). It is in fact more a gun than a howitzer (although the distinction between these two types has long since been blurred with the general increase in range and the use of a number of charges for both guns and howitzers) as it has a long gun-like barrel and very long range.

For over half its length the M 1955 barrel has a massive circular jacket. A square breech ring houses a screw-type breech block. The barrel retracts over the trail for towing. The buffer recuperator is mounted below the barrel.

A variable bag charge is used, and like the M 115 and M 110 the shell is nuclear or HE. Shell weight is 11 kg heavier than the American equivalent.

The box section, split trail carriage, is supported on double road wheels on single axles, and a two wheeled limber supports the trail legs. The AT-T fully tracked tractor is used to tow the gun.

In the Soviet Army, the M 1955 is held at Army or Corps level as a general support weapon.

Employment:

Albania	Egypt	Poland
Bulgaria	East Germany	Rumania
China	Hungary	USSR
Czechoslovakia		

Howitzers travelling behind their AT-T tractors.

Miscellaneous

A number of elderly equipments are reputed to continue in service as shown. They do not warrant a full description but are included here in synopsis form:

	Calibre (mm)	Rate of fire (rds/min)	Weight (kg)	Range (m)	Muzzle velocity (m/sec)	Ammunition (kg)	Traverse	Elevation	Country of origin	Country of use
Field gun 75/22	75		764	10,500	480		7°	0° + 40°	Spain	Spain
Howitzer M 1902	75								Sweden	Turkey
Gun M 1902/30	76	8	1,350	12,000	717	6·4	2°	−5° + 37°	USSR	Finland Vietnam
Howitzer M 1927	76	14	780	8,570	387		6°	−6° + 25°	USSR	
M 36	76		1,620	13,600	706	6·4	60°	−5° + 75°	USSR	Finland
Mountain gun M 1938	76	14	786	10,000	503	6·23	10°	−8° + 70°	USSR	Vietnam
Howitzer M 1943	76	14	600	4,200			60°	−8° + 25°	USSR	Vietnam
M 37–10	105								USSR	Finland
Field gun M 1941	105	7	1,800	13,400	600	14·9	53°	−6° + 45°	USSR	Cuba Guinea Vietnam Finland
Field howitzer M 39	150	4–6	5,720	14,600	580	41·5	45°	−5° + 66°	Sweden	Sweden
Field howitzer FH 18	150	5	6,500	15,000	580	42	45°	−5° + 65°	Sweden	Switzerland
Medium field howitzer M 40	150	4	5,530	13,300	520	43·5	60°	0° + 45°	Germany	Finland

IV. Self-propelled Field Guns

The previous section dealt with towed field guns, and the technical problems of field gunnery and indirect fire. The equipments described in this chapter are employed in the same way as their towed equivalents.

The advantages and disadvantages of SP weapons have been discussed in Section III. In summary, the SP is expensive to develop, manufacture and maintain: it is heavy and therefore difficult to move by air and requires careful route reconnaisance: training is a problem with enclosed fighting compartments: the whole weapon is vulnerable to automotive breakdown. Set against these disadvantages, the SP field gun is more mobile, quicker to deploy and move, often automated, and in some measure independant of an ammunition vehicle. The immunity from direct attack which indirect fire techniques give to field artillery generally is supplemented in the case of most SPs by the protection against all but a direct hit afforded to the detachment and equipment by armoured fighting compartments.

Three types of mounting are found: the open chassis, e.g. M 107, the built-up casemate which offers limited traverse, but is generally more spacious than a turret, e.g. the VK 155 L/50 and the rotating turret, e.g. Abbot.

105 mm SP howitzer AMX 105/50

France

Calibre	105 mm
Barrel length	23 calibres
Muzzle brake	Double baffle
Ammunition type	Separate
Charges	8
Ammunition options	HE (Mk 63) (16·15 kg)
	HE (M 1) (14·9 kg)
	HESH
	Smoke
	Chemical
	Illuminating
	Carrier
	Blank
Rate of fire	—
Muzzle velocity	568 m/sec (Mk 63 ammunition)
Maximum range	14,000 m (,, ,,)
Elevation limits	−4°30′ + 70°
Traverse on carriage	20°
Detachment	4
Chassis—Type	AMX 13
Engine	SOLAM, flat 8, petrol
Power	270 bhp
Speed	60 km/hour
Endurance	—
Ammunition carried	52
Height × length × width	2·7 × 5·2 × 2·65 m
Weight	16,500 kg

This weapon is also referred to as the AMX 105/A. It entered service in 1952 and is still used in the artillery regiments of non-mechanised brigades and in the divisional artillery reserve units.

The gun was designed to use the standard American M 1 ammunition which gives a maximum range of 11,500 m. This performance has been improved by the introduction of the French Mk 63 ammunition: the HE shell is of a hollow base design and the new HEAT round penetrates 360 mm of armour. A new double charge system comes in two cartridge cases—one to five and six to eight. The claimed burst fire rate is six rounds in 20 seconds.

The weapon's chief limitation is the poor top traverse due to the fixed casemate mounting. The recoil system beneath the barrel, and horizontal equilibrators project beyond the casement. A distinctive recognition feature is the square shield, drilled in the top left corner for the direct fire telescope's line of sight, which elevates with the recoiling mass.

The chassis is one of 23 derivatives of the AMX 13 light tank. It provides good cross country mobility and a stable gun platform for this size of gun so that a spade is not needed. This contrasts with the extensive changes necessary to mount a 155 mm on this chassis (see entry relating to 155 mm SP Mk III).

The Dutch AMX 105/50 is fitted with a longer 30 calibre barrel. This barrel, which increases range to 15,000 m is also fitted in the newer 105 B French gun.

Employment France
Morocco
Netherlands

The weapon is mounted in a fixed casemate. Note the shaped armour covering for the buffer/recuperator beneath the barrel, and the unusual shield with its aperture for direct laying of line of sight.

105 mm SP howitzer AMX 105B
France

Calibre	105 mm
Barrel length	30 calibres
Muzzle brake	Double baffle
Ammunition type	Separate
Charges	8
Ammunition options	HE (16·15 kg)
	Smoke
	Illuminating
Rate of fire	—
Muzzle velocity	675 m/sec
Maximum range	15,000 m
Elevation limits	—
Traverse on carriage	360°
Detachment	4
Chassis—Type	AMX 13
Engine	SOLAM, flat 8, petrol
Power	270 bhp
Speed	60 km/hour
Endurance	—
Ammunition carried	80
Height × length × width	2·7 × 6·4 × 2·5 m
Weight	17,000 kg

The AMX 105B is an improved version of the AMX 105/50. The main difference lies in the provision of a turret giving 360° traverse: because the 105/50 already has a fully enclosed casement this new equipment, with turret, is only 500 kilogrammes heavier. A commander's cupola is fitted, and mounts a machine gun.

The longer barrel, as fitted to the Dutch 105/50 is used with the original muzzle brake. The recoil and equilibrator systems are housed inside the turret.
used with the original muzzle brake. The recoil and equilibrator systems are housed inside the turret.

The ammunition system is the eight charge Mk 63 type used in the 105/50, but performance is improved to 15,000 m by the longer barrel. The vehicle carries 80 complete rounds of ammunition which is an important improvement over the 105/50. It is not known if the new barrel accepts American M 1 ammunition.

Chassis details are as for the 105/50.

Employment   Switzerland

105 mm SP gun 'Abbot'—FV433
United Kingdom

Calibre	105 mm
Barrel length	325 cm
Muzzle brake	Double baffle
Ammunition type	Semi-fixed
Charges	8
Ammunition options	HE
	HESH
	Smoke
	Illuminating
	Practice
Rate of fire	12 rds/min
Muzzle velocity	708 m/sec
Maximum range	17,000 m
Elevation limits	−5° + 70°
Traverse on carriage	360°
Detachment	4 (including driver)
Chassis—Type	FV 430
Engine	Rolls Royce K60
Power	240 bhp
Speed	48 km/hour
Endurance	480 km
Ammunition carried	40
Height × length × width	2·5 × 5·8 × 2·6 m
Weight	16,556 kg

Abbot is the first British gun to be designed as an SP from its inception. The barrel is new and the chassis is a derivative of the APC FV 430 series. It came into service in 1965 as the standard close support weapon of the Royal Artillery, except in specialist and airportable functions, replacing the towed 25 pounder.

The gun's performance is exceptional. With the latest Mk II ammunition, maximum range is 17,000 m. Accuracy at that range is twice that of previous designs and barrel life is at least 10,000 rounds.

A semi-automatic loading system with powered ramming produces a sustained rate of fire of 12 rounds/minute. The spent cartridge is ejected automatically on run-out and the vertical sliding breech closes when a fresh cartridge is loaded. The cartridge is brass, and is fired electrically. Eight charges are available. Cartridges are supplied with five charge bags. These are removed and the cartridge re-made for sub charges A and B. Super charge is delivered in a special cartridge case.

The gun accepts American M 1 ammunition using Abbot Mk I charges (range limited to 15,000 m), and its own range of HE, HESH, SH practice, illuminating and smoke shells. A nylon driving band is under development to provide exceptional consistency and increased range while reducing mechanical wear to a minimum.

The turret rotates through 360° and provides protection against small arms fire and shell splinters. The crew are protected against chemical attack and nuclear fall out. The pressurized crew compartment is air-conditioned, and a fume extractor is fitted to the barrel.

105 mm SP gun—'Abbot'.

The Abbot prepared for swimming, with the floatation screen erected and the exhaust pipe extension fitted.

Sighting is conventional and laying is electrically power assisted. Fire control is effected by a sophisticated communications kit. Communication within the turret is by an induction loop feeding special head sets. A subsidiary loop communicates outside the vehicle. Radio and sighting systems are compatible with developments in automatic data transmission.

The Rolls Royce K60 engine is a turbo-charged vertically opposed six cylinder multi-fuel type. Its 240 bhp gives a power to weight ratio of 15 bhp/ton. The Allison Tx 200 automatic transmission is fitted. Electrical power is provided by two alternators running off the main engine to 24 volt batteries of 200 amp/hour capacity.

The road wheels have torsion bar suspension. No spade is fitted. Ground pressure is 0·81 kg/cm². The vehicle wades to four feet without preparation, and swims propelled by its tracks when a permanently fitted flotation screen is raised.

A less sophisticated 'value engineered' version is made by the manufacturer (Vickers Ltd) called the Vickers Abbot. It is recognisable by the absence of external stowage bins. Models now in production are fitted with the General Motors V6 petrol engine which powers the American M 113 APC.

The Vickers private venture Falcon twin 30 mm air defence gun is mounted on the Abbot chassis.

Employment   India
United Kingdom

105 mm SP howitzer M 52

United States of America

Calibre	105 mm
Barrel length	—
Muzzle brake	Nil
Ammunition type	Semi-fixed
Charges	7
Ammunition options	HE (14·9 kg)
	HEAT
	Smoke WP
	Chemical
	Illuminating
	Carrier
	Blank
Rate of fire	3 rds/min
Muzzle velocity	472 m/sec
Maximum range	11,200 m
Elevation limits	−9° + 60°
Traverse on carriage	60°
Detachment	5
Chassis—Type	M 41 light tank
Engine	OAS 895
Power	500 bhp
Speed	56 km/hour
Endurance	150 km

Ammunition carried	105
Height × length × width	3·1 × 5·8 × 3·3 m
Weight	24,040 kg

The M 52 was introduced into service in 1954 as part of a new family of SP equipments. Previous American SPs had been open mountings on a tracked chassis: the M 52 has a fully enclosed casemate superstructure. It was the smallest member of the family and is the only one to be in service still.

The gun was designed to use the M 1 ammunition which was originally intended for the M 101 towed howitzer. The breech is a vertical sliding type. No muzzle brake is fitted, but a long slim fume extractor is fitted.

The chassis used for the M 52 was first developed for the 155 mm M 44. The use of a smaller gun greatly increases the stowage available for ammunition, and does away with the need for a spade. The chassis is fully described under the M 44.

Employment	Japan	ʿTunisia
	Jordan	USA (Reserve)
	Spain	

105 mm SP howitzer M 52.

105 mm SP howitzer M 108

United States of America

Calibre	105 mm
Barrel length	—
Nuzzle brake	Nil
Ammunition type	Semi-fixed
Charges	7
Ammunition options	HE
	Illuminating
	Carrier
	Smoke
	Chemical
Rate of fire	3 rds/min
Muzzle velocity	—
Maximum range	12,000 m
Elevation limits	−6° + 75°
Traverse on carriage	360°
Detachment	6
Chassis—Type	Individual
Engine	General Motors 8V 71 T
Power	420 bhp
Speed	55 km/hour
Endurance	350 km
Ammunition carried	87
Height × length × width	3·04 × 6·09 × 3·14
Weight	22, 452 kg

The 105 mm M 108 was introduced in 1964. It consists of the M 52 barrel mounted on a special chassis which it shares with the 155 mm M 109.

The barrel is not fitted with a muzzle brake, but has a small fume extractor near the muzzle. The ammunition is the M 1 type developed for the M 101A1, but unlike that weapon, the M 108 has a vertical sliding breech inherited from the M 52. The power assisted loading system is shared with the larger M 109, and results in a low rate of fire.

Sighting is by conventional dial sight and elevation quadrant. There is a direct fire elbow periscope. Laying in elevation and azimuth is hydraulically powered.

Extensive use of aluminium keeps the weight down. The turret gives protection to the detachment against small arms fire, and splinters. The turret is very spacious, with good access from side and rear hatches.

The chassis runs on 14 road wheels, using torsion bar suspension. No return rollers are used for the 15 inch wide track. The engine is the General Motors 8V 71 T turbo-charged diesel delivering 420 bhp through an Allison XTG 411-2A automatic transmission. There are four gears: steering is by clutch brake on the lower two, and by geared steering on the higher ratios. Power for the hydraulic firing functions is provided by a pump driven off the main engine. As a back-up service there is a manual pump for elevation and traversing hand wheels.

The vehicle can swim when fitted with flotation bags in canvas retainers. Four are fitted each side, and one at either end. Wave barriers at side and front are also fitted. A blower inflates the bags in 75 seconds to two pounds/square inch. This pressure can be maintained in the event of minor damage. Propulsion in the water is by track motion at a speed of six kilometres/hour.

Employment	Belgium	Turkey
	Khmer Republic	USA
	Spain	

105 mm M 108 SP howitzer.

122 mm SP gun

Union of Soviet Socialist Republics

Calibre	122 mm
Barrel length	47 calibres
Muzzle brake	Double baffle
Ammunition type	Separate
Charges	—
Ammunition options	HE (25·5 kg)
	APHE
	Smoke
	Illuminating
Rate of fire	—
Muzzle velocity	900 m/sec
Maximum range	21,900 m
Elevation limits	—
Traverse on carriage	360°
Detachment	—
Chassis—Type	PT 76
Engine	2 × 6 cylinder Otto
Power	480 bhp
Speed	44 km/hour
Endurance	—
Ammunition carried	—
Height × length × width	Width 3·14 m
Weight	—

This is a new 122 mm SP gun which was seen for the first time at the 30th Anniversary of the Polish Peoples Republic celebrations in 1974. It is the first Soviet SP field gun. As yet little is known, and much of the detail quoted is speculative. It is the D 74 gun in a 360° turret, mounted on a new chassis, the front of which resembles the BMP. The driver sits to the left of the engine compartment.

The general layout of the running gear is that of the PT 76 tank with an extra wheel, making a total of 7 per side.

The D 74 gun carries the same double-baffle muzzle brake (and is assumed to give the same performance) as the towed version. Range would be 21,900 m with a 22 kg shell and an anti-armour capability to defeat 230 mm of plate at 1000 m. A rocket assisted round has been rumoured.

If the PT 76 chassis is used this weapon will probably share that tank's inherent buoyancy and in-water speed of 10 kilometres propelled by two hydro-jets. The two six-cylinder 240 bhp engines drive through a five-speed gearbox and give a speed of 44 kilometres/hour. Suspension is by torsion bars with two hydraulic dampers per side.

Employment
Poland
USSR and probably other WTO countries.

This picture was taken at the gun's first public showing in July 1974, at the parade to celebrate the 30th Anniversary of Poland's liberation. The similarity of the hull to that of the PT 76 tank is very clear.

155 mm SP howitzer Mk III

France

Calibre	155 mm
Barrel length	33 calibres
Muzzle brake	Double baffle
Ammunition type	Separate
Charges	10
Ammunition options	HE (43·75 kg)
	Smoke BE and WP
	Illuminating
Rate of fire	4 rds/min
Muzzle velocity	647 m/sec
Maximum range	21,600 m
Elevation limits	0 + 67°
Traverse on carriage	50°
Detachment	11
Chassis—Type	AMX 13
Engine	SOLAM, flat 8, petrol
Power	270 bhp
Speed	60 km/hour
Endurance	—
Ammunition carried	Nil
Height × length × width	2·2 × 6·2 × 2·75 m
Weight	16,700 kg

This equipment consists of the AMX 13 chassis on which is mounted a modified 155 M 50 howitzer. Barrel length has been increased by 10 calibres to 33, and a newer double baffle muzzle brake fitted. Some early models were fitted with the un-modified gun.

The breech is a screw type, with integral obturation for the bag type charge system. Conventional laying arrangements are on the left of the barrel, and the buffer/recuperator beneath it.

The effect of the lengthened barrel is to increase muzzle velocity to 765 m/sec and range to 21,600 m using the TA 68 hollow-base shell. This equipment accepts two charges (9 and 9A) more than the M 50, so that its performance with older types of ammunition is better.

The gun fires French 155 mm ammunition (Type 56 and TA 68) as well as NATO types—including the American M 107 which gives a limited range of 18,000 m. The illuminating round is American. Two types of propellant are used in the charge system: charges one to six are fast burning, and charges five to 9A slow burning.

The gun is large for the size and weight of its chassis, and is therefore mounted at its extreme rear, so that the firing stresses can be passed directly to the ground via two spades which form a miniature split trail. This arrangement allows 50° top traverse, (30° to right and 20° to left): laying in azimuth is power assisted. The positioning of the breech provides excellent access for loading—a task which is possible at the highest elevation (67°). However, the physical effort of loading the separate ammunition keeps the rate of fire to four rounds/minute—as for the towed version.

The equipment does not swim but wades to a depth of 0·7 m. To accommodate the gun and spade mounting the rear sprockets of the tank running gear have been removed, leaving five bogie wheels and the front driving sprocket. Otherwise the layout and performance of the chassis is unchanged.

Normally two crew members (driver and commander) travel with the gun in protected compartments. The commander has a small cupola. Three other members of the detachment can be carried for short distances, but they will normally travel with the remainder in the support vehicle with the first-line ammunition (this second vehicle is the AMX 13 VCA).

A radio is fitted and can be used for fire orders.

Employment	Argentina
	France
	Venezuela

The 155 mm M 50 howitzer mounted on the AMX 13 tank chassis. The trunnions are mounted at the extreme rear over the spade system. Note absence of crew space.

155 mm GCT SP gun

France

Calibre	155 mm
Barrel length	40 calibres
Muzzle brake	Multi-baffle
Ammunition type	Separate (combustible cartridge)
Charges	7
Ammunition options	HE (43·75)
	Smoke BE and WP
	Illuminating
Rate of fire	9 rds/min
Muzzle velocity	810 m/sec
Maximum range	23,600 m
Elevation limits	−5° + 66°
Traverse on carriages	360°
Detachment	4
Chassis—Type	AMX 30C
Engine	Hispano-HS 110
Power	720 bhp
Speed	60 km/hour
Endurance	450 km
Ammunition carried	42
Height × length × width	3·0 × 10·4 × 3·1 m
Weight	41,656 kg

The GCT gun (Grand Cadence de Tir) is a new weapon mounted on the well tried AMX 30C tank chassis. It was first seen in 1973.

The long, 40 calibre, barrel improves the range of the Mk III SP. A new, vertical sliding breech block is fitted. Recoil is constant at 0·95 m despite elevation to 66°. At some traverse angles, elevation is limited to 12°, but not in the main forward arc of fire.

The barrel is chambered to accept existing ammunition such as the American M 107 and French Type 56.

However, it is particularly designed to fire the new hollow base TA 68 shell. The charge is contained in a combustible cartridge case. The virtue of this system is that the facility for automated handling and loading, which is not possible with a bag charge, does not lead to the problem of disposing of a spent cartridge case. Older bag charges can be used, but not automatically loaded.

A rocket assisted projectile will increase range to 30,000 m.

42 complete rounds are carried in the vehicle. They are loaded through wide-opening doors in the rear of the turret into a magazine. From the magazine, loading by a hydraulic mechanism is fully automatic. The cyclic rate of fire is nine rounds/minute, which gives a burst fire rate of six rounds in 40 seconds. Manual loading limits the rate to 2–3 rounds/minute.

The AMX 30 chassis is powered by the Hispano-Suiza HS 110 engine. It is a flat 12, multi-fuel super-charged diesel developing 720 bhp, or 18 bhp/ton. The five speed gearbox has a manual shift. The centrifugal clutch is electrically operated by the movement of the gear lever. Five double-wheels per track have torsion bar with resilient bump stops. Hydraulic dampers are fitted to the suspension of the front and rear wheels.

The vehicle wades to 2·2 m, but does not swim.

The equipment is scheduled for service in 1978.

The GCT gun and turret has been fitted to the German Leopard tank chassis as a private cooperative venture between the manufacturers of these two weapons.

Employment   Trials only

The great size of the turret of this equipment, mounted on a main battle tank chassis (AMX 30), is apparent from this picture. Although the gun is taken from the earlier Mk 111 SP, the only noticeable similarity is the muzzle brake.

155 mm SP howitzer L 33

Israel

Calibre	155 mm
Barrel length	33 calibres
Muzzle brake	Single baffle
Ammunition type	Separate
Charges	8
Ammunition options	HE (43·7 kg)
	Smoke
	Illuminating
Rate of fire	—
Muzzle velocity	725 m/sec
Maximum range	21,525 m
Elevation limits	−3° + 52°
Traverse on carriage	60°
Detachment	8
Chassis—Type	M 4 Super Sherman
Engine	Cummins diesel
Power	460 bhp
Speed	36 km/hour
Endurance	260 km
Ammunition carried	54
Height × length × width	3·46 × 8·55 × 3·33 m
Weight	42,250 kg

The L 33 is the first heavy artillery weapon to be designed and built in Israel by SOLTAM. It consists of the Tampella designed M 68 howitzer mounted on a modified M 4 Super-Sherman tank chassis.

The barrel is fitted with a semi-automatic breech, and this in conjunction with a pneumatic handling and loading system allows a 'very high' rate of fire; no figures have been released. The barrel is chromium plated to prolong its life: replating is possible and restores a worn barrel to a new condition. The range of the weapon is believed to be greater than the published figure.

The gun is mounted in a fixed casement which forms a high superstructure on the chassis. The recoil system, mounted below the barrel, and the equilibrators, extend beyond the casemate. A fume extractor is fitted.

The aiming system includes direct fire sights.

The Super Sherman tank has been in Israel's service since 1950. Local modifications included the fitting of a Cummins diesel engine. The original horizontal volute suspension is retained. There is little doubt that as a tank this is no longer a viable weapon, and that the serviceable chassis are being put to good use as SP artillery carriages. The crew of eight are served with an induction-loop internal communications system, and are all provided with seat belts.

It is claimed that fuel and ammunition for 20 hours is carried in the vehicle. The weapon is used extensively in the counter-battery role, and considerable thought has been given to its tactical handling. The sighting and fire control techniques have been developed to take advantage of the gun's mobility to change gun positions rapidly, and so avoid enemy counter-battery fire.

Employment   Israel

The hull of the original Sherman tank can be seen beneath the new superstructure.

155 mm gun SP 70

Tri-national: Federal Republic of Germany, Italy, United Kingdom

Calibre	155 mm
Barrel length	39 calibres
Muzzle brake	Double baffle
Ammunition type	Separate
Charges	8
Ammunition options	HE (43·5 kg)
	Smoke BE
	Illuminating
Rate of fire	—
Muzzle velocity	827 m/sec
Maximum range	24,000 m
Elevation limits	—
Traverse on carriage	360°
Detachment	6
Chassis—Type	individual
Engine	—
Power	—
Speed	—
Endurance	—
Ammunition carried	—
Height × length × width	—
Weight	—

This is in fact a picture of a full-scale mock-up of SP 70.

SP 70 is a project being undertaken by Germany, Italy and the United Kingdom in parallel with the FH 70 towed gun project. SP 70 will be the FH 70 ordnance mounted on a purpose designed chassis. The breakdown of development work is:

Italy	Recoil system
	Loading system
	Some chassis elements
Germany	Chassis and running gear
	Ordnance
United Kingdom	Turret
	Sights

Performance will be directly comparable with FH 70. Existing 155 mm ammunition and a purpose-built type (HE, smoke and illuminating), will be used. The rocket assisted projectiles which are under development will increase range to 30,000 m. Further details will be found under FH 70.

Employment Under development:
Germany
Italy
UK

155 mm automatic gun VK 155 L/50

Sweden

Calibre	155 mm	
Barrel length	—	
Muzzle brake	Pepper pot	
Ammunition type	Semi-fixed	
Charges	—	
Ammunition options	HE (48 kg)	
Rate of fire	15 rds/min	
Muzzle velocity	865 m/sec	
Maximum range	25,000 m	
Elevation limits	−3° + 40°	
Traverse on carriage	30°	
Detachment	4	
Chassis—Type	Individual	
Engine	Rolls Royce	Boeing
	K60	502–10MA
Power	240 bhp	300 bhp
Speed	35 km/hour	
Endurance	—	
Ammunition carried	14	
Height × length × width	3·25 × — × 3·3 m	
Weight	51,000 kg	

The requirement for a gun of long range was stated in 1950, the prototype appeared in 1960 and production was between 1966 and 1968. This highly advanced Swedish SP from AB Bofors features fully automatic firing at a rate of 15 rounds/minute. To achieve this remarkable performance the all-round traverse featured in most modern SP designs has been sacrificed: only 30° of traverse is possible without moving the vehicle itself: there is no spade to delay this action.

The magazine holds 14 rounds. The ammunition is delivered to the gun in clips of five rounds, which are loaded into the magazine mechanically. Fuze and charge options are selected before the magazine is loaded.

Recoil forces are used to cock the spring action of the loading system which consists of two movements: offering the round to the breech, and ramming. From the magazine, rounds are fed by gravity into the two feed trays. The feed trays serve a loading tray behind the breech.

Range is very good—25,000 m, and it is believed that a rocket assisted projectile is being developed which should produce at least 30,000 m.

Laying is manual except that electrical power is used for coarse elevation setting, and for raising and lowering the barrel to and from the loading angle.

All automatic and powered functions have manual back-up systems, for which the detachment in the two cabins is increased to seven. The vehicle is enormously heavy. Two engines are fitted: Rolls Royce K60 (as fitted in Abbot) is a turbo-charged six cylinder two stroke diesel producing 240 bhp: a Boeing 502-10MA gas turbine plant produces 300 bhp. The vehicle runs on 12 road wheels and the track returns along the top of these without rollers. The hydro-pneumatic suspension is locked for firing.

22 mm of armour plate is fitted to the magazine and cabin which is fully proofed to protect the crew from chemical attack and nuclear radiation.

Employment Sweden

The SP VK 155 mm L/50 showing the massive magazine mounted over the turret.

155 mm SP howitzer M 44

United States of America

Calibre	155 mm
Barrel length	20 calibres
Muzzle brake	Nil
Ammunition type	Separate
Charges	7
Ammunition options	HE (43·2 kg)
	Smoke WP and BE
	Illuminating
	Chemical
Rate of fire	1 rd/min
Muzzle velocity	569 m/sec
Maximum range	14,600 m
Elevation limits	−5° + 60°
Traverse on carriage	60°
Detachment	8
Chassis—Type	M 41 light tank
Engine	OAS-895
Power	500 bhp
Speed	56 km/hour
Endurance	120 km
Ammunition carried	24
Height × length × width	3·1 × 6·09 × 3·3 m
Weight	28,550 kg

The M 44 is now an outdated equipment, relegated to the reserve by the United States' Army, and largely phased out by previous users. It was the last of the American SP guns to have an open topped casemate.

The howitzer is the M 114, but with a modified recoil system which does not project beyond the casemate.

The interrupted screw type breech block and percussion firing system are retained.

The ammunition used is the M 107 family which was developed for the M 114. A hydraulic ram is fitted. The rate of fire is quoted as one round/minute: this is slower than the rate of the towed version and reflects the problems of handling ammunition in the confines of the casemate.

The gun is mounted in an open platform with high sides but no top. Traverse is good for the style of mounting. Stability in action comes from a large, hydraulically operated spade, over which the rear of the casemate opens to extend the platform floor, and ease ammunition supply.

The chassis is based on the M 41 light tank, and is also used for the M 52 SP. The running gear has six road wheels, four return rollers, and a single (driving) sprocket. The engine is a supercharged horizontally opposed six cylinder, and is air cooled. An unusual feature is the driving position which is to the left of the breech in the casemate. The engine and transmission fill the whole of the front of the hull; more recent designs offset the engine and sit the driver beside it.

The main weaknesses in the design are the lack of overhead protection for the detachment, the small onboard ammunition store and the limited radius of action.

Employment	Belgium	Japan
	Ecuador	Spain
	Italy	United States (Reserve Army)

155 mm M 44 SP howitzer. Crew member showing is the driver. Note fixed casemate.

155 mm medium howitzer M 109

United States of America

Calibre	155 mm
Barrel length	20 calibres
Muzzle brake	Double baffle
Ammunition type	Separate
Charges	7
Ammunition options	Nuclear
	HE (43·2 kg)
	Smoke BE and WP
	Illuminating
	Chemical
	Cannister
Rate of fire	3 rds/min
Muzzle velocity	564 m/sec
Maximum range	14,600 m
Elevation limits	−3° + 75°
Traverse on carriage	360°
Detachment	6
Chassis—Type	Individual
Engine	General Motors 8V 71 T
Power	420 bhp
Speed	55 km/hour
Endurance	320 km
Ammunition carried	28
Height × length × width	3·04 × 6·09 × 3·14 m
Weight	20,050 kg

The M 109 has become a standard workhorse for general support in the western world. Its size, spacious turret and reliable chassis make it an ideal vehicle for development of other projects. The M 109G and M 109U are national variants developed by Germany and Switzerland respectively. The M 108 is a 105 mm version, and the M 109 A1 a long barrel development now entering service as a retrofit conversion. The Italians have modified one as a development vehicle for SP 70.

In its original form the M 109 range is only 14,600 m. However, within that limitation its charge system gives excellent overlap and high angle fire is instantly available. The breech is semi-automatic interrupted screw type with integral obturation for the bagged charge. The firing mechanism is percussion using a lanyard. A hydraulic, semi-automatic power ram operates at a set loading angle. A loading tray and the rammer are deployed from the rear of the turret for each operation. Although elevation is fully powered the rate of fire is only 3 rounds/minute, or 45 rounds/hour.

The M 114 ammunition is used, but with the addition of a cannister round. The Americans are known to have developed a 155 mm nuclear shell which may be fired from this weapon.

Sighting is by conventional dial sight and elevation quadrant. There is a direct fire elbow periscope. Hydraulic power rotates the turret and is used for elevation. Power for the hydraulic firing functions is provided by a pump driven off the main engine. As a back-up service there is a manual pump for elevation and traversing.

The M 109 has the same chassis and turret as the 105 mm M 108. It can be distinguished by the heavier barrel and bulky six valve fume extractor mounted close to the muzzle brake. The M 109 also has two small spades behind the tracks for additional stability on reverse slopes and when firing high charges at low angles of elevation.

The chassis runs on 14 road wheels, using torsion bar suspension. Non-return rollers are used for the 15 inch

This picture shows the small spades deployed and gives an impression of the spaciousness of the turret. Note the side access panel to the fighting compartment.

The interior of the German M 109G showing the horizontal sliding breech and to its left the Zeiss periscopic sight.

The new long-barrelled M 109 A1.

wide track. The engine is turbo-charged diesel delivering 420 bhp through an Allison XTG 411-2A Automatic transmission. There are four gears: steering is by clutch brake on the lower two, and by geared steering on the higher ratios. The power to weight ratio of 18 bhp/ton gives the vehicle a good performance.

The vehicle can swim when fitted with flotation bags in canvas retainers. Four are fitted each side, and one at either end. Wave barriers at side and front are also fitted. A blower inflates the bags in 75 seconds to two pounds/square inch. This pressure can be maintained in the event of minor damage. Propulsion in the water is by track motion at a speed of six kilometres/hour. The three variants of the basic design are:

M 109 A1: This equipment is the standard M 109, rebarrelled, and using a new charge system. The re-barrelling programme has started in America and the conversion is available to other users. The retention of the fume extractor keeps the original look of the equipment. The original shell is used. The new barrel is 33 calibres in length and raises the muzzle velocity to 635 m/sec. Range is in excess of 18,000 m.

M 109G: This is a German modification which gives a range of 18,000 m—a performance which predates and pre-empts the fitting of the M 109 A1 barrel. The modifications lead to an increase in the rate of fire to six rounds/minute, but this increase is largely due to the fact that the German gunners dispense with the assisted loading system.
Modifications are:

(a) New muzzle brake.
(b) New breech ring and block. The screw type is replaced by a horizontal sliding semi-automatic type. The chamber accepts existing ammunition.

(c) The addition of an eighth charge giving a range of 18,000 m with a muzzle velocity of 686 m/sec.
(d) Locally manufactured Zeiss sights.
(e) Secondary armament replaced by the German MG 1 (formerly known as MG 42).
(f) New track with removable rubber pads as used by the Leopard tanks.

M 109U: This Swiss version is known locally as the Panzerhaubitz 66. It replaces a towed 105 mm howitzer as the artillery weapon organic to the mechanized division. Modifications are:

(a) A new electrical system
(b) A modified loading system which operates at all angles of elevation
(c) The 0·50 machine gun is replaced by a 12·7 mm anti-aircraft gun.

Employment:

Austria	Iran	Spain
Belgium	Israel	Switzerland
Canada	Italy	(M 109U)
Denmark	Libya	United Kingdom
Federal Republic of	Netherlands	USA (M 109 A1)
Germany (M 109G)	Norway	

175 mm SP gun M 107

United States of America

Calibre	175 mm
Barrel length	60 calibres
Muzzle brake	Nil
Ammunition type	Separate
Charges	3
Ammunition options	HE (66·6 kg)
	Chemical
Rate of fire	1 rd/min
Muzzle velocity	·914 m/sec
Maximum range	32,700 m
Elevation limits	− 2° + 65°
Traverse on carriage	60°
Detachment	13
Chassis—Type	Individual
Engine	General Motors 8V 71 T
Power	420 bhp
Speed	54 km/hour
Endurance	725 km
Ammunition carried	1
Height × length × width	3·47 × 11·3 × 3·14 m
Weight	28,165 kg

This is a true gun with a high muzzle velocity and flat trajectory. Since it came into service in 1962, it has boasted the longest range of any gun or howitzer. It is an important counter battery weapon. It is a highly sophisticated weapon: every operation is power assisted.

The performance stems from the great length of barrel, but at the cost of a barrel life of only 1,200 EFC's. The interrupted screw type breech block provides obturation for the bag charge system. A variable length hydro-pneumatic recoil system is mounted below the barrel.

Split function laying is used. The azimuth layer sits to the left of the barrel, the elevation layer to the right.

Loading is fully mechanized: the hydraulic systems are controlled from the platform behind the breech. The shell is delivered to the gun in a carrying tray. A hoist lifts the carrier and round to a loading tray which is offered to the breech for power ramming. One round is carried on the equipment.

The vehicle layout is non-tactical in that the chassis is open and the gun mounted without casement or turret: thus the overall weight of the weapon is kept within reasonable limits. Of the detachment of 13, five travel on the equipment. The driver sits down in the chassis and is offered some protection by a hatch. The massive spade is raised and lowered hydraulically. Stability in action is assisted by locking the road wheel suspension. The barrel is retracted for travelling.

The running gear consists of five large diameter road wheels per side: the track returns along their upper rims. Ground pressure is 0·95 kg/cm². Hydraulic power is produced by a pump run off the main engine—a super-charged diesel which is common to the M 108 and M 109.

Employment:

West Germany	Italy	United Kingdom
Greece	Netherlands	USA
Iran	Spain	Vietnam
Israel		

175 mm SP gun M 107. Note hydraulic spades at rear.

8 inch SP howitzer M 110

United States of America

Calibre	203 mm
Barrel length	25 calibres
Muzzle brake	Nil
Ammunition type	Separate
Charges	7
Ammunition type	Nuclear
	HE (90·7 kg)
	HE spotting
	Chemical
Rate of fire	½ rd/min
Muzzle velocity	594 m/sec
Maximum range	16,800 m
Elevation limits	−2° + 65°
Traverse on carriage	60°
Detachment	13
Chassis—Type	Individual
Engine	General Motors 8V 71 T
Power	420 bhp
Speed	54 km/hour
Endurance	725 km
Ammunition carried	1
Height × length × width	2·6 × 7·48 × 3·14 m
Weight	26,308 kg

The M 110 consists of the M 115 towed 8 inch ordnance on the 175 mm SP mounting of the M 107. A full description of the two parts will be found under those equipments. The complete interchangeability of the 175 mm and 203 mm barrels is demonstrated by the Israeli M 107 batteries which carry 8 inch barrels, to be quickly interchanged for precision shoots, or long range engagements.

The barrel has an interrupted screw type breech with a variable length recoil system mounted below it. Details of the nuclear round are classified. Two charge systems

The long-barrelled 8 inch SP M 110 (A1).

are used—charges one to five green bag and five to seven white bag. The weapon is noted for its extreme accuracy.

Firing functions are fully power assisted, including the loading sequence. Split function laying is used.

The chassis is powered by a General Motors supercharged diesel engine. Hydraulic power is supplied by a pump run off the main engine. The suspension of the five road wheels per side is locked for firing, but the weapon's stability stems mainly from the huge hydraulically powered spade.

A new, long barrel version (M 110 A1) is shortly to be introduced by the United States. Few details have been released, but range will obviously be improved. Its barrel length is believed to be 37 calibres, and will retract for travelling as does the M 107.

Employment	Belgium	Italy
	Federal Republic	Netherlands
	of Germany	United Kingdom
	Iran	USA
	Israel	

8 inch M 110 SP howitzer. Note exposed crews and hydraulic spades.

V. Mortars

A mortar is basically a specialised form of howitzer, designed to fire solely at high-angle, i.e. 45–80°, and using graded charges of propellant to vary its trajectory. The piece, generally smooth bore, is supported at the muzzle end by a bipod and rests on a circular steel base plate which takes all the shock of discharge. Typical mortars have no buffer-recuperator mechanism, which enormously simplifies manufacture. Recoil is kept low by using relatively small propellant charges as compared with a howitzer, which enables the whole equipment to be light and, in the smaller natures, man-portable, but limits the range. The noise of discharge is almost inaudible in battle conditions, and the high angle of projection makes the mortar easy to deploy, particularly in jungle or in mountains. The steep angle of descent enables deep valleys, reverse slopes and jungle clearings to be searched.

The projectile is a finned bomb which is loaded and fired by simply dropping it down the muzzle by hand, the primer hitting a fixed firing pin at the bottom of the breech. (Alternatively, in some models as mentioned below, trigger firing is possible; 'controlled' as opposed to 'automatic' discharge.) The thin walled bomb has excellent blast fragmentation and is also a good smoke and chemical vehicle.

Laying is indirect in the ordinary way, a small dial-sight referring to an aiming post stuck in the ground a few yards off.

The mortar is a quick-reaction weapon. It is normally deployed well forward and fire-control can either be by voice from an observation post a short distance ahead, or by man-pack radio. The zone of dispersion is a broad ellipse or even near-circular and relatively large in terms of range as compared with a breech-loading rifled piece, but the rate of fire is high—20 rounds per minute from well trained crews—and as a simple, inexpensive device for bringing down a saturating area concentration within its limits of range the mortar is unequalled. Used in ones and twos close behind the attacking troops it is extremely useful for rapid close support on small targets in squad and platoon action. The great advantage of the mortar is its small size, mobility, cheapness and simplicity. Not surprisingly it is the favourite weapon of guerrillas, being extremely difficult to locate and counter-bombard. As will be seen in the ancillary section pp. 141–143 a specialised locating equipment has been developed for the location of enemy mortars.

The mortar is the chosen self-operated close support weapon of the infantry (who took to it whole heartedly in World War II, discarding the infantry howitzers and guns in the cannon-companies of the infantry regiments where these existed in its favour). Nevertheless the larger natures, say, from a calibre of 105 mm upwards, have true artillery characteristics regardless of the affiliation of the operating arm. The Israeli army has a 160 mm mortar, and 120 mm mortars can now range up to 9,000 m, or 5·4 miles. Except for the British, who have set their face against any but light infantry mortars, they are deployed by many armies as an essential complement to the other two members of the indirect fire artillery family—the guns and rockets.

The passion for sophistication has also overtaken mortar designers. Mortars are being made more accurate by improving their sights and ballistics. Mortar ammunition is becoming more and more expensive as lethality is increased and range and consistency improved by rifling, and plastic driving bands, which expand on discharge to seal the bore effectively; the bomb must, of course, be a loose fit so as to slide down the barrel in the act of loading. There is also a demand for the greater ranges provided by the rocket-assisted projectile principle. Hotchkiss-Brandt, for instance, have developed their *Projectile*

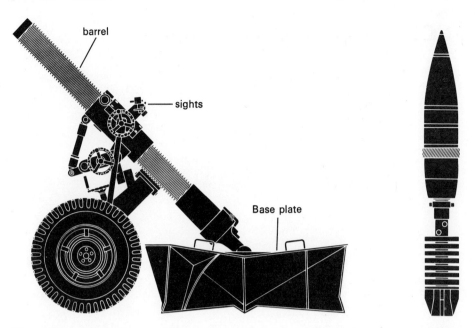

Figure VIII(a): Typical heavy mortar.

Figure VIII(b): PEPA mortar round.

Figure VIII(c): Example of a breech-loading mortar.

Empenné á Propulsion Additionelle (**PEPA**) to improve the range of their 120 mm mortar from 6,650 m to 9,000 m and the Soviet artillery has a huge breech-loader.

Here, of course, we have a characteristic design dilemma. The general utility of mortars —their cheapness, simplicity of operation, mobility, flexibility of deployment, high power and lethality—have made demands for bigger mortars, more accuracy, and more range so that cost and complication increase and indeed some of the rare, very large mortars that have been designed are really more like high-angle howitzers. This in turn generates a demand for sophisticated fire control procedures and target acquisition equipment. The opinion of artillerymen as a whole is to resist this trend and to maintain the distinction between the crude, simple mortar and sophisticated, rifled, breech-loading ordnance.

105 mm EC1A 105-L medium mortar

Spain

Calibre	105 mm
Barrel length	1,500 mm
Barrel weight	—
Baseplate weight	—
Bipod weight	—
Total weight in action	105 kg
Ammunition options	HE (9·2 kg)
	Smoke (9·2 kg)
	Practice (9·2 kg)
Range	7,050 m
Rate of fire	12 rds/min
Elevation limits	—
Traverse limits	—
Detachment	4

105 mm EC 1A in firing position.

This mortar is of similar design to the ECIA 81-L mortar. The differences are in calibre, the strength of the various parts, and a differently shaped baseplate, which is round in this case.

The barrel is mounted on the baseplate by a ball and socket joint, and is supported by a tripod instead of the more usual bipod.

Due to the extra weight over the 81-L, two types of trailer have been designed for this weapon. The normal trailer of box-type construction is capable of carrying the complete weapon, its accessories and twelve rounds of ammunition. It weighs 239 kilogrammes without ammunition. A light cart is available for airborne operations; it weighs only 110 kilogrammes, and will carry the whole weapon, but no ammunition. Though it is normally transported on a trailer, this mortar can be carried by three men or by one mule.

The HE round has a damage radius of 150 m from its 1·75 kilogrammes charge of TNT. A smoke round is available.

Employment Spain

The 105 mm EC 1A on its trailer with 12 rounds of ammunition.

107 mm mortar M 30

United States of America

Calibre	107 mm
Barrel length	1,520 mm
Barrel weight	71 kg
Baseplate	100 kg (M 24)
Total weight in action	295 kg
Ammunition options	HE (M 329) (11·2 kg)
	HE (M 3)
	Smoke WP
	Chemical
	Illuminating
Range	5,420 m
Rate of fire	20–25 rds/min
Elevation limits	+45° +85°
Traverse limits	16°
Detachment	5–6

The M 30 is a muzzle-loaded rifled weapon, introduced into service in 1951, which has two mountings. The difference lies in the basplate: M 24 is an inner baseplate of magnesium with an outer baseplate ring: M 24 A1 is a one-piece steel assembly and weighs 104 kilogrammes. The whole equipment weighs 295 kilogrammes, and breaks into six parts for transporting: barrel with integral tube cap and firing pin; baseplate; base ring; bridge; rotator; monopod support or standard. The monopod support is an important recognition feature.

Two types of HE ammunition are available: M 329 (and M 329-B1) ranges to 5,420 m with a muzzle velocity of 293 metres/second: M 3 (and M 3A1) gives a muzzle velocity of only 257 metres/second and achieves a range of 4,600 m. The chemical round gives the same performance as M 3. This mortar is used in an SP configuration when mounted in a modified M 113 APC known as the M 106.

Employment	Austria	Netherlands
	Italy	Philippines
	Japan	USA
	South Korea	Zaire

107 mm mortar M 30.

107 mm heavy mortar M 1938 and M 107

Union of Soviet Socialist Republics

Calibre	107 mm
Barrel length	1,670 mm
Barrel weight	—
Bipod weight	—
Baseplate weight	—
Total weight in action	170 kg
Ammunition options	HE (9 kg)
	HE light (7·9 kg)
Range	6,300 m
Rate of fire	15 rds/min
Elevation limits	+45° +80°
Traverse limits	6°
Detachment	6

The 107 mm mortar of two marks, M 1938 and M 107, is a scaled down version of the Soviet 120 mm mortar, reduced in weight and size to suit its normal role, as the regimental mortar of mountain units. The mortar is usually transported by pack animals in difficult terrain, but is towed on a two-wheeled carriage over normal roads. For animal-packing, the weapon breaks down into three loads; barrel, bipod and baseplate.

The M 107 is the improved model of this mortar and has replaced the M 1938 in the Soviet Army, although the earlier version is still to be found in the non-Soviet Warsaw Pact countries and in South-East Asia.

Employment	China	North Korea
	Ethiopia	Poland
	East Germany	USSR
	India	Vietnam
	Jordan	

The 1938 model 107 mm mortar deployed.

The M 107 mortar in travelling position.

4·2 inch mortar Mk 3

United Kingdom

Calibre	107 mm
Barrel length	1,980 mm
Barrel weight	41·3 kg
Bipod weight	20·8 kg
Baseplate weight	84 kg
Total weight in action	550 kg (including carriage)
Ammunition option	HE (9·1 kg), Smoke (10·2 kg)
Range	3,750 m
Rate of fire	12 rds/min
Elevation limits	45° −80°
Traverse limits	7° − 21°
Detachment	6

The British 4·2 inch mortar first saw action at El Alamein and proved to be a most effective weapon in World War II. It is still in service in five armies. It consists of a steel tube with a cap and breech piece screwed onto it, a bipod, a cradle with elevating and traversing gears, sights and a base plate. It has a two charge ammunition system. There are six men in the detachment with two ¾ ton type towing vehicles: one towing the mortar and the other towing a 10 cwt two wheeled ammunition trailer, which holds up to 44 bombs.

Employment	Ethiopia	Nepal
	Laos	Turkey
	Malaysia	

The 4·2 inch mortar in action: note square spade attached to base plate.

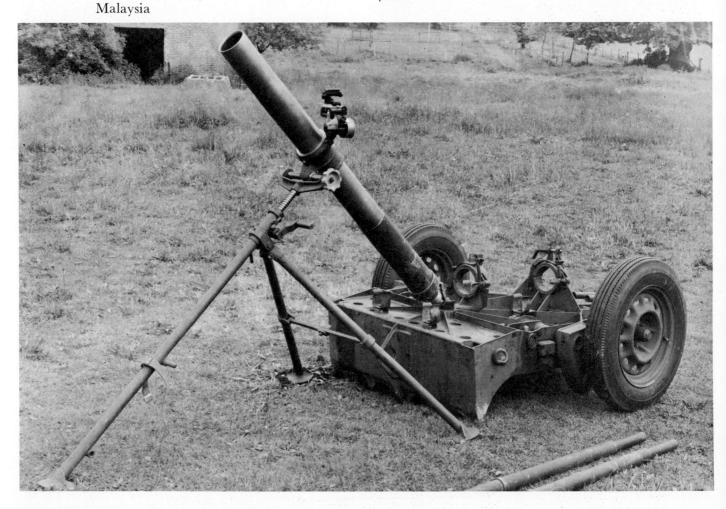

120 mm mortar M 60

Austria

Calibre	120 mm
Barrel length	1,500 mm
Barrel weight	—
Bipod weight	—
Baseplate weight	—
Total weight in action	296 kg
Ammunition options	HE (15·8 kg)
Range	5,700 m
Rate of fire	15 rds/min
Elevation limits	+45° +80°
Traverse limits	6°
Detachment	6

This Austrian weapon of unknown ancestry consists of a conventional baseplate, bipod and buffer design. It is removed from its heavy two wheel trailer for firing. Unlike many other designs, the weapon does not form part of the trailer carriage, to be towed by its muzzle, but rather sits on a complete trailer.

The barrel is mounted by ball and socket to the baseplate to allow 360° traverse. The baseplate is dish-shaped with locating spade like extensions beneath; it has two integral lifting handles.

Employment   Austria

---

120 mm standard Tampella mortar (M 65)

Finland

Calibre	120 mm
Barrel length	1,940 mm
Barrel weight	84 kg
Bipod weight	69 kg
Baseplate weight	72 kg
Total weight in action	225 kg
Ammunition options	HE (M 58F) (12·9 kg)
	HE (ST)
	Smoke
	Illuminating
	Practice
Range	8,300 m
Rate of fire	5–10 rds/min
Elevation limits	+37° +87°
Traverse limits	360°
Detachment	3–4

120 mm Tampella mortar mounted on the M 3 half-track.

The 120 mm standard Tampella is a smooth-bore mortar made to high tolerances and is designed for simplicity in both operation and maintenance. Though normally towed, it can be carried by mule, or man-handled over very short distances.

The barrel is made of high-tensile steel alloy and has a close tolerance bore. It is internally threaded at the breech end to take the breech block which contains the firing mechanism. The firing mechanism is of the spring-loaded striker type actuated by a lanyard and has a safety lever. The bipod incorporates the recoil buffer with the barrel collar, elevation, azimuth and correction gears. Leg spread is limited by an adjustable chain. Welded sheet steel is used for the 960 mm diameter baseplate, in the centre of which is a socket to take the breech-piece ball end. The mortar can be traversed 360° without moving the baseplate. The sight unit consists of an elevation and azimuth mechanism, one range and two cross-levelling bubbles and a collimator. Quick releases for large adjustments are fitted and the mils-graduated dials can be freed for rapid and large adjustments. A quick release dovetail mount on the bipod facilitates removal of the sight, though this is not necessary when firing. A steel box chassis two-wheel trailer is normally used to move the weapon. It weighs 129 kilogrammes.

Four types of ammunition are available, though any 120 mm mortar ammunition can be used. The M 58F round is a HE bomb containing 2·3 kilogrammes of TNT and utilises up to eight secondary charges. Three types of smoke round of the same designation are available (FM, PWP and WP) also illuminating and practice rounds. With the Super Tampella (ST) bomb, a range of 8,300 m is possible.

The Israeli Army until recently relied almost entirely on mortars for close support artillery, and it is this weapon—made under licence by Soltam—which is used. It is carried in, and often fired from, the M 3 half-track and is deployed in regiments of 12 mortars with each infantry brigade.

Employment   Finland
Federal Republic of Germany
Israel

120 mm Tampella mortar on normal ground base-plate.

120 mm light Tampella mortar

Finland

Calibre	120 mm
Barrel length	1,726 mm
Barrel weight	43 kg
Bipod weight	31·5 kg
Baseplate weight	62 kg
Total weight in action	136 kg
Ammunition options	HE (M 58F) (12·9 kg)
	HE (M 58FF) (13 kg)
	Smoke
	Illuminating
	Practice
Range	6,250 m
Rate of fire	5–10 rds/min
Elevation limits	+45° +70°
Traverse limits	—
Detachment	3

The 120 mm light Tampella mortar is a smooth-bore weapon with a retractable firing pin. The barrel is made of steel alloy, and is externally threaded at the breech to take the breech block containing the firing pin. A ball extension on this block makes the joint with a central socket in a circular welded baseplate and enables the mortar to be fully traversed without re-bedding. The bipod is of similar design to all the Tampella mounts, and incorporates a recoil buffer, and dustproof gearing for elevation, azimuth and fine adjustment. The sight unit is the same as that of the 120 mm standard, and of the 81 mm Tampella mortar, and is covered in the description of the former.

The optional carriage is of tubular construction and weighs 130 kilogrammes. It can be towed at speeds up to 40 kilometres/hour. The weapon, all its accessories and six rounds of ammunition can be carried. The mortar can be man-packed by three men or one mule.

A special range of ammunition designated M 58FF has been produced for this mortar, though it will also fire the M 58F ammunition. The HE bomb is filled with 2·8 kilogrammes of TNT. Other rounds include three types of smoke, and illuminating and practice bombs. All rounds have the same ballistic properties, so only one range table is necessary.

This mortar, like the Standard Tampella M 65, is made in Israel.

Employment   Finland
              Israel

20 mm light Tampella mortar deployed.

In travelling position.

120 mm MO-120-AM 50 heavy mortar

France

Calibre	120 mm	*Traverse limits*	17°
Barrel length	1,746 mm	*Detachment*	4
Barrel weight	76 kg (with towing ring)		
Bipod weight	—		
Baseplate weight	80 kg		
Total weight in action	402 kg (242 kg without under-carriage)		
Ammunition options	HE (PEPA/LP) (13·4 kg)		
	HE (M 44) (13 kg)		
	Coloured smoke (13 kg)		
	Illuminating (Mk 62 ED) (13·6 kg)		
	Smoke WP (Mk 62) (13 kg)		
	Practice		
Range	9,000 m (with PEPA ammunition)		
Rate of fire	8–12 rds/min		
Elevation limits	+45° +80°		

This is a smooth-bore mortar capable of both automatic and controlled fire. A bipod is provided for greater stability during sustained fire, but it can also be fired from its road wheels which are equipped with a special locking device to stop the weapon moving when it is fired without its bipod. In its travelling position a screw-on ring mount is attached to the muzzle end of the tube, and the whole unit is towed by a suitable vehicle. The AM 50 fires the same family of ammunition as the other Hotchkiss-Brandt 120 mm mortars, including the rocket assisted PEPA round which produces the maximum range of 9,000 m.

Employment   France

Note the triangular base plate and the use of the wheeled carriage to form a 'bipod support'.

120 mm MO-120-60 (light) heavy mortar

France

Calibre	120 mm
Barrel length	1,632 mm
Barrel weight	34 kg
Bipod weight	25 kg
Baseplate weight	33 kg
Total weight in action	92 kg
Ammunition options	HE (PEPA/LP) (13·4 kg)
	HE (M 44) (13 kg)
	Coloured smoke
	Illuminating (M 62)
	(13·6 kg)
	Smoke WP
	Practice
Range	5,500 m 6,550 m (PEPA)
Rate of fire	8–15 rds/min
Elevation limits	+40° +85°
Traverse limits	17°
Detachment	3

The MO-120-60 is the lightest of a range of 120 mm mortars manufactured by Hotchkiss-Brandt. Its total weight of 94 kilogrammes permits it to be broken down into a three-man load. It is also APC mounted in AMX VCL. It is a conventionally designed smooth bore weapon with most refinements eliminated in order to reduce as much weight as possible. A unique buffer absorbs some of the shock of firing, and has probably been evolved to reduce the stress on the very light construction. The barrel weight of 34 kilogrammes indicates that it is thin-walled and the maximum charge (4) suggest that this light barrel structure imposes a limitation on range. Nevertheless, a wide choice of ammunition is available for this weapon. The M 44 HE bomb is the primary round; others include coloured HE, smoke, illuminating and training. The bombs weigh between 13·8 kilogrammes and 13 kilogrammes. The rocket assisted PEPA round is available, which ranges to 6,550 m.

Employment   Argentina
              France

Hotchkiss-Brandt 120 mm (MO-120-60) mortar

120 mm MO-120-M 65 heavy mortar

France

Calibre	120 mm
Barrel length	1,640 mm
Barrel weight	44 kg
Bipod weight	24 kg
Baseplate weight	26 kg
Total weight in action	104 kg
Ammunition options	HE (PEPA/LP) (13·4 kg)
	HE (M 44) (13 kg)
	Coloured HE
	Illuminating (Mk 62)
	(13·6 kg)
	Smoke WP
	Practice
Range	9,000 m
Rate of fire	8–12 rds/min
Elevation limits	+40° +85°
Traverse limits	17°
Detachment	2–3

The MO-120-M 65 is an attempt to combine some of the lightness of the MO-120-60 with the fire power of the MO-120-AM 50. Normal transportation is achieved by putting the weapon on a light trailer which can be towed by a vehicle or pulled by two men. However, due to the relatively light weight, it is possible to manpack the weapon in three roughly equal loads, using special harness.

This is a smooth-bore weapon fired from a tripod and baseplate and capable of either automatic or controlled operation. In addition, the breech is equipped with a safety device to prevent accidental percussion when, for example, the weapon is being unloaded. The weapon is capable of firing any 120 mm ammunition, including the PEPA/LP (projectile empenne à propulsion additionelle/longue portee) HE round with additional propulsion.

Employment France

Hotchkiss-Brandt 120 mm (M 65) mortar on its light trailer.

120 mm MO-120-RT-61 heavy rifled mortar

France

Calibre	120 mm
Barrel length	2,080 mm with breech
Barrel weight	114 kg
Bipod weight	—
Baseplate weight	190 kg
Total weight in action	582 kg
Ammunition options	HE (PRPA) (15·6 kg)
	HE (PR 14) (15·7 kg)
	Preclair illuminating (15·7 kg)
Range	13,000 m with PRPA, 8,350 m
	with PR14
Rate of fire	6–10 rds/min
Elevation limits	+30° +85°
Traverse limits	14°
Detachment	3

The Hotchkiss-Brandt 120 mm rifled mortar is one of the largest mortars available today. It is mounted and towed on a specially designed pair of road wheels from which it is also fired. Stabilisation is achieved by the baseplate, which is effective both on hard and marshy ground. The manufacturers claim that the weapon can be brought into action in 1½ minutes and out again in two minutes.

The mounting, consisting of the cradle and carriage, is of advanced design. The traversing gear and cross levelling gear are similar to those found in the Hotchkiss-Brandt standard 120 mm mortar, but the elevating system is unique, in that quick, rough elevation is obtained by varying the position of the axis of the cradle relative to the axis of the wheels, and this having been done, fine adjustment is obtained by varying the position of the cradle, in relation to the barrel.

The weapon is capable of either automatic or controlled fire and has its own range of ammunition. The PR 14 HE bomb is comparable in its effect to the standard 105 mm artillery shell. The bomb weighs 15·7 kg and has a maximum range of 8,350 m. In addition, the PRPA (Projectile Rayé a Propulsion Additionelle), which weighs 15.6 kg, has a maximum range of 13,000 m due to the incorporation of a rocket motor which is initiated during flight. The Preclair illuminating round has a range of 8,000 m, and candle power of 1,050,000 for one minute or 1,600,000 for 40 seconds. Firing of conventional ammunition requires the use of range conversion tables since the other Hotchkiss-Brandt bombs are calibrated for different barrel lengths. The barrel of this mortar is rifled from breech to muzzle with 40 grooves with a uniform twist of 10·5°. The screw-on breech piece has a spherical ball butt flattened on one side which is locked into a socket in the baseplate. The firing mechanism is completely watertight and can be used submerged.

Employment France

Note the simplicity of design; it is towed by the muzzle.

120 mm ECIA 120-SL and 120-L heavy mortar

Spain

	120 SL	120 L
Calibre	120 mm	120 mm
Barrel length	1,600 mm	1,600 mm
Barrel weight	—	—
Baseplate weight	—	—
Bipod weight	—	—
Total weight in action	123 kg	213 kg
Ammunition options	HE (N Type) (16·7 kg)	HE (N Type) (16·7 kg)
	HE (L Type) (13·2 kg)	HE (L Type) (13·2 kg)
	Smoke (N Type) (16·7 kg)	Smoke (N Type) (16·7 kg)
	Smoke (L Type) (13·2 kg)	Smoke (L Type) (13·2 kg)
	Practice (N & L Types)	Practice (N & L Types)
Range	5,940 (L type)	6,600 (L type)
Rate of fire	12 rds/min	10 rds/min
Elevation limits	—	+45° +85½°
Traverse limits	—	—
Detachment	4	4

In firing position.

There are two versions of the EC1A 120 mm mortar.

The ECIA 120-SL has a similar configuration to other ECIA mortars such as the 81-L and 105-L; it has the same tripod support. A feature of this mortar, not apparent on the other members of the ECIA family, is an adjustable chain for limiting the leg spread of the tripod. Although normal transport is by trailer, the manufacturer claims that it is possible for the weapon to be manpacked by three men.

Two types of ammunition designated N and L are available for this weapon. The N type bombs are heavier and longer, and carry a bigger charge (3·2 kilogrammes of TNT or smoke composition), than the L bomb (2·3 kilogrammes).

The range of the N type is 900 m less than the L type for both weapons. Packaging of ammunition is the same in each case. Two rounds are packed in individual containers in a wooden case.

The ECIA 120-L is a longer range version of the 120-SL. The basic configuration is the same, although it has a larger baseplate and a heavier barrel. It fires the same ammunition as the 120–SL and is transported on a 146 kilogramme trailer. It is too heavy for man-packing. The other difference between the two mortars is that the 120-L does not have the adjustable chains to limit tripod leg spread.

Employment Spain

Mounted on its trolley.

120 mm mortar M 41C

Sweden

Calibre	120 mm
Barrel length	2,000 mm
Barrel weight	—
Bipod weight	66 kg
Baseplate weight	—
Total weight in action	285 kg
Ammunition options	HE (M 58F) (12·9 kg)
	Smoke
	Illuminating
	Practice
Range	6,400 m
Rate of fire	12 rds/min
Elevation limits	+45° +80°
Traverse limits	360°
Detachment	4

This is a Second World War weapon originally designed and produced in Finland as the Tampella M 1940. In 1960, the original base plate was replaced by the Hotchkiss-Brandt M 52, locally manufactured under licence from France.

The bipod is the same as that fitted to the Tampella M 65. It incorporates the twin recoil buffer and laying gear. A cross bar in front of the barrel collar carries the sight at its left end and traversing hand wheel at the right. Leg spread is limited by an adjustable chain. The carrying trailer is detached for firing.

The barrel carries lifting handles near its base and is mounted into the centre of the baseplate. The whole equipment is traversed about the baseplate mounting to give 360° traverse.

The M 41C is 65 kilogrammes heavier than the later M 65, with which it has shared a common sight since 1972. The M 58F range of ammunition can be fired but it is not known if the longer range super-Tampella round is accepted. The ammunition types include three different smoke rounds.

Employment   Eire
              Sweden

120 mm mortar MW 41

Switzerland

Calibre	120 mm
Barrel length	—
Barrel weight	—
Bipod weight	—
Baseplate weight	—
Total weight in action	262 kg
Ammunition options	HE (13 kg)
Range	5,000 m
Rate of fire	10 rds/min
Elevation limits	—
Traverse limits	—
Detachment	6

The MW 41 is an elderly and heavy weapon characterized by the convex baseplate with four hinged carrying handles. The barrel is fixed to the baseplate by a conventional ball and socket joint. The bipod, mounted to the barrel with a recoil buffer, is also of a conventional pattern. It allows limited traverse, and elevation from about 45° to 80°.

Reconnaisance battalions and armoured regiments of mechanised brigades are equipped with this mortar.

Employment   Switzerland

120 mm heavy mortars M 1938 and M 1943

Union of Soviet Socialist Republics

Calibre	120 mm		Smoke (16 kg)
Barrel length	1,850 mm		Incendiary (16·7 kg)
Barrel weight	—	*Range*	5,700 m
Bipod weight	—	*Rate of fire*	12–15 rds/min
Baseplate weight	—	*Elevation limits*	+45° + 80°
Total weight in action	500 kg	*Traverse limits*	8°
Ammunition options	HE (15·4 kg)	*Detachment*	5–6

These two weapons are almost identical. Detailed modifications have been made, but do not affect the MP-41/MP-42 collimating sight. The 120 mm mortar M 1938 was the standard Soviet infantry mortar until it was replaced recently by the 120 mm M 1943. A unique design when originated, the mortar can be quickly broken down into three parts, barrel, bipod and baseplate, for movement over short distances. For normal travel the whole weapon folds together and is towed on a two-wheeled tubular carriage or, if necessary, can be animal-packed in its three parts. The mortar can be either drop or trigger-fired by lanyard, as required, and an anti-double-loading device is provided for attachment to the muzzle.

Although the 120 mm mortar M 1943 has virtually replaced the M 1938 as the regimental mortar of the Soviet infantry both are found in the other countries listed. The M 1943 is manufactured in communist China as the 120 mm mortar type 55, and exported to Pakistan and Tanzania.

Whilst the ballistic and performance details and methods of handling are the same for both models, the outward appearance differs slightly: the shock absorber cylinders of the M 1943 are much longer than those of the M 1938, and in the later model the elevating and traversing gear is rather more sophisticated.

The outer casing of the HE ammunition can be made of either wrought or cast iron, the latter being more effective against personnel but being slightly reduced in maximum range.

The Austrians refer to this mortar as M 60.

120 mm heavy mortar M 1943.

Employment:

Afghanistan	Egypt	Syria
Algeria	East Germany	Tanzania
Albania	Iraq	USSR
Austria	Lebanon	Vietnam
Bulgaria	Morocco	Yemen
China	North Korea	Yugoslavia
Congo	Pakistan	
Czechoslovakia	Romania	

120 mm UBM 52 heavy mortar

Yugoslavia

Calibre	120 mm
Barrel length	1,290 mm
Barrel weight	—
Bipod weight	—
Baseplate weight	—
Total weight in action	400 kg
Ammunition options	Heavy HE (15·9 kg)
	Light HE (12·25 kg)
	Smoke
	Illuminating (12·2 kg)
Range	6,000 m (with the lighter shell)
Rate of fire	25 rds/min
Elevation limits	+45° +85°
Traverse limits	60 at 45° elevation
Detachment	5

120 mm heavy mortar UBM 52

The Yugoslav 120 mm mortar UBM 52 can fire the same ammunition as the Soviet 120 mm mortars but is an adoption of a Western weapon, the MO-120-AM 50 made under licence. The UBM 52 was designed as a heavy mobile weapon for use both in normal operations and in mountainous terrain. It is thus semi-permanently mounted on its own two-wheeled carriage for firing, but can be taken apart for pack transport by five mules. It also possesses a muzzle attachment to permit towing by either two mules or a vehicle. The cleverly designed spiked rectangular baseplate and hydro-elastic recoil system allow the mortar to be halted and fired almost

immediately, no ground preparation for the baseplate being necessary. In spite of its shorter barrel, the UBM 52 can outshoot the Soviet M 1943: using its light HE ammunition, it has an extra 300 m range and a far higher rate of fire.

Employment Burma
                  Yugoslavia

160 mm Tampella heavy mortar

Finland

Calibre	160 mm
Barrel length	3,066 mm
Barrel weight	—
Bipod weight	—
Baseplate weight	250 kg
Total weight in action	1,700 kg
Ammunition options	HE (40 kg)
	Smoke
Range	9,600 m
Rate of fire	5–8 rds/min
Elevation limits	+43° +70°
Traverse limits	360°
Detachment	7

This is a smooth-bore weapon which incorporates a number of novel features. It is mounted on a two-wheeled carriage, but the baseplate is removed and loaded in the towing vehicle for travelling. In action, the wheels are swung inwards so as to be at a tangent to the baseplate centre. This endows the weapon which

is too heavy for the detachment to lift, with 360° traverse. The movement of the carriage wheels is used for both coarse and fine azimuth laying: for fine laying a hand wheel and reduction gear is fitted to the left hand wheel.

The barrel, breech piece and recoil buffer are of conventional design.

The HE round contains five kilogrammes of explosive (TNT) and is fitted with an impact fuse. A primary and nine secondary charges are used. The barrel is lowered for loading: a semi-automatic lowering device and a counter-balance mechanism enable the detachment to produce a high rate of fire for the size of the equipment.

The weapon is made under licence in Israel by Soltam Ltd. Many of the Israeli 160 mm mortars are mounted on a modified Sherman tank chassis. A ramp is used to present ammunition to the barrel for loading from its on-board stowage.

Employment Finland
                  Israel

160 mm Tampella heavy mortar.

160 mm mortar M 43

Union of Soviet Socialist Republics

Calibre	160 mm
Barrel length	3,230 mm
Barrel weight	—
Bipod weight	—
Baseplate weight	—
Total weight in action	1,270 kg
Ammunition options	HE (40·8 kg)
Range	5,150 m
Rate of fire	3 rds/min
Elevation limits	+45° +80°
Traverse limits	25°
Detachment	4–8

The weapon is sometimes distinguished from the newer M 53 by the term 'non-nuclear.' It is a smooth-bore, breech-loaded weapon. It is permanently mounted on a two-wheel axle, which serves as a bipod. A long cradle carries the barrel on trunnions mounted at its top end.

Elevation and traverse are provided for at the attachment point of the cradle to the axle. The base plate is attached to the bottom of the cradle: it is 1,524 mm in diameter, dish-shaped with protruding webs beneath to give stability. There are four lifting handles round the rim. The baseplate is folded over the cradle and barrel for travelling, and the mortar is towed by its muzzle.

The barrel is swung to the horizontal for loading. A single equilibrator is fitted to the right, opposite the sights and laying gear.

The M 43 is no longer in use in the Soviet Army.

Employment:

Afghanistan	Egypt	Syria
Albania	East Germany	Vietnam
China	India	
Czechoslovakia	North Korea	

The 160 mm heavy M 1953 mortar with its long barrel being manhandled into the firing position.

160 mm mortar M 53

Union of Soviet Socialist Republics

Calibre	160 mm
Barrel length	4,480 mm
Barrel weight	—
Bipod weight	—
Baseplate weight	—
Total weight in action	1,300 kg
Ammunition options	Nuclear (41·5 kg)
	HE (40·8 kg)
Range	8,040 m
Rate of fire	2–3 rds/min
Elevation limits	+50° +80°
Traverse limits	24°
Detachment	7–9

The M 53 is a newer mark of weapon than the M 43. The general arrangement of the two weapons is the same and they share the 1,524 mm diameter baseplate with its distinctive carrying handles. The barrel of the

M 53 is altogether stronger and longer. Range is improved to 8,040 m. It is breech-loading.

Details of the nuclear round are highly classified. It is probably a sub-kiloton yield device which has not been supplied to other users of the weapon. The Russians no longer use the M 53. The Chinese refer to this mortar as the Type 60.

Employment   China
              Iraq
              Egypt
              Syria

The mortar being loaded.

The 160 mm mortar M 53 being laid.

240 mm mortar M 53

Union of Soviet Socialist Republics

Calibre	240 mm
Barrel length	5,340 mm
Barrel weight	—
Bipod weight	—
Baseplate weight	—
Total weight in action	3,610 kg
Ammunition options	Nuclear (130 kg)
	HE (100 kg)
Range	10,000 m
Rate of fire	1 rd/min
Elevation limits	+45° +65°
Traverse limits	17°
Detachment	8

This is the largest mortar in service today, but is believed to be obsolete in the Soviet Army. It is a breech loaded weapon made up of baseplate, two-wheeled carriage, barrel and cradle. The baseplate is a conventional disc with a diameter of 2,130 mm. The wheeled carriage supports the cradle and barrel, serving in place of the bipod of smaller mortars. Elevation is adjusted by gearing at the attachment of cradle to carriage. The barrel is mounted at its centre of gravity in trunnions set in the top of the cradle: this allows the barrel to be swung to the horizontal for loading.

The general arrangement allows reasonable elevation, but limits traverse. Large switches present a problem because of the size of the weapon. The fin-stabilised bomb is loaded through a vertically sliding breech block. Lifting the bomb to the breech is a four-man task using a giant Stilson clamp with two long handles. The breech stands over five feet from the ground in the loading position. A small trolley is used to move rounds about the baseplate position.

Little is known about the nuclear round, which is probably comparable with the American 8 inch howitzer shell. The short range of the mortar must present a problem in deployment in the nuclear role.

Employment   Algeria   India
                Bulgaria Iraq
                China   Rumania
                Hungary USSR

240 mm mortar M 53 being loaded.

VI. Artillery Rockets

This section deals with a wide variety of rockets, both guided and free flying, with ranges from a few thousand metres to hundreds of kilometres, and warheads from two or three kilogrammes to megaton nuclear devices. The criteria for inclusion in this chapter is that the weapon should be truly mobile and intended to influence the immediate battle rather than targeted for strategic effects. The Attila rockets are hardly in the same class as the Scaleboard or Shaddock: nor are the multiple launchers strictly comparable in purpose with single guided weapons, except that there is an interesting link weapon in the Japanese 30 rocket. All types of rocket are included together for convenience.

Some missiles have guidance systems, and most have fins, but these are added to the two basic components—rocket motor and warhead. For small missiles, especially those for which only one type of warhead is available the two parts will be pre-assembled and delivered as a complete unit. Larger missiles in the Honest John/Lance class will almost certainly be delivered to the users as separate components. The assembly area can be away from the launch site for security, and the time of assembling is also used for checking out the various missile systems.

In the case of liquid fuel motors, fuelling is usually left until the last moment. It is a hazardous and complex task requiring bulky equipment. Warhead mating and fuelling will probably be at the launch site (an exception is Lance whose liquid fuel is pre-packed and ready for use) because of the difficulty of moving the missile after fuelling.

Many rockets have wings, or more accurately fins. These are not aerodynamic and do not generate lift, but are control surfaces. Unguided rockets use them to give stability in flight: they are slightly offset from the axis of the rocket and sustain, in flight, the spin imparted at launch. Guided missiles employ moveable control surfaces which effect changes in the missile's course.

Either solid or liquid fuels are used to power the rocket motor, each having its own advantages and disadvantages. Liquid fuel is dangerous to handle, difficult to store and requires a sophisticated control and motor design, yet it has a greater energy output for its weight, thrust can be varied and the motor stopped and restarted. The solid fuels have the opposite qualities. In general, the smaller and cheaper rockets are solid fuelled.

A free flight rocket is inherently less accurate than a projectile fired from a gun. The sources of inaccuracy can be minimised in design and manufacture, although this increases the cost of the weapon, to a point where it is economically sensible to adopt a guidance system. As a result the tactical handling of rockets is designed to take advantage of the weapon's characteristics.

What are the sources of inaccuracy?

First, the behaviour of the rocket motor. Unless some of the advantages in warhead design (which will be explained later) are compromised, or the launch rail is excessively long, the motor will continue to burn while the missile is in free flight. This means that the missile is subjected to the influence of crosswind and low-level air eddies while the centre of gravity and thrust is changing because the propellant is being consumed. This effect is magnified by any misalignment or thrust due to manufacturing tolerances.

Second, the missile which consists of rocket motor and warhead is much larger than a shell, and therefore more susceptible to the effects of crosswinds. Stabilization in flight normally depends on fins which increase the area against which the wind operates, and are especially productive of errors to the intended trajectory just after launch when the rocket is still accelerating.

Third, the burning time of the fuel is many times greater than that of a gun's propellant, so that small variations in the rate of burning have a more noticeable effect on the maximum velocity of the missile. This effect is exaggerated by the head or tail component of the wind: the wind acts against a shell only after it has achieved its maximum muzzle velocity in the protection of barrel, while the wind affects the missile's acceleration (and maximum velocity) as well as its unpowered flight.

Despite the relatively low accuracy of free flight rockets, they do have real advantages over the gun as a weapon delivery means. The rocket itself is not a cheap device, but its launcher is relatively simple compared with a gun. The production techniques of gun and shell require great industrial expertise in the construction of shell cases, barrels and stress bearing carriages. At the same time, they require sophisticated light industry for a host of ancillaries, from sights to hydraulics. The rocket requires only skilled light industry. As a result, rockets have been especially popular with the lesser industrial nations who have sought a measure of independence in their military needs: Brazil, Spain and Switzerland come to mind.

They have advantages too for the more sophisticated armies, which have them in service as well as guns. The Soviet Army especially has long seen their utility, and new Western weapons (LARS and RAP 14) will reflect the belief in a judicious mixture of the two weapon systems. The simple, unstressed rocket launcher can be assembled in banks, and once loaded, a large number of rockets can be ripple fired in a salvo lasting a few seconds. The shock effect at the target is great; only the mortar approaches it in this respect. No gun can achieve the same rate of fire, even the sophisticated Swedish L 50.

The rocket is less subject to limitations of calibre, is subject to smaller firing forces and therefore is less limiting to the warhead designer. As a result early nuclear weapons for the battlefield were rocket delivered. Multiple warheads and guided sub-munitions are more easily fitted to rockets. The motor shell provides a useful vehicle for controlled flight. Carrier warheads for smoke, incendiary, propaganda and chemical agents have a better payload than a shell of equivalent size.

The rocket's lack of accuracy can even be turned to advantage. The weight of fire which the multiple launcher produces allows the instantaneous saturation of a large area. This is especially effective with smoke, incendiary or chemical agent warheads, or against large or poorly defined targets. The effect of one salvo from a battery of LARS is equivalent to one round per gun from 10 battalions of guns.

There is a requirement to impose attrition on massed armoured attacks as early as possible in order to relieve pressure on direct fire weapons. The problem is that armour can only be defeated by a direct hit. Neither gun nor rocket can guarantee the accuracy required without resorting to some form of terminal guidance. The rocket's saturation capability, coupled to the freedom it allows the warhead designer provides an elegant solution. A multiple warhead consisting of small anti-armour devices not only increases the degree of saturation, and thus increases the chance of a hit, but attacks armour at its most vulnerable points—the roof and belly. Two types of sub-warhead are being worked on: the hollow charge bomblet or high energy solid shot attacking the roof, and perhaps more practical, the shaped charge minelet attacking the belly. This last has the additional advantage that it remains active after the critical moment of delivery. This concept is most advanced in the Pandora and Medusa warheads for LARS.

What has been said so far refers to small rockets which are directly comparable in range and warhead performance with guns. Post-war development has produced the giant 'single shot' weapons. These have more than filled the position in the order of battle once occupied by the super heavy artillery. They extend the ability of the army commander to influence the battle from his own resources beyond the range of conventional artillery.

The earliest 'battlefield missile' was a direct product of the World War II German work on the V2 type weapon. Guidance was achieved by radio signal. The process required the monitoring of the rocket's flight path by radar which increased the size of the handling unit, and was subject both to enemy jamming and deliberate misdirection. The latest types have inertial guidance systems which, being pre-programmed and independent of external signals, overcome both the earlier shortcomings. Today's battlefield missile is launched by a small section with few vehicles and is much more battle-worthy as a result.

Samurai

Italy

Calibre	76 mm	Reload time	—
Rocket length	1,200 mm	Detachment	—
Rocket weight	10·6 kg		
Fuel	Liquid		
Stages	One		
Guidance	Nil		
Range	18,000 m		
Warhead	HE (3 kg)		
Tubes/Rails	—		
Traverse limits	—		

The liquid propellant used in this inexpensive small calibre rocket is self pressurising and burns for 300 seconds. Maximum speed is 1,100 metres/second. The weapon is designed as a surface-to-surface, or air-to-surface weapon.

The cruciform fins at the rear have a 200 mm span.

Employment   Trials only, Italy

80 mm 108-R rocket

Brazil

Calibre	80 mm	Detachment	—
Rocket length	—		
Rocket weight	—		
Fuel	Solid		
Stages	One		
Guidance	Nil		
Range	12,000 m		
Warhead	HE		
Tubes/Rails	16 tubes		
Traverse limits	—		
Reload time	—		

Very little is known about this small Brazilian rocket. Its calibre is in the order of 80 mm and it is fired from a multiple launcher.

The 16 tubes are arranged in three rows of five, six and five, and are mounted on a Land Rover type vehicle. It has no fins but is stabilised in flight by spin imparted by angled main motor vents.

Employment   Brazil

81 mm Dira rocket

Switzerland

Calibre	81 mm
Rocket length	1,300 mm
Rocket weight	16 kg
Fuel	—
Stages	—
Guidance	Nil
Range	8,700 m
Warhead	—
Tubes/Rails	30 tubes
Traverse limits	360°
Elevation limits	—
Reload time	—
Detachment	—

The DIRA rocket is spin and fin stabilised. It fires from an Oerlikon multiple launcher which is a 30 tube configuration and can be mounted on the M 113 APC. The tubes are arranged in two bundles of 15. It is also employed in a naval role and is suitable for deployment with airborne forces in a towed version.

Missile velocity is 490 metres/second and a warhead payload of 7 kilogrammes can be carried.

Employment   Switzerland

81 mm Dira rocket.

82·5 mm Attila Mk 11 rocket

Italy

Calibre	82·5 mm
Rocket length	1,400 mm
Rocket weight	14 kg
Fuel	Liquid
Stages	One
Guidance	None
Range	4,500 m
Warhead options	Incendiary UIS-3 (3 kg)
	Anti-personnel US-3 (3 kg)
Tubes/Rails	One rail or 40-rail
Traverse limits	—
Reload time	—
Detachment	—

The Attila Mk II is a development of Attila Mk I, but remains a short range weapon with a small warhead. It is reliable, robust and easy to handle. A single rocket can be used as a man-pack weapon, and there is also a trailer-mounted multiple launcher which will hold 40 rockets.

The unusual motor uses pre-packed hypergolic fuels to generate high pressure steam which provides the thrust. The motor is not powerful and the rocket's speed is only 200 metres/second. However, this method of propulsion has the tactical advantage that the efflux dissipates quickly and is invisible to infra-red scanners.

The rocket is stabilised by four narrow fins with a span of 225 mm. Because of its weight and lack of 'signature' Mira would be most suitable for use in difficult or broken terrain and for guerrilla operations.

A 'Super Attila' rocket is under development. It is an altogether larger weapon, 1·93 m long with a diameter of 104 mm. It will have a warhead payload of 5 kg.

Employment   Trials only, Italy

Attila II rocket on single rail for test firing.

---

107 mm rocket launcher Type 63

China

Calibre	107 mm	*Warhead*	HE
Rocket length	837 mm	*Tubes/rails*	12
Rocket weight	19 kg	*Traverse limits*	32°
Fuel	Solid	*Reload time*	—
Stages	One	*Detachment*	—
Guidance	Nil		
Range	8,300 m		

The Type 63 rocket launcher was introduced into

Chinese Army in 1963. It can be fired with all 12 tubes together or in separate two-tube sections. It can be mounted in a vehicle or it can be broken down into components for carrying by men or animals. It is thus a most suitable weapon for guerrilla warfare.

Employment   China

Type 63 wheeled launchers.

Type 63 rockets packed ready for launching in pairs.

Type 63 rocket and tubes.

108 mm Mira artillery rocket

Italy

Calibre	108 mm
Rocket length	2,960 mm
Rocket weight	50 kg
Fuel	Liquid
Stages	One
Guidance	Nil
Range	5,000 m +
Warhead	HE (10 kg)
Tubes/Rails	Single or 12 Rails
Traverse limits	—
Reload time	—
Detachment	—

The Mira is related to the Italian Bora and Attila II rockets and shares the same motor design: thrust is generated by steam produced by pre-packed hypergolic fuels. Maximum speed at motor shut down is 280 metres/second which produces a range of over 5,000 m.

The rockets are fired singly or in salvos from a 12 rail trailer. A single man pack rail has also been developed.

Employment   Trials only, Italy

108 mm Mira rocket on single rail for test firing.

108 mm R-6 rocket

Spain

Calibre	108 mm
Rocket length	768·5 mm
Rocket weight	16·3 kg
Fuel	Solid
Stages	One
Guidance	Nil
Range	7,800 m
Warhead options	HE
	Smoke
	Incendiary
Tubes/Rails	18
Traverse limits	45°
Reload time	8 mins
Detachment	—

The R-6 is the smallest of five rockets which have been developed in Spain. It has a solid IMI motor, is spin stabilised and has a claimed delivery error of one per cent of the range. 3·1 kilogrammes of propellant are used, and the HE warhead contains 1·75 kilogrammes of explosive.

The rocket is launched from a cage whose helical rails impart spin. The L-18/R-6 launch vehicle is a one-ton truck which carries 18 cages on a pedestal mounting. The rockets are fired electrically at one-second intervals. The launchers are grouped into batteries of six: a battery salvo puts down 250 kilogrammes of explosive.

Employment   Spain

108 mm R-6-B-2 launcher elevated.

R-6-B-2 rocket

Spain

Calibre	108 mm
Rocket length	935 mm
Rocket weight	19·4 kg
Fuel	Solid
Stages	One
Guidance	Nil
Range	10,000 m
Warhead options	HE (8·8 kg)
	Smoke
	Incendiary
Tubes/Rails	32 cages
Traverse limits	45°
Reload time	—
Detachment	—

The R-6-B-2 is a member of a family of Spanish surface-to-surface free flight rockets. Characteristics which are common to the whole family include the use of IMI motors, spin stabilisation, and a claimed delivery error of one per cent of range. The launching cages incorporate helical rails which impact spin. The motors are initiated electrically, and these R-6-B-2 rockets are launched at one second intervals.

The 32 launching cages are arranged in four rows of eight on a pedestal mounting standing on a flat platform one-ton truck. A stabilising jack is fitted to the vehicle.

Six launchers make up a battery.

Employment Spain

113

110 mm Lars

Federal Republic of Germany

Calibre	110 mm
Rocket length	2,260 mm
Rocket weight	35 kg
Fuel	Solid
Stages	One
Guidance	Nil
Range	14,000 m
Warhead	HE (17·2 kg)
	Smoke
	Incendiary
	Anti-vehicle
	Anti-armour minelets
Tubes/Rails	2 boxes of 18 tubes
Traverse limits	210°
Reload time	15 mins
Detachment	5

Lars is a vehicle mounted rocket system designed to produce a high concentration of fire very rapidly.

The long rocket motor produces a velocity of 635 metres/second resulting in a flat trajectory and a minimum range of 6,500 m. The rockets are spin stabilised; the spin imparted by grooves in the launch tubes is sustained by offset fins which deploy after launch. The launch tubes are laid out in two banks each with 18 tubes in rows of five, six, six and one. Each tube is 3·9 m long.

The weapon is laid from a seat set between the bundles of launch tubes. The sights consist of a conventional periscope dial sight (the Panoramic Sight Type 39) and elevation scale. Laying is mechanical.

Firing control allows single rounds, part or whole salvos to be fired. The full salvo is despatched in 18 seconds; reloading takes 15 minutes with mechanical handling. Two ammunition handlers assist the detachment of three men.

At present only the anti-personnel warhead is in service. The anti-vehicle warhead will contain eight Pandora AT I mines. Under development still is the anti-armour warhead which will contain between three and five Medusa AT 2 hollow charge mines. The rocket has a high payload for its size which gives plenty of scope for the design of highly effective warheads.

The launch vehicle is the Maginus Jupiter 7·5 ton 6 × 6 truck. The cab is armour plated and contains the electrical firing control gear: this arrangement precludes firing in an arc 25° either side of the rear of the vehicle.

Two steady jacks are manually lowered behind the rear wheels of the vehicle. All-up weight is in excess of 15,000 kilogrammes. A two wheel trailer launcher has been developed, but has yet to enter service. It weighs 19,000 kilogrammes and carries 15 tubes. The system was introduced in 1970, and each German division is scaled to two batteries of eight vehicles.

The meteorological correction of the moment for a Lars Battery is obtained by the Conar Fire Control System consisting of a radar and a computer. A single rocket is fired on the estimated range and bearing to the target which 'self-destructs' $\frac{3}{4}$ way down the trajectory. It is tracked by the radar and the computer extrapolates

The 110 mm West German rocket launcher, showing the unusual laying position.

from it the necessary data to be applied to all launchers nominated to engage the target. As there has been no adjustment of fire on the target the first salvo arrives in the target area without any loss of surprise effect.

Employment West Germany

The Conar radar used in conjunction with Lars to determine the correction of the moment.

110 mm T Type rocket

Spain

Calibre	110 mm
Rocket length	1,224 mm
Rocket weight	23·94 kg
Fuel	Solid
Stages	One
Guidance	Nil
Range	12,000 m
Warhead	—
Tubes/Rails	—
Traverse limits	—
Reload time	—
Detachment	—

The T Type rocket is still experimental, and few facts have been released. It is known to be spin stablilised by offset tail fins. Unlike many rockets of this size, the fins are fixed and do not deploy under spring action after launch. The result is a large diameter cage-type launcher which prevents the use of multiple launchers as in the German Lars. There is presumably some cost saving in manufacture, although the type of operational launcher is planned to be different.

Employment Trials only, Spain

The Type T rocket prepared for test firing.

114 mm rocket

Brazil

Calibre	114 mm
Rocket length	2.0 m
Rocket weight	—
Fuel	Solid
Stages	2
Guidance	Nil
Range	25,000 m
Warhead	HE
Tubes/Rails	5
Traverse limits	360°
Reload time	—
Detachment	—

This weapon has been developed by the Department of Studies and Technological Research. It is fired from a four wheel trailer adapted from a 40 mm anti-aircraft gun. The five launch rails are widely spaced in a two, one, three configuration. The wheels are removed for firing, giving the weapon all round traverse.

Each stage carries cruciform fins which impart and sustain spin.

Employment Brazil

Rocket launcher BM 21

Union of Soviet Socialist Republics

	Light		Heavy
Calibre	122 mm		
Rocket length	1·905 m	or	3·23 m
Rocket weight	46 kg	or	77 kg
Fuel	Solid		
Stages	One		
Guidance	Nil		
Range	14,000 m or 20,000 m		
Warhead	HE		
Tubes/Rails	40		
Traverse limits	240°		
Reload time	10 mins		
Detachment	6		

The BM 21 is the smallest of a family of Russian multiple rocket launchers: these weapons have been a prominent feature of the Soviet order of battle since the introduction of the Katyusha rocket in 1941. The BM 21 was first seen in 1964. The single stage, solid fuel rocket is given an initial spin by the helical groves in the launch tube. Fins to sustain the spin are spring loaded to deploy after launch. The motor has a six jet nozzle, and a conventional nose fuse can be set to impact or delay action.

The BM 21 consists of a bank of 40 tubes arranged in four rows of ten, and mounted on a URAL 375 truck.

The mounting is a simple turntable set over the rear wheels. A tubular extension to the left rear of the mounting carries the sight bracket: it turns down to bring the sight to a convenient height for a man standing on the ground to operate. The truck cab is retained and not protected. This lack of protection, and the downward turn of the sight bracket limit traverse to two arcs—140° to the left and left rear, and 90° to the right.

It will be noted that there is both a light and heavy version of this rocket in service.

The rockets are normally fired in a battery salvo to take full advantage of their shock and saturation effects.

A single tube adaption of this rocket is used by the North Vietnamese. The 2,460 mm tube and its tripod mount are man packed as two loads of 22 kilogrammes and 28 kilogrammes respectively.

There is a Czechoslovak version of this equipment called the M 1972 consisting of the BM 21 launcher with a 40 rocket automatic reloading system mounted on a TATRA 813 lorry.

Employment

Afghanistan	German Peoples' Republic	Syria
Angola	Hungary	USSR
Czechoslovakia	Iran	Vietnam
Egypt	Poland	

Left: A BM-21 captured in Vietnam, used by the Viet Cong sometimes as a single shot weapon.

Above: The BM 21 multi-launcher mounted on a URAL-375 truck.

Below: The Czech version showing the automatic loading system.

128 mm rocket launcher RM 130 (M 51)

Czechoslovakia

Calibre	128 mm
Rocket length	800 mm
Rocket weight	24·2 kg
Fuel	Solid
Stages	One
Guidance	Nil
Range	8,200 m
Warhead	HE (24·2 kg)
Tubes/Rails	32 tubes
Traverse limits	30°
Reload time	2 mins
Detachment	6–8

This is undoubtedly the same weapon as the Yugoslavian M 63. The launch pack of 32 tubes mounted in four rows of eight is either trailer or vehicle mounted. (The Yugoslavian version is not vehicle mounted.) All 32 rockets are fired electrically in 12 seconds. They are spin stablised. The trailer version is very similar to an obsolete American equipment, the 145 mm M 21. The chief similarity is the arrangement of the launch tubes on a two wheel carriage with split trail legs, like a field gun. Conventional elevating and traversing gear is used; traverse being limited without moving the carriage. An eight man detachment is employed, most of whom are loading numbers.

The vehicle mounted version is usually seen on the PRAGA V3S 5 ton 6 × 6 vehicle. Rumania uses the ZIL 157 truck. Traverse is limited to 240°. The arrangement of the vehicle and launch tubes is similar to the Russian BM 21.

There is a similar Russian equipment—the 16 tube BM 13—firing a longer rocket. This is no longer in service, but is believed to be used as a training expedient in East Germany and Poland.

Employment	Austria	Czechoslovakia	Rumania
	Bulgaria	Egypt	Yugoslavia
	China		

The launcher mounted on a LICW Praga V-3S vehicle.

140 mm RAP 14 rocket launcher

France

Calibre	140 mm
Rocket length	2,000 mm
Rocket weight	52 kg
Fuel	Solid
Stages	One
Guidance	Nil
Range	16,000 m
Warhead	HE (19 kg)
	Incendiary
	Smoke
	Illuminating
Tubes/Rails	22 tubes
Traverse limits	360°
Reload time	1 min
Detachment	—

The RAP 14 is a new weapon system, still undergoing trials. It is a trailer mounted equipment being developed by Constructions Navales et Industrielles de la Mediterranée.

The rocket's speed is in excess of Mach 2, and is achieved in the two second motor burn time. Helical rails within the tubes impart spin: in-flight, stabilisation is assisted by cruciform fins which deploy after the rocket leaves the launch tube and give a total span of 360 mm. Delivery error is quoted as one per cent of range, and the beaten zone of a salvo is given as 25 acres.

The pre-fragmented HE warhead can be fitted with impact or air burst fuzes. A new air burst fuze which gives an outstandingly accurate height of burst is being developed. A safety pin, which is removed when the rockets are loaded, is fitted to the fuzes. The warhead and rocket motor are packed and stored separately and are mated together before loading.

A single round can be fired, or a full salvo in 10 seconds. Mechanized reloading from a container takes only one minute: by hand four minutes.

The rockets are set in layers of five, six, five and six tubes in a box-like container, and mounted on a trailer which is towed conventionally.

For firing, the two wheel trailer is lifted onto four jacks or legs which form a cruciform platform beneath the launcher, rotate about a bearing at the centre of the cross allowing 360° traverse. Elevation is by hydraulic ram. The jacks are also hydraulic, and one man can bring the equipment into and out of action in two minutes. All up weight of the loader launcher is 4,500 kilogrammes. It is helicopter and air portable and suitable for all climates.

An improved version (RAP 14S) is already under development, to range to 20 kilometres. A naval mounting carries only 18 rockets, and the weapon is also suitable for coast defence.

Employment   Trials only France

RAP 14—single rocket after launch.

140 mm rocket launcher M-1965

Union of Soviet Socialist Republics

Calibre	140 mm	*Reload time*	—
Rocket length	1,092 mm	*Detachment*	—
Rocket weight	39·6 kg		
Fuel	Solid		
Stages	One		
Guidance	Nil		
Range	10,500 m		
Warhead	HE (41 kg)		
Tubes/Rails	16		
Traverse limits	28°		

The M 1965 is a special light weight weapon suitable for airborne forces. It is mounted on a carriage with split trails and consists of four rows of four launchers. The launcher tubes are similar to those of the BM-14, and it has the same performance as the earlier version.

Employment   USSR

140 mm M-1965 launcher being loaded.

Rocket launcher BM-14

Union of Soviet Socialist Republics

	14/8	*14/16*	*14/17*
Calibre (mm)	140	140	140
Rocket length (mm)	1,092	1,092	1,092
Rocket weight (kg)	39·6	39·6	39·6
Fuel	Solid	Solid	Solid
Stages	One	One	One
Guidance	Nil	Nil	Nil
Range (m)	10,600	10,600	10,600
Warhead	HE	HE	HE
Tubes/Rails	8 tubes	16 tubes	17 tubes
Traverse limits	30°	30°	210°
Reload time (mins)	2	3/4	4
Detachment	5	5–7	6

The BM 14 is fired from four mountings, but is always characterised by the short launch tubes. The options are:

14/8 (eight tube launcher). A trailer mount weighing 600 kilogrammes. It is used by the airborne forces of Poland and was first seen in 1963. Reload time is very short. Traverse is limited to 30°, but the elevation gives the same range as other mountings. The trailer is towed by the GAZ 63. The weapon is known in Poland as the WP 8.

14/16 (16 tube towed launcher). Known as the BM 14/16 or M 1965, this configuration consists of a 1,500 kilogramme trailer with split trail legs like a gun. The tubes arranged in four rows of four are mounted in a simple U-shaped cradle. It has a detachment of five, and two extra loaders to keep down the reload time.

14/16 (16 tube SP launcher). This is an arrangement of 16 launch tubes in two rows of eight mounted on a ZIL 151 truck chassis.

14/17 (17 tube launcher). This seems to be the original arrangement of tubes and was first seen in 1959, mounted on a GAZ 63. Traverse is limited by the need to protect the front of the vehicle from the rocket efflux.

All varieties of this weapon are known as the BM 14, so that it is not possible to distinguish which user nations have which version.

Employment:

Algeria	German Peoples' Republic	Syria
China	Hungary	USSR
Czechoslovakia	Poland	Vietnam
Egypt	Rumania	

145 mm rocket launcher RAFALE

France

Calibre	145 mm	*Traverse limits*	—
	3,200 mm	*Reload time*	—
Rocket length			
Rocket weight	78 kg		
Fuel	Solid		
Stages	One		
Guidance	Nil		
Range	—		
Warhead	19 kg Anti-Personnel (35 fragmentation bomblets) Anti-tank (56 shaped *charge* bomblets or 5 minelets)		
Tubes/Rails	18		

RAFALE is still under development in France and little is known about its performance except that accuracies are claimed of 1·1% of range for length zone and ·4% of range for lateral spread. This is achieved by firing a meteorological sighting missile before a salvo, which is tracked by radar to deduce the meteorological correction of the moment for each target. The 18 rail launcher is currently mounted on a Berliot lorry.

Employment   Development in France

158 mm BREDA BR 51 GS

Italy

Calibre	158 mm		
Rocket length	30/38 cm		
Rocket weight	123 kg		
Fuel	Solid		
Stages	One		
Guidance	Nil		
Range	24,000 m		
Warhead weight	—		
Warhead	Preformed fragmenting (60 kg) Canister Incendiary Anti-armour		
Tubes/Rails	10		
Traverse limits	—		
Reload time	—		
Detachment	—		

The BR 51 GS is in an advanced stage of development. Accuracy is quoted as 0·75 per cent of range. At the maximum range this produces a range spread of 180 m, thus a salvo of rockets should produce a good saturation effect. The anti-armour round is of the multiple warhead type, and increases the overall rocket length from 300 mm to 380 mm. Range is adjusted by air brakes, which are pre-set before launch and if fully deployed reduce the maximum velocity from 750 metres/second to 690 metres/second. The minimum range is unusually high—7,500 m.

A multiple launcher mounted on a tracked chassis or wheeled is planned, and each launcher will be able to fire 300 rockets per hour, from ten launch frames arranged in two rows of five.

Employment   Trials only, Italy

194 mm BORA artillery rocket

Italy

Calibre	194 mm	*Traverse limits*	—
Rocket length	4.7 m	*Reload time*	—
Rocket weight	226 kg	*Detachment*	—
Fuel	Liquid		
Stages	One		
Guidance	Nil		
Range	10,000 m +		
Warhead	HE (20 kg)		
Tubes/Rails	3 rails		

The Bora is the largest of three Italian rockets which use high pressure steam to provide thrust. Like the other two members of the family (Attila II and Mira) the hypergolic fuels are pre-packed and stable when separate. Maximum speed is 390 metres/second and the range is modest for the size of the rocket. However the propulsion system has the tactical advantage of being invisible to infra-red viewers and the efflux disperses quickly. The stabilising fins have a span of 474 mm.

The warhead is described as being 'fragmentation semi-armour piercing'. An impact fuze is fitted.

The rocket is launched from a triple rail, two wheel trailer. The trailer is a triangular frame with a towing eye at the apex. The launch rails are built on a framework of tubular members. Traverse is limited, but the whole trailer can be easily manhandled through large switches in azimuth. Elevation is by twin jack pillars beneath the launch rail framework.

Note. The Italians are developing another member of this family called FLIT: calibre 152 mm, same propulsion system, 15 kg semi armour piercing HE fragmentation warhead, range, 10,000 m.

Employment   Trials only, Italy

194 mm Bora on single rail launcher about to be test fired.

Battlefield missile 'Wolf'

Israel

Calibre	150–200 mm?	
Rocket length	—	—
Rocket weight	—	—
Guidance	Nil	Nil
Range	1,000 m	4,500 m
Warhead	HE (170 kg)	(HE 70 kg)
Tubes/Rails	—	—
Traverse limits	—	—
Reload time	—	—
Detachment	—	—

There are two new Israeli battlefield rockets which are both called Wolf (Ze'ev). They were used in the 1973 Yom Kippur War. They are not accurate but reputedly effective against large concentrations of men or materiel. It would be logical to use a multiple launcher for a weapon with such characteristics. It is believed that a cage-type launcher is used.

There is no indication of the size of the rockets, but the weight of the warheads suggests a calibre of 150/200 mm.

Employment   Israel

200 mm rocket launcher BMD 20

Union of Soviet Socialist Republics

Calibre	200 mm	*Reload time*	6–10 mins
Rocket length	3·11 m	*Detachment*	6
Rocket weight	194 kg		
Fuel	Solid		
Stages	One		
Guidance	Nil		
Range	18,000 m		
Warhead	HE		
Tubes/Rails	4 frames		
Traverse limits	20°		

This is a very elderly equipment which has been relegated to a training role by Warsaw Pact countries. It is, however, believed to be active in North Korea. It is is mounted on either the ZIL 151 for ZIL 157 trucks.

Employment   North Korea
Warsaw Pact countries (training only)

216 mm E-3 rocket

Spain

Calibre	216 mm
Rocket length	1,406 mm
Rocket weight	101 kg
Fuel	Solid
Stages	One
Guidance	Nil
Range	14,500 km
Warhead	HE (37·5 kg)
	Incendiary
	Smoke
Tubes/Rails	21 cages
Traverse limits	90°
Reload time	14 mins
Detachment	—

The E-3 rocket belongs to the same family as the R-6-B-2.

It too has an IMI solid fuel motor, is spin stabilised and has a quoted delivery error of one per cent of range. The rockets are fired electrically at two second intervals.

The 21 launch cages are mounted on a pedestal which is laid manually. Elevation of the launching assembly is by screw jack.

The pedestal and launch cages are mounted on a Banieros Pante III truck—the L-21/E-3 launcher. The vehicle is a 6 × 6 wheeled chassis with an open cab and platform body. A steady jack is lowered to provide a stable firing platform: it consists of a framework of tubular members which hinges up when not in use.

A trailer mounting is believed to exist.

Employment   Spain

216 mm E 3 rocket launcher.

240 mm rocket launcher BM 24

Union of Soviet Socialist Republics

Calibre	240 mm
Rocket length	1·180 m
Rocket weight	113 kg
Fuel	Solid
Stages	One
Guidance	Nil
Range	11,000 m
Warhead	HE
Tubes/Rails	12 cages
Traverse limits	210°
Reload time	3–4 mins
Detachment	6

This stubby rocket is launched from an arrangement of two rows of six cages mounted on the ZIL 151 truck. The layout is very similar to that of the BM 21, including the sight mounting. In this case, however, the cab is protected by folding steel screens which cover the windows. Steady jacks are fitted behind the rear wheels.

The Soviet Army has a version mounted on the AT-S medium tracked chassis, but this has yet to be exported.

Employment	Algeria	Israel	Syria
	Egypt	Poland	USSR
	East Germany		

The BM-24 deployed. Note blast shields on wind-screen of truck.

250 mm rocket launcher BMD 25

Union of Soviet Socialist Republics

Calibre	250 mm
Rocket length	5·822 m
Rocket weight	455 kg
Fuel	Solid
Stages	One
Guidance	Nil
Range	30,000 m
Warhead	HE
Tubes/Rails	4 cages
Traverse limits	—
Reload time	—
Detachment	—

BMD 25 on JAAS-214 truck.

The BMD 25, first seen in 1957, is a large rocket, fired from a cage. The four fins are permanently deployed and engage in helical rails in the launch cage to impart spin. The four cages are arranged in a single row, mounted on a ZIL 151 truck. KrAZ 214 is an alternative chassis. The cab is projected by folding screens and rear steady jacks are fitted. The arrangement is exactly that of the BM 24.

A version with six launch cages is believed to exist.

Employment　USSR

300 mm 30 rocket

Japan

Calibre	300 mm
Rocket length	4·5 m
Rocket weight	—
Fuel	Solid
Stages	One
Guidance	Nil
Range	25,000 m
Warhead	—
Tubes/Rails	2 rails
Traverse limits	—
Reload time	—
Detachment	—

The Type 30 rocket is the largest of a family of rockets produced by the Nissan Motor Company's Space and Aeronautical Department. No details of other members of this family are available. This weapon has an excellent range for its size. Small cruciform fins are fitted and the rocket appears to have spin motors.

The general arrangement of the Hino launch vehicle is similar to the Honest John, except that there are two launch rails. There are three hydraulic steady jacks, one at the rear, and one at each side forward of the eight wheel twin rear axles. Like the Honest John launcher there is no driver's cab and traverse is limited.

Employment Japan

300 mm D-3 rocket

Spain

Calibre	300 mm
Rocket length	1·898 m
Rocket weight	247·5 kg
Fuel	—
Stages	One
Guidance	Nil
Range	17,700 m
Warhead	HE (89·4 kg)
	Smoke
	Incendiary
Tubes/Rails	10 cages
Traverse limits	90°
Reload time	—
Detachment	—

The D-3 rocket is a larger version of the E-3. It is claimed to have the same delivery accuracy—one per cent of range. The rate of fire is the same for both equipments—one round in two seconds.

The rockets are launched from cages, which are only 22 mm longer than the rocket. Ten cages arranged in two rows of five are mounted on the Banieros Pante III truck to make the L-10/D-3 launcher. The pedestal mount and screw jack elevating gear are from the E-3 system.

A mechanical re-loading system is used.

Employment Spain

300 mm D-3 being fired from L-10/D-3 launcher.

381 mm G-3 rocket

Spain

Calibre	381 mm
Rocket length	2·657 m
Rocket weight	527·5 kg
Fuel	Solid
Stages	One
Guidance	Nil
Range	23,500 m
Warhead	HE (217 kg)
Tubes/Rails	8
Traverse limits	45°
Reload time	—
Detachment	—

Little is known about the G-3 rocket that is not tabulated above. It is the largest of the Spanish rockets, and boasts a very large warhead. It is launched from a short cage, which is only 163 mm longer than the rocket. Accuracy of one per cent of range is claimed.

The L-8/G-3 launcher is self propelled and wheeled.

Employment Spain

---

557 mm battlefield missile Lance

United States of America

Calibre	557 mm
Rocket length	6·146 m
Rocket weight	1,285 kg
Stages	One
Fuel	Liquid
Guidance	Inertial
Maximum speed	—
Range	112 km
Warhead	Nuclear
Tubes/Rails	One
Traverse limits	—
Reload time	—
Detachment	6

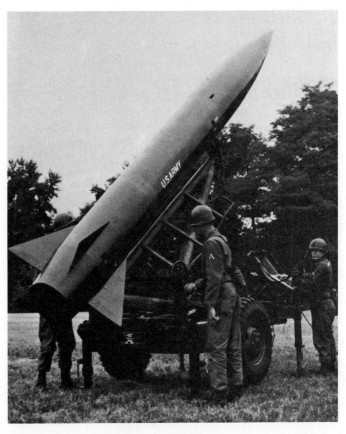

Lance and launcher on wheeled mountings.

American battlefield guided missiles trace their ancestry back to the German V2 rockets of World War II. The first was Corporal, then Sergeant and now Lance, which also replaces Honest John and thus simplifies the order of battle. Basic research started in 1959: first firings were in 1965 and the weapon entered service in 1972.

The missile is made up of three basic assemblies: warhead, main rocket assemblage and control surfaces. The main rocket assemblage contains the guidance module, propellant tanks and rocket motors. The propellant consists of two hypergolic agents: an oxidiser (inhibited red fuming nitric acid), and the fuel (assymmetrical dimethylhydrazine).

Advanced storage techniques combine the convenience of storage and handling associated with solid propellants with the power and fine thrust control possible with liquid fuels.

At launch a boost motor accelerates the missile to the required speed over a period of between 1·5 and 6 seconds: it then shuts down and a sustainer motor continues to propel the rocket in a state of zero acceleration. The duration of the boost depends on the required range. An accelerometer determines the point at which the boost motor is shut down, and then controls the infinitely variable thrust of the sustainer motor.

During the boost phase, the rocket is guided by vector thrust control. In flight, the weapon is stabilised by spin which is imparted by tapping off gases from the solid propellant gas generator (the 'starter motor' for the main motors). This system is active for 1·5 seconds, and spin is maintained by the fins.

The inertial guidance system is immune to all known enemy counter measures. It automatically compensates for meteorological influences and gives the missile a 'fire and forget' characteristic. The missile is laid in azimuth like a gun. Target range data is fed to the missile before firing by a monitor programmer. This solid state device also supplies pre-launch electrical power, monitors the firing sequence and controls the arming of the firing mechanism, yet it is only 42 × 51 × 43 cm.

At present only a nuclear warhead is available. However, the rocket's payload (up to 450 kilogrammes) and size make it suitable for conventional weapons of the cluster-bomb or multiple warhead type.

A Distance Measuring Warhead (DME) is under development for super-accurate delivery. It consists of a semi-active homing device which requires the deployment of two ground stations and is based on the civilian aircraft ground approach equipment. The new warhead carries four canard control surfaces.

The compact rocket is launched from a tracked vehicle derived from the M113 AFV. The engine and running gear are unchanged except for the addition of suspension locks to provide a stable launch platform.

Traverse, and elevation to the firing angle, are manual. The vehicle with its six man detachment is capable of 64 kilometres/hour and swims at 10 kilometres/hour.

The launch rail assembly can also be mounted on a light two wheel trailer weighing 3,000 kilogrammes complete with rocket. This can be air dropped, and gives air delivered and air mobile forces a nuclear weapon.

The launcher vehicle is accompanied by a loader/transporter carrying two rockets. It is fitted with a hydraulic handling unit or crane which both loads the launcher and handles the mating of warhead to motor. Control surfaces in the shape of four rear mounted fins are fitted at the launch site during deployment.

Belgium	Netherlands
Federal Republic of Germany	USA
Israel	United Kingdom
Italy	

557 mm Lance missile and launcher mounted on M 113.

650 mm Pluton

France

Calibre	650 mm
Rocket length	7·59 m
Rocket weight	2,350 kg
Fuel	Solid
Stages	One
Guidance	Inertial
Range	120 km
Warhead	Nuclear (500 kg)
Tubes/Rails	One
Traverse limits	N/A
Reload time	—
Detachment	4

Issue of Pluton to six regiments, each to be of six launchers began in 1975. The missile is delivered as three major components: motor, warhead and guidance module. The motor is single stage, solid fuel. The weapon is assembled onto the launch vehicle using the motor's delivery container as the launch tube.

The rocket flies free for the first five seconds before the pre-programmed guidance system takes over. Changes in course are effected by control surfaces at the tips of the fins. After launch the inboard computer adjusts the flight path using inputs from an accelerometer and gyro reference. A simple, but effective back-up inertial guidance system is mounted in parallel to the primary system. This second system serves to monitor the weapons performance and acts as a safety device. Before the warhead is initiated a comparison of data between both guidance systems must agree within predetermined limits.

The launch position command post is equipped with an IRIS 35M computer. This produces target data for direct input to the missile guidance system based on firing position survey data and target coordinates. A second IRIS 35M computer mounted on the launcher vehicle monitors the weapon and firing sequence and automatically carries out pre-flight checks. It also accepts orientation for the missile from a north seeking gyro.

The warhead is the airforce AN 52 which is said to have 10 kiloton and 25 kiloton options.

The weapon systems reaction time is 30 minutes.

The missile launch vehicle is based on the AMX chassis, which runs on five road wheels with five return rollers. It is powered by the Hispano Suiza HS 110 Flat-12 cylinder diesel, which is multi-fuelled, supercharged, and produces 720 bhp. The centrifugal clutch is operated electrically by movement of the mechanical five speed gear change. The main engine is supplemented by a small turbine which provides pre-launch power for the missile and launcher functions. Protection of the crew from nuclear and chemical attack is provided using the same air filtration and pressurisation equipment as the AMX 30 tank.

A dual purpose hydraulic crane is fitted over the right hand track. It handles the weapon assembly and when laid flat extends under the launch container as the means of elevation. There is no provision for laying in azimuth; placing the vehicle within 10° of the line of fire is sufficient for the guidance system to be effective.

Employment France

Pluton missile in its container/launcher ready to deploy. For firing the container launcher elevates in the vertical plane.

762 mm Honest John

United States of America

Calibre	762 mm
Rocket length	7·5 m
Rocket weight	2,040 kg
Fuel	Solid
Stages	One
Guidance	Nil
Range	37,000 m
Warhead	Nuclear
	HE
Tubes/Rails	One
Traverse limits	4°
Reload time	—
Detachment	4

Honest John is a simple, unguided surface-to-surface rocket, designed to be fitted with nuclear or conventional warheads. It has a single stage, solid fuel motor. Super-

sonic speed is reached during the four second motor burn time.

The missile is stabilised in flight by four tail fins. Two spin motors ignite as it leaves the launcher and neutralise any eccentricity in the motor performance. Accuracy throughout its range band (7·5 to 37 kilometres) compares favourably with an equivalent heavy artillery piece.

Sighting is by standard clinometer and dial sight, mounted at the left rear of the launch vehicle. Laying is manual, but top traverse is limited to 4°: thus great care must be exercised in deploying the launcher for its target.

Developmental policy has been one of continual improvement. No modifications have greatly changed the shape or size: it is still 7·5 m long and weighs over 2,000 kilogrammes at launch. After 15 years operational

762 mm Honest John rocket elevated ready for firing, but note jacks on vehicle have not yet been lowered.

service, production has stopped, and most but not all users are phasing Honest John out of their order of battle in favour of Lance.

The warhead, motor, and fins are assembled together into a complete missile in the field. Once assembled, the missile is loaded onto the 6 × 6 International Harvester launch vehicle. This vehicle has no cab superstructure: the windscreen folds flat during firing to avoid damage. Four steady jacks are deployed to provide a stable launch platform. The vehicle has excellent battlefield mobility, both loaded and unladen.

The launching party consists of the launcher, a command post vehicle and a windset trailer which measures the low level wind at launch.

Simplicity is the great virtue of the whole weapon system. It leads to robust and reliable equipment, and requires few techniques which are not common with conventional guns. It is now being replaced by Lance.

Employment	Belgium	Netherlands	UK
	Denmark	South Korea	USA
	France	Taiwan	
	Greece	Turkey	

Battlefield missile MD 660

Israel

Calibre	—
Rocket length	—
Rocket weight	450–650 kg
Fuel	—
Stages	Two
Guidance	—
Range	280–450 km
Warhead	HE
	Nuclear
Tubes/Rails	—
Traverse limits	—
Reload time	—
Detachment	—

It is known that Israel is involved in the development of a long range missile system, or systems. A project called 'Jericho' and another known as MD 620 may all be related to the MD 660. The French Dassault Company was involved in early development, and 50 missiles were ordered in 1969. It is believed that only two have been delivered, but the present status of the weapon is in doubt.

Range and weight quotes vary widely and the weight figures are very low. They may refer to the warhead payload.

The existence of a nuclear warhead is equally open to doubt, although MD 660 would be a suitable delivery means for such a weapon.

Employment   Probably trials only

790 mm Sergeant battlefield support missile

United States of America

Calibre	790 mm
Rocket length	10·5 m
Rocket weight	4,536 kg
Fuel	Solid
Stages	One
Guidance	Inertial
Range	45–140 km
Warhead	Nuclear
Tubes/Rails	One
Traverse limits	N/A
Reload time	—
Detachment	—

The Sergeant is a second generation equipment to Corporal. It is now being phased out of service in favour of Lance, having been in service for 10 years.

It consists of four sub-assemblies: warhead, guidance pack, rocket motor and control surfaces. These are assembled before firing, but not necessarily at the launch site.

The firing unit consists of four vehicles, including the launcher and missile transporter. This was a big advance over Corporal. The inertial guidance, operating control tabs at the rear of the stabilising fins, represented an equally important advance over Corporal because of its immunity to enemy interference.

All pre-fire sequences can be simulated by the XM 68 E2 trainer missile.

Employment	Federal Republic of Germany
	USA

790 mm Sergeant on its launch trailer.

FROG missile system

Union of Soviet Socialist Republics

'FROG' (Free Rocket Over Ground) is the NATO designation for a family of unguided Russian missiles. The Russians name may be LUNA. Each of the six types represents a continuing development programme, and the rocket diameter is not constant: for convenience all FROGS have been grouped together.

FROG is similar to Honest John—the nearest equivalent Western weapon. They are free flight missiles built round a solid fuel motor. Stabilisation is by spin which is sustained in flight by fins. Like Honest John, the missiles are fired from a launcher/transporter.

The FROG family are all nuclear weapons. However, the size and payload could allow conventional multiple warheads to be fitted. The HE warheads used by Egypt and Syria in the Yom Kippur War were ineffective because the delivery error exceeded the radius of damage.

In the Soviet Army FROG is deployed with tank and motor rifle divisions in battalions of four launchers.

Employment:

Algeria (4)	East Germany (7)	Poland (7)
Bulgaria (7)	Hungary (7)	Syria (7)
Cuba (4)	Iraq (7)	USSR (1–7)
Czechoslovakia (7)	North Korea (5 & 7)	
Egypt (3 & 7)	Romania (7)	

FROG 1

Union of Soviet Socialist Republics

Calibre	850 mm
Rocket length	10·0 m
Rocket weight	3,000 kg
Fuel	Solid
Stages	One
Guidance	Nil
Range	25–65 km
Warhead	Nuclear
	HE
	Chemical
Tubes/Rails	One
Traverse limits	—
Reload time	—
Detachment	—

FROG 1 is an obsolete weapon, first introduced in 1957. It is launched from a ribbed box container. This could, like the French PLUTON system, be the delivery container for the motor section of the missile. The container certainly forms a heater jacket to maintain a constant temperature for the solid fuel. The six-fin tail, and the warhead project out of the container at either end. A tubular framework protects the warhead which overhangs the vehicle when travelling and is of much greater diameter than the motor body.

The missile is transported on, and fired from, a vehicle based on the JS 3 tank chassis. It has six road wheels, and three return rollers. The engine is a V 12 diesel which produces 520 bhp. All-up weight is in the order of 36,000 kilogrammes.

The built-up superstructure of the vehicle incorporates an enclosed cabin. The carrying cradle is also the launch rail, and is elevated by a hydraulic ram. There are steadying jacks at the rear so that the suspension does not lock for firing as it does with newer Western equipments. Traverse is probably very limited.

FROG 2

Union of Soviet Socialist Republics

Calibre	600 mm
Rocket length	9·0 m
Rocket weight	2,400 kg
Fuel	Solid
Stages	One
Guidance	Nil
Range	25 km
Warhead	Nuclear
	HE
	Chemical
Tubes/Rails	One
Traverse limits	—
Reload time	—

FROG 2 is a lighter, smaller rocket than its predecessor. It has a simpler cruciform tail fin assembly and the warhead is still of greater diameter than the motor section. The missile is carried on a framework of U-

FROG 2.

shaped ribs and longitudinal side members. A tubular frame supports the front of the launch rail for travelling. An 'A' Frame under the launch rail is used to elevate the rail and missile to the launch angle. Split function laying is used.

The vehicle is the tracked PT 76 chassis with six road wheels and no return rollers. It has a six cylinder diesel engine developing 240 bhp. The superstructure of FROG 1 is missing and the careful designing has resulted in a weight of only 15,000 kilogrammes. The PT 76 is an inherent swimmer, riding high in the water propelled by hydro-jets. The FROG 2 mounting may well possess this quality also. It has a road speed of 35 kilometres/hour, and an endurance of 250 kilometres.

FROG 3

Union of Soviet Socialist Republics

Calibre	550 mm
Rocket length	10·5 m
Rocket weight	2,280 kg
Fuel	Solid
Stages	Two
Guidance	Nil
Range	40 km
Warhead	Nuclear (250 kg)
	HE
	Chemical
Tubes/Rails	One
Traverse limits	—
Reload time	—
Detachment	—

When introduced in 1960 the FROG 3 was the first rocket of its type to have two stages. The first stage is fitted with four stabilising fins, in line with those of the second stage. The first stage motor is made up of 12 jets built around a central nozzle. The warhead is less shaped than its predecessor, consisting of a simple cylinder and conical nose cone.

The vehicle and mounting are exactly the same as FROG 2, except that two track return rollers are fitted above the road wheels.

FROG 3 being prepared for firing.

FROG 4 and 5

Union of Soviet Socialist Republics

Calibre	400 mm
Rocket length	10·2 m
Rocket weight	2,040 kg
Fuel	Solid
Stages	Two
Guidance	Nil
Maximum speed	—
Range	45 km
Warhead	Nuclear (300 kg)
	HE
	Chemical
Tubes/Rails	One
Traverse limits	—
Reload time	—
Detachment	—

Although the range is quoted as much greater than FROG 3, these weapons appear to be identical to it except in the shape of the warhead, which is a simple cone fitting flush with the motor body. FROG 5 has a further modification to the nose cone, but is otherwise a FROG 4. The figures quoted for warhead weight are greater than for FROG 3.

It is believed that FROG 4 and 5 launchers may have a built-in north-seeking gyro to assist in laying.

FROG 5 with its conical nose section being prepared for firing.

FROG 4.

FROG 6

Union of Soviet Socialist Republics

FROG 6 is a training vehicle with dummy rocket. It has rarely been seen in public. Its production may have been made necessary because of the increasing complexity of the sighting systems attributed to FROGs 4 and 5.

FROG 7

Union of Soviet Socialist Republics

Calibre	600 mm
Rocket length	9·0 m
Rocket weight	6,300 kg
Fuel	Solid
Stages	One
Guidance	Nil
Maximum speed	—
Range	60 km
Warhead	Nuclear
	HE
	Chemical
Tubes/Rails	One
Traverse limits	—
Reload time	—
Detachment	—

FROG 7 has probably been in service since 1965, but was first shown to the public in 1967. It is the latest of the FROG range of missiles and the first to have a wheeled launch vehicle.

It is altogether bigger than preceding types. It reverts to being a single stage rocket. The main motor venturi is surrounded by a ring of 20 smaller nozzles. The warhead is flush with the motor body, and the fins are both narrower and longer.

The launcher/transporter is the eight wheeled ZIL 135. Steadying jacks fold down to provide a stable firing platform. For the first time, the missile sits on its launch rail (which is of triangular cross section like Honest John's), and not in a cradle. For travelling, the rocket is restrained by two straps. The cab of the ZIL 135 is a conventional lorry type, suggesting that some sort of screen is used to protect the glass when the missile is launched.

The nuclear warhead is in the 25 kiloton class.

A tender based on the ZIL 135 carries three missiles ready and prepared for firing. A crane vehicle is required to transfer them to the launch rail.

Above: FROG 7 was the first of the series to have a wheeled launcher. Note cylindrical body, conical nose and resemblance in layout to Honest John.

Left: ZIL 135 truck carrying three FROG 7 rockets.

Battlefield missile—SCUD A (SS-1B)

Union of Soviet Socialist Republics

Calibre	850 mm
Rocket length	10·5 m
Rocket weight	4,500 kg
Fuel	Liquid
Stages	One
Guidance	Radio command
Range	150 km
Warhead	Nuclear
Tubes/Rails	One
Traverse limits	N/A
Reload time	—
Detachment	—

SCUD is the NATO name for this huge rocket which was first seen in 1957. It is launched vertically, and guided by radio command during flight. Course corrections are effected by control surfaces at the rear of the motor, which also act as stabilising fins. The launch vehicle is basically that of FROG 1. Based on the JS 3 tank chassis, it has a built-up superstructure which contains a cabin for the detachment.

The missile is carried in a frame of tubular members which extends forward round the nose cone to protect

SCUD A on tracked launchers.

SCUD A on wheeled launchers.

it. This frame raises the rocket to its vertical launch position behind the chassis, and provides a ladder for access to the warhead during final check-out procedures. It is lowered for firing.

Although details of the launch procedure have not been released, the fuelling and guidance check-out must involve a considerable number of men and vehicles at the launch site. The weapon is most unlikely to travel after fuelling. The radar and radio vehicles needed by the type of guidance used increases the size of the firing unit. Reaction time is claimed as one hour, and the warhead is reputedly in the 100 kiloton class.

The following list of users refers to SCUD A and B as no definite indication is available.

Employment	Bulgaria	Hungary	Syria
	Czechoslovakia	Iraq	USSR
	East Germany	Poland	
	Egypt	Rumania	

Battlefield missile SCUD B (SS-1C)

Union of Soviet Socialist Republics

Calibre	850 mm
Rocket length	11·0 m
Rocket weight	6,300 kg
Fuel	Liquid
Stages	One
Guidance	Inertial
Range	165–280 km
Warhead	Nuclear
Tubes/Rails	One
Traverse limits	N/A
Reload time	—
Detachment	—

SCUD B.

SCUD B is a direct development of SCUD A, and considerably heavier. It continues to use the tail fins as control surfaces. Its fuel is described as 'storable'.

It was first seen on the SCUD A tracked launch vehicle. The new vehicle is an eight wheel MAZ 543, first seen in 1965. The nose of the missile, protected by a single tubular rail, sits between two cabs: one for the driver, the other for the missile control console and operator. The body of the vehicle contains the detachment and control gear. The launch pad is integral to the erector frame. The rear of the vehicle is supported on jacks while the missile is elevated to the vertical for launching.

The missile is held in the erector frame by clamps behind the warhead.

SCUD is deployed in brigades of nine launch sections and attached to fronts.

There have been rumours of a SCUD C weapon, but it is believed that these arise from confusion over the two launch vehicles used for SCUD B.

Employment   East Germany
            USSR

Battlefield missile—Scaleboard (SS-12)

Union of Soviet Socialist Republics

Calibre	850 mm +
Rocket length	11·0 m +
Rocket weight	—
Fuel	Liquid
Stages	One
Guidance	Inertial
Range	700–800 km
Warhead	Nuclear
Tubes/Rails	One
Traverse limits	N/A
Reload time	—
Detachment	—

Scaleboard is the largest Soviet battlefield missile, and was first introduced to the public in November 1967.

The missile is transported in a heavily ribbed container which is only removed after erection to the vertical launch position behind the erector/launcher vehicle. It is believed that the motor is liquid fuelled, and that the warhead is in the megaton class, but few facts about this important weapon have been released.

The container and missile are transported on a MAZ 543 wheeled erector/launcher similar to that used for SCUD A and FROG 7.

Employment   USSR

Scaleboard (SS-12).

Battlefield support missile Pershing (MGM 31)

United States of America

Calibre	1,000 mm
Rocket length	12·2 m
Rocket weight	4,600 kg
Fuel	Solid
Stages	Two
Guidance	Inertial
Range	160–750 km
Warhead	Nuclear
Tubes/Rails	One
Traverse limits	N/A
Reload time	—
Detachment	—

The original Pershing was brought into service in 1962, and was deployed to Europe in 1964. With the introduction of an improved version in 1969, the two types became known as 1 and 1A. Pershing 1 is no longer in service.

The first stage motor is fitted with four tiny triangular stabilising fins. The second, sustainer stage has four control surfaces.

The Pershing 1A is carried on an articulated M 656 wheeled erector/launcher, which is fitted with a launch pad for the vertical take-off. The rocket can be carried complete after warhead mating—an improvement over the earlier model. The launch equipment consists of:

(a) Erector/launcher.
(b) Programme test and power generator on a second M 656.
(c) Control truck.
(d) Radio terminal vehicle with pneumatically raised aerial.

An automatic count-down process has reduced reaction time but the rocket is unchanged for 1 and 1A systems.

The whole system is airportable in C 130 Hercules aircraft, and is operated in battalions of four firing batteries.

Employment USA

The Pershing missile after war-head mating ready for launch.

VII. Ancillary Equipment for Surface-to-surface Artillery

As artillery weapons have become more sophisticated, so they have become dependent on a variety of ancillary equipments in order to realise their full potential. A field gun firing in the simplest indirect fire role has always required an observer, communications, a command post equipped to produce gun-sight data, and an adequate supply of ammunition. The more sophisticated and longer range systems of today require in addition the means of acquiring targets 'well over the hill'; night observation aids, range finders and other survey instruments for their observers; and the means of measuring meteorological changes and muzzle velocities. Furthermore they need computers to assess and collate the mass of target information and to provide almost instantaneous firing data at the guns and rockets tasked to engage each target. In this chapter some of the specialist equipments used by artilleries today are described in six categories: target acquisition and locating, observation post aids, survey instruments, meteorological instruments, muzzle velocity measurement, and artillery computers.

1. TARGET ACQUISITION AND LOCATING

The basic artillery problem is to achieve accurate location of the target and the guns in relation to each other. This is a reasonably simple problem, when the target can be seen from a ground observation post, but the acquisition and accurate locating of targets deep in enemy held territory, and well out of sight of ground observers is more difficult. The devices used to provide information about this kind of target fall into two categories. First, those which provide general surveillance and hence target acquisition in depth; these include drones or remotely piloted vehicles and long range surveillance radar. Secondly those which locate enemy guns, mortars and rocket launchers; this includes flash spotting, sound ranging and mortar/rocket locating radars.

Drones

AN/USD (Midge)

Canada

The AN/USD 501 is a reliable airborne reconnaissance system which flies preplanned missions out to 150 km. The drone can have either a camera or an infra-red line-scan sensor which permits detection, recognition and identification of small, low contrast ground objects. The system includes a supply of re-usable drones and facilities for flight planning and handling, launching and recovering the drones. Photographic processing and interpretation can also take place at the drone troop location. Terminal guidance and recovery is effected by a radio beacon, which causes a parachute to open for a safe descent at the troop position.

It has some advantages over manned aircraft reconnaissance in that its flight response time is short, it can operate from unprepared sites, and it is so fast and has so small a radar echoing area that it is relatively immune to anti-aircraft defences. However it is not able to send back information in flight, its mission has to be preplanned and cannot be altered once it has been launched, its sensor payload is limited, and, most important of all, its target information response time is slow, because its photographs can only be interpreted after the mission has been completed. Its detailed characteristics are still classified.

Employment Belgium
Canada
United Kingdom

The Midge being launched.

R 20

France

R20 is a monoplane drone, propelled by a Marbore II jet engine. It is launched by means of a solid fuel propelled cradle from a modified standard 3–4 ton vehicle. It is guided from the ground by a tracking and control radar when it is within range, but for the major part of its course it is controlled by its own computer and gyroscopic controls. Its sensors include camera for day and night photography, infra-red line-scan, and radio activity detectors (cyclope).

Characteristics

Length	5·7 m
Wing space	3·7 m
Weight	850 kg
Engine thrust	400 kg
Speed Mach	0·65
Radius of action	160 km
Overflight accuracy	300 m
Guidance	Preset inertial

Employment France

The R-20 French drone.

Developments

It is likely that remotely piloted vehicles, which can be controlled during flight and which can send back real-time target information by television, will eventually replace the drone in its target acquisition role.

Surveillance Radars

The problem with a radar system is that it can only detect moving targets in the line of sight. Its application for target acquisition in depth in broken country, such as is normal in North West Europe, is therefore limited. It does, however, have the advantage of being unaffected by weather and extreme climatic conditions. Two examples are:

RATAC

France

This reliable light radar is now in full production for the French Army. It has been designed primarily as a target acquisition radar, but it can also be used for the direction of artillery fire, guiding reconnaissance patrols and aiding helicopter navigation. Its details are still classified.

AN/TPS-58

United States of America

This is a vehicle mounted system weighing 3,500 pounds. It has an accuracy of 50 m with a detection range of 12 km for personnel and 20 km for vehicles.

Locating

There are only two methods of locating enemy guns and rocket launchers in service at the moment—flash spotting and sound ranging. Flash spotting provides the location of the gun by plotting the bearings to its muzzle flash as seen from a number of observation posts. Sound ranging uses a device to measure the difference in time of arrival of the sound of discharge at a number of microphones whose locations are fixed by survey.

It has always been possible to find the positions of enemy guns by their muzzle flash and this still remains the most simple method of locating. Observations are made from a number of accurately surveyed posts using a theodolite-type instrument to the gun flash. The coordinates of the gun can then be determined by computation or graphical intersection. There are however practical difficulties in ensuring that all observers record the same flash and that bearings are taken with sufficient accuracy to produce dependable results as the batteries are usually sited in defilade and direct observation is impossible. These can be overcome by a high standard of observer training. Flash spotting has been a generally neglected art in many armies in recent years, but the Egyptians demonstrated in 1973 that it is still a worthwhile system.

Sound ranging was first used effectively in World War I and has the advantage over flash spotting in that it can locate well beyond the field of view of an observer and it is not affected by the visibility. A series of accurately surveyed microphones is established across the front at intervals of 300–700 m for 'short base' locating, and 1,000–2,000 m for 'long base' locating. The whole system is called a 'sound ranging base', and a pair of microphones is termed a 'sub-base'. The time of arrival of the sound of an enemy gun or rocket launcher firing is recorded electrically by each microphone and, since each pair of microphones constitutes two known points with a known time interval, the direction of the explosion from each sub-base can be calculated. In practice the recordings of at least three microphones are needed to give an accurate plot, and more are desirable at longer ranges. It is a fairly simple matter to design a plotting board which, having allowed for meteorological corrections, will show the location of an enemy gun at the intersection of the bearings from each microphone. Accurate location of guns can be obtained by this method out to $1\frac{1}{2}$ times the base length for a Long Base (e.g. out to 15,000 m for a 10,000 m base) and out to $2\frac{1}{2}$ times the base length for the Short Base (e.g. out to 3,750 m for a 1,500 m base).

Mortar Locating Radars

These radars operate by 'observing' the flight of a hostile projectile and extrapolating its trajectory back to the source. The mortar bomb's fin is an excellent radar reflector and its high trajectory brings it above the horizon early in its flight before any ballistic variables have had time to influence it. The vertical attitude of the bomb in flight presents the optimum reflecting shape, and the steep trajectory enables several observations needed to determine its shape to be clearly separated in elevation. Only mortars can be located at present, but the extension of this concept to the location of multiple rocket launchers is a future possibility. A satisfactory radar able to track the far flatter trajectories and smaller echoing areas of shells from guns is not yet in service although one is believed to be under development in the United States.

Green Archer

United Kingdom

Green Archer, an X-band mortar locating radar entered service in the British Army in 1962. It is mounted on a four-wheel trailer incorporating levelling jacks and is supplied with power by a specially silenced generator mounted on a similar trailer. The radar, mounting and its trailer, weigh 2,915 kg. Green Archer can be mounted on an APC: the British Army used the FV 432, and the German, Dutch and Danish Armies the American M 113. The radar head is mounted on the roof of the APC, with the control equipment inside, and the generator is towed behind. Maximum range is about 17 km and mortar location is achieved in 30 seconds. An electronic target simulator is available for training.

The principles on which the equipment works are quite simple. The radar reflector has two pre-set angles. After receiving an echo at the lower angle, the reflector is raised, and a second echo from the same bomb received. An analogue computer extrapolates the trajectory back to the firing position by comparing the information from each echo and the time interval between them. The radar beam must be extremely narrow, and sector scanning of 40° in azimuth is made possible by a scanner which operates fast enough to prevent a bomb passing through the observed sector undetected.

Employment	Denmark	South Africa
	Federal Republic of Germany	Sweden
	Italy	Switzerland
	Israel	
	Netherlands	

Cymbeline

United Kingdom

Cymbeline is a replacement for Green Archer, and is an altogether smaller and lighter equipment. It is mounted on a two-wheel trailer complete with generator and weighs only 980 kg. The radar head operates on the trailer: there are three levelling jacks and the reflector folds flat for travelling. It can also be mounted on an APC. The normal switched single beam can be supplemented by a double-beam operation at short ranges.

As well as locating mortars with extreme accuracy, Cymbeline can be used for observing and adjusting the fire of friendly guns, coastal surveillance and some light aircraft control functions. As a mortar locating radar, its maximum range is in the order of 20 km, although the exact range depends on the calibre of the mortar. There is a minimum range of one km. Its reaction time is 15–20 seconds. A target simulator for training purposes is built-in, and so is a self-test facility. A data storage system is available to enable one operator to handle several simultaneous locations.

The control assembly can be deployed up to 15 m from the radar head. It consists of a cathode ray tube and numerical display on which the echo is displayed together with the co-ordinates of its point of origin. In action, the equipment can be operated by one man. Two set elevations are used to provide single beam readings of the target bomb's trajectory. A third lower elevation can be selected to provide a warning to the operator.

Employment Entering service in British Army now

Mortar locating radar Cymbeline mounted on the British FV 432.

AN/MPQ-10A

United States of America

This is now an elderly and cumbersome equipment which weighs 2,700 kg. It uses a parabolic reflector. The AN/MPQ-10A operates from 460 m to a maximum range of 18,300 m. It scans up to 45° in azimuth.

The radar operates in conjunction with a mortar-locating computer and produces the co-ordinates of hostile mortar positions or the point of impact for bombs being tracked. There is a visual display of information.

AN/MPQ-4

United States of America

AN/MPQ-4 is similar to the British Green Archer System, and consists of two two-wheel trailers. One carries the radar head and associated circuitry, while the other carries a power generator. The primary trailer weighs 2,300 kg.

The maximum detection range is 10 km, at which range an accuracy of 50 m is claimed. It scans 25° in azimuth.

The radar is operated by one man at the radar trailer, or with the control console remoted.

It is likely to be replaced by the AN/TPQ-36 for which data is not yet available.

SNAR-2, Small Yawn, Porktrough

Union of Soviet Socialist Republics

Little is known about these three radars, which are used for mortar and to a certain extent rocket location. They are all mounted on an AT-L tracked vehicle and use the X-band. The effective range of SNAR-2 is thought to be about 9,000 m.

Employment   Warsaw Pact countries
Egypt
Syria

---

2. OBSERVATION POST AIDS

The basic aids for an artillery observer are of course his binoculars, his map and his compass. Of the other aids towards achieving accuracy of target location and the swift application of artillery fire on to it three must be given special attention, as they have brought significant advances both in observer efficiency by day and night, and also in closing the survey loop between the guns and the target. These are the laser range finder, the night observation device and the short range radar.

Laser Range Finders

Accurate range and azimuth measurement by the observer is an essential ingredient of accurate target location. The artillery laser range finders are in general small, compact and of rugged construction. By adding the ability to measure angles the one equipment can be used to establish the co-ordinates of its own and target positions within 5 m. Where data links are provided to fire control computers, the computer can resolve the bearing and distance calculation to establish target co-ordinates. Some examples of laser range finders in service are given below.

VAL 11501 artillery laser

Multi-National (Sweden and Yugoslavia)

Sweden and Yugoslavia have co-operated to produce the VAL 11501. It is related to the VAL 11210 tank laser. Both use a neodynium glass rod laser medium, and the main difference lies in the range: the artillery laser measures distances up to 5 km. The instrument measures two target ranges (only one of which is displayed under the operator's control) and records the total number of echoes within the beam. Angular measurements in azimuth and elevation are also displayed. Direct data output to a fire control computer is possible.

Laser Rangefinder—'LAR'

Netherlands

LAR is a two man portable 34 kg equipment which measures ranges up to 10 km. The laser source is neodynium glass. Power at 24 volt d.c. is supplied by a rechargeable nickel-cadmium battery pack and is sufficient for 150 measurements. A range finding pulse, when reflected from the target is processed into an electric signal resulting in a digital display or data output direct to a fire control computer. The pulse rate is 6 per minute. Azimuth and elevation angles are also measured, and with range information can be stored for a short time or displayed immediately. Ranges of two targets (separated by a minimum of 30 m) which fall within the beam can be measured, and both can be stored. Accuracy to 5 m is claimed.

Simrad laser rangefinder LP 3

Norway

The LP 3 is tripod mounted, man portable equipment weighing only 11 kg. The laser source is neodymium-doped glass and the pulse rate is 12 per minute. Maximum range is 20,000 m (minimum 200 m), range accuracy is claimed as 5 m, and range discrimination between echoes is about 30 m. Angles of azimuth and elevation can be measured to a resolution of one mil. Output is displayed on a digital indicator. A 7× magnification sighting telescope is fitted. The LP 3 can be fitted on to the British night observation device for use in conjunction with it.

Simrad mounted on British night observation device NOD-B.

Laser rangefinder VAL 11105

Sweden

The VAL 11105 is available as a portable direct operating unit mounted on a tripod, or in a vehicle mounted periscope configuration. It operates to nearly 15 km. A neodymium glass laser source is used, powered by 12 rechargeable nickel-cadmium cells which are sufficient for 250 operations. There is a digital display of range and angles of azimuth and elevation, and a direct data output to fire control computers. The VAL 11105 is made by L. M. Ericsson, who also make the Naval VAL 10102. This heavy equipment (33 kg) has a Ruby laser source and has a range of 30 km with a claimed accuracy to 10 m. It has been adapted experimentally for land use.

AN/GVS-3

United States of America

The AN/GVS-3 weighs only 14 kg. It has a maximum range of 10 km, and a minimum range of 250 m. Range measurement is accurate to 5 m. There is provision for angular measurement in azimuth.

TM 12

France

This is another lightweight laser (15 kg). Its measurement range is between 300 m and 10 km with an accuracy of 5 m range, 2 mils in azimuth and 1 mil in elevation.

Night Observation Devices

An artillery observer must be able to cover his zone of observation by day and night. The night observation devices which are currently being developed are image intensifiers. These make possible identification of moving targets out to about 2,000 m with even greater range in moonlight, but the snag is that any white light on the battlefield renders them temporarily useless, although in-built automatic brightness control is overcoming this problem. The next generation of night observation devices is likely to rely on thermal imaging, which will also have the advantage of being able to see through battlefield smoke and mist. Many different varieties of device will soon be available, although few are yet in service. They will all tend to be bulky due to the need for a large viewing lens. The usefulness of the passive night observation device is greatly increased if it can be used in conjunction with a laser range finder.

Short Range Surveillance Radar

A short range radar is useful to the artillery observer by night or in poor visibility. It is able to scan out to the limit of line of sight and to distinguish between moving vehicles and men. Its effective arc of surveillance is about 60° with detection ranges being possible out to 10 km. The radar will produce bearing and distance to the target, and it is then a simple matter for the observer to find its co-ordinates. Operator fatigue is a problem, but this can be alleviated to some extent by incorporating an audio alarm signal.

Examples of short range surveillance radars are: Radar No 14 GS Mk 1 (ZB 298) (United Kingdom), Rasura DR-PT-2A (France), Rasit 72 A1 (Rapier) (France).

3. SURVEY INSTRUMENTS

Accurate survey of the locations of guns, observers and targets is an essential step towards achieving first salvo accuracy—they must all be on the same survey grid. Up to now this has been achieved only after laborious and time-consuming instrumental measurement and manual computation by artillery surveyors. The introduction of an inertial survey instrument—the Position and Azimuth Determining System (PADS)—will transform this situation. PADS is a distance and azimuth gyroscopic instrument, which in the British version shortly to be introduced, is basically the same as that developed for the Harrier fighter/ground attack aircraft. It will give an instant digital display of a vehicle's coordinates with an accuracy of a few metres, and it is intended to be issued to all observers, gun position command posts and target acquisition devices. Its limitations are that its survey data base has to be up-dated frequently, and every 10 miles or so, against the data of previously surveyed bearing pickets. The United States and France are known to be developing survey instruments which are similar to the British PADS.

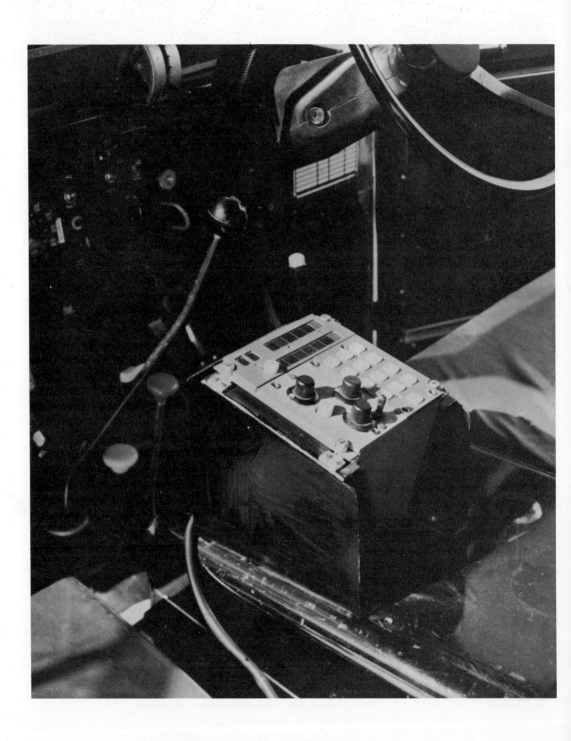

PADS display in Landrover.

Even with a wide distribution of PADS instruments, there will still be a requirement for skilled artillery surveyors to provide the data for bearing pickets (i.e. a post, or picket, clearly marked with its co-ordinates and the bearing to various natural reference objects to enable an azimuth angle measuring instrument—theodolite or director—to be set up) and for those who require survey but do not have PADS throughout the area of operations. Above all they require very accurate distance measuring instruments and these are normally commercial instruments adapted for military use. A British example is given below.

Landrover mounted PADS system.

Tellurometer MRA 5

United Kingdom

The equipment comprises a control unit, an antenna unit and various cables and connectors. It can all be carried in a landrover. Two instruments are required to make a measurement, a master and a remote set. The accuracies obtained are better than 1 in 100,000. Microwaves are transmitted to a reflector at an identical out-station, and the time interval between transmission and reception provides an extremely accurate measure of the distance between the two stations. The result in metres is displayed instanteously at the master station.

The Tellurometer set up for use.

4. METEOROLOGICAL INSTRUMENTS

Information about meteorological variations essential to compute or 'predict' variations in the trajectory due to abnormal wind, temperature and barometric pressure must be regularly received by the artillery command posts. It must be gathered at frequent intervals by the meteorological station and disseminated quickly. The usual method is to measure the rate of ascent and wind blown track of a balloon. Radar tracking is used and the resulting readings are processed by computer into several 'standard' measurements, each tailored for a specific type of equipment, i.e. guns, missiles, sound-ranging, drone systems, etc. The message can be disseminated by voice, teleprinter, or as a direct data transmission to fire control computers. Examples of some meteorological systems in service are given below.

Artillery Meteorological System—'AMETS'

United Kingdom

AMETS is a self-contained, mobile, upper air meteorological station, designed to provide up-to-date information rapidly. Many of the component parts of AMETS are common with FACE, the British Artillery fire control computer—an advantage in production and maintenance.

The AMETS system is completely mobile and largely automatic in operation. A single AMETS will normally provide the meteorological data required in a divisional area.

The balloon-carried radiosonde needs no pre-flight calibrations and is automatically tracked by a modified Plessey WF 3 radar, after initial visual tracking.

Information is processed by the Marconi 920B computer and can be printed out for voice transmission, or produced as a punch tape suitable for direct data transmission to FACE. A meteorological message covering up to an altitude of 20,000 m can be produced hourly. A message for any given height can be produced within three minutes of the radiosonde passing that height. Information messages can be produced for guns, drones, sound-ranging, and fall-out calculations for chemical and nuclear defence.

AMETS lightweight system deployed in the field.

AN/UMQ-7

United States of America

The AN/UMQ-7 is a mobile equipment system which has its own 45 kilowatt generator, hydrogen generator tracking radar and computer. Accuracy of tracking up to 160 km is 16 m for range and 0·05 m in elevation. It produces all standard meteorological messages.

The observation and computation of data and the production of standard messages is fully automatic.

Sirocco

France

The Sirocco system is currently undergoing trials in France. It comprises a meteorological balloon tracking radar (QR-MX-2) and a telemetry receiver providing wind speed and direction and air temperature at a series of standard altitudes. It passes standard messages on a teleprinter or over radio links to field artillery units.

This may either be fed directly into the Atila fire control computer, or used for manual computation of firing data. Maximum range of the radar is in excess of 130 km with a tracking accuracy of 5 m for range and better than 1 mil angular accuracy. A wind speed measurement accuracy of better than 1 kt is claimed.

---

5. MUZZLE VELOCITY MEASUREMENT

Before the advent of radar, muzzle velocity (MV) was calculated from a series of test firings to observe the fall of shot on a measured range, by firing through screens, photographing the projectile as it left the muzzle and by extrapolation from wear measurements made in the bore or by the number of rounds fired. The need for greater accuracy of fire demands measurement on the operational site; repeated at intervals to establish the performance of a gun as its wears. Variation in muzzle velocity is caused by small manufacturing variations in the weight of projectile and propellant, and by propellant temperature as well as by the gradual wear of the bore. The variations are significant in their effect on the fall of shot and must therefore be considered in the calculation of gunsight data. A number of velocity measuring devices are now available which can be used at the gun position to monitor changes in muzzle velocity. Some feed information directly to the command post computer. They all work on the Doppler principle and consist of a radar head and small computer which translates the shift in frequency between the outgoing radar pulse echo from the shell into velocity.

In order to avoid geometrical errors, the radar head must be close to the muzzle. This exposes the mechanism to the shock of firing, so that the equipment must be robust. At the moment of leaving the barrel the propellant gases create an ionizing effect so that measurement must be made after the shell has travelled some distance from the muzzle. To achieve the highest accuracy several measurements are made and the results compared electronically to extrapolate the muzzle velocity.

DR 513 ballistic radar

Denmark

The remarkable feature of this doppler radar is its rugged construction and high shock and vibration resistance which enable it to be placed very close to, or even on, the gun being examined. This ensures the least possibility of geometrical error in the result. It is a compact and self-contained equipment suitable for both field and range use. A test unit is incorporated in the design. Over 14 countries have been supplied with the DR 513.

Velocities from 50 to 2,000 m/sec can be measured to an accuracy of 0·1 per cent. There is a visual readout of muzzle velocity on a tape which can be fed to a computer and is sufficient to extrapolate the shell's performance at any point on the trajectory.

The horn antenna incorporates both transmitter and receiver and can be placed on any non-recoiling part of the gun or on a tripod. The data box is remoted from the antenna. Measurements are made automatically at 30 and 40 m from the muzzle.

Note transmitter to left of wheels—antenna beyond.

DR 810 ballistic radar

Denmark

The DR 810 is designed specifically for field use. Like the DR 513 it can be mounted on or very near the gun being examined. The antenna weighs 13 kg, and the data box 22 kg. 24 volt d.c., or 220 volt a.c. electrical supply can be used without recourse to additional equipment.

The DR 810 measures velocities from 50 to 1,750 m/sec. The projectile velocity is measured at several points along the trajectory and the muzzle velocity calculated and displayed immediately. The first measurement point can be varied to avoid the disturbing effects of muzzle flash. The Nixie tube display in metres/second can be of one firing, or an average of up to eight previous firings.

There are selectors for the velocity band, one of three first measuring points (30, 60 or 120 m), and the offset of the antenna. Compensation for parallax is automatic.

Isidor muzzle velocity meter

Sweden

The Isidor meter is intended for field use. It consists of a light solid state antenna (four kilogrammes) and a data unit. It can be mounted on the gun being examined.

The Isidor measures velocities from 175 to 1,150 m/sec. The read-out can be the measurement of one firing, or an average of several shots. The equipment operates to a range of 2,000 times the calibre of the weapon being measured. Accuracy of 0·5 per cent is claimed.

The direct read-out is expressed as the difference between the nominal performance of the gun which is pre-set by the operator, and the actual velocity measured.

Projectile velocity measuring radar—'Pacer'

United Kingdom

Pacer is designed for use in the field. It is small and operates from a 24 volt d.c. or mains voltage a.c. electrical supply. Unlike the Scandinavian systems, Pacer is not intended for semi-permanent attachment to the gun, but is deployed (by one man) when necessary. It weighs 130 kg.

Pacer measures velocities between 200 and 1,600 m/sec to an accuracy of 0·3 m/sec. It can measure down to 100 m/sec with reduced accuracy. There is a built-in automatic test facility.

The operator must select the anticipated muzzle velocity to within 20 m/sec: the radar is then automatically activated by the muzzle flash, and after the measurement is made, automatically switches off: the result of the measurement is shown on a Nixie tube display. The only other actions required by the operator is the initial setting up of the radar head within 2 m of the barrel between muzzle and breech, and aiming it along the line of fire.

Pacer—transmitter (*on left*) and computer/display units.

Projectile velocity measuring equipment (PVME)

United Kingdom

PVME is complementary to Pacer, and is designed for experimental, research and proofing uses. It is both more complex and more accurate. Both PVME and Pacer are manufactured by Ferranti Ltd. and a combination of parts of the two equipments is possible so that the rugged and shock resistant Pacer antenna can operate with the PVME data handling equipment.

An accuracy of 1/10,000 is claimed. All measurements are duplicated by two transceivers operating in different radar bands. The points of measurement on the trajectory are variable and controlled by the operator. There is an oscilloscope display of velocity against time and a stored display of the timings of the projectile at the three measuring points. A tape for subsequent print-out or computer input can be provided.

6. FIRE CONTROL COMPUTERS

The development of the computer for field use has been the most important technical innovation in gunnery since World War II. In most cases the military computer has been developed from a commercial design, and specially adapted to cope with the tough battlefield environment.

The field artillery computer is used to resolve firing data for the gun sights from the co-ordinates of gun position and target to include allowance for all known ballistic variables. The computer programme includes all known performance facts for the type (or types) of gun being served. Variables such as individual gun muzzle velocities, changes in temperature and meteorological conditions can be fed into the computer manually, by tape or by direct data link from a suitable instrument.

Manual input requires a keyboard, often associated with a matrix of light symbols which indicate which part of the computer programme or memory is being used.

The computer is a flexible instrument which can be programmed for any type of gun or for many other artillery problems: survey meteorological calculations, sound-ranging and logistic problems can all be automated. Most small field service computers need to be re-programmed before tackling each type of task; only the largest can handle all calculations using one programme. Programmes are usually fed into the computer by tape—a simple process which can be performed in the field by the operator: in some cases the matrix must also be changed.

Computers are expensive, but they are fast and highly accurate: they have in-built test and error detection facilities, require less training for the operator and do not suffer from battle fatigue or human error.

Falke computer

Federal Republic of Germany

Falke is based on the Telefunken TR-8 family of digital computers and is known as the TR-84M. It is one of a family of military computers. It produces gun-sight data, calculates meteorological data, resolves sound-ranging and flash-spotting observations into hostile battery co-ordinates and assists fire control.

Field artillery computer—Saab ACE-380

Sweden

The ACE-380 is a field artillery computer weighing only 50 kg. It is based on the Datasaab D5-30 and is designed to be used in a battery command post. It calculates firing data from one gun position, taking into account the existing ballistic variables. Meteorological corrections are added from data processed by the computer itself based on measurements at any 30 levels of atmosphere. There is an automatic error detection device.

After manual entry of gun position information and meteorological data, target data can be fed into the computer automatically or semi-automatically by the observer, or manually by the operator. A keyboard is used which has six function areas: battery co-ordinates, target data, change of target, fire adjustment and function controls such as 'compute', 'test' and 'store'. Muzzle velocities are automatically entered from measuring devices on the guns.

Keyboard and display panel.

There is a visual display of firing data in the command post and a direct data link to the gun sights.

A ferrite core memory stores up to 16,000 words. This is sufficient to handle 500 targets together with 20 target records corrected for current conditions. Stored data can be recalled, displayed, up-dated and restored, as required.

Field artillery fire control equipment—9FA 101

Sweden

The 9FA 101 is intended to be a simple battery command post computer. The system can be extended to include automatic input by forward observers with a data link direct to the guns. The basic computer weighs 31 kg.

The main function is the production of gun sight data from target and gun position co-ordinates. 9FA 101 also produces fuze settings and gun corrections from observations of the fall of shot.

Target co-ordinates are fed to the computer by keyboard, while other relevant data is set on multi-position switches. A direct radio link input device for forward observers called HADAR is under development.

All firing data is displayed numerically, but can be augmented by repeater stations at each gun. The repeater units incorporate speech facilities for the passage of supplementary orders.

Field artillery computer—'FACE'

United Kingdom

FACE is a digital computer based on the commercial Marconi-Elliott 920B. It has been in service with the British Army since 1969. The system is rugged and suitable for rough combat zone use. It runs off a 24 volt d.c. electrical supply, and can be mounted in a Landrover. It has been sold to three other countries.

FACE can be programmed to produce gun or a free flight rocket firing data, or to solve survey problems. It is also incorporated into AMETS. In its gun control role it can handle calculations for three battery positions, each of eight guns. Only one type of equipment can be handled by each programme. The programme can be changed by the operator in the field, and when a new display matrix is required, this too can be changed

FACE layout in FV 432 command post vehicle.

by the operator. The programme includes the drill sequences, so that after each input the next piece of information is requested by an illuminated panel in the display matrix.

The required programme including the ballistic data of an individual weapon, is entered via a sealed cassette tape. Target data and variable factors such as individual gun muzzle velocities are fed into the memory by the operator using a key console. Meteorological data is inserted by punched tape (available from the teleprinter) or via the key console.

Data is shown on a Nixie tube visual display. A printed record, or punch tape read-out is possible using the built-in teleprinter. In the gun control role, firing

data for each gun is displayed in sequence. Alternatively individual gun sight data can be transmitted to each gun by the Artillery Weapon Data Transmission System (AWDATS) which operates by FM radio frequency signal over existing radio or line equipment.

Besides the programme, initial battery position, individual gun data, and meteorological data, the FACE memory will hold 40 recorded targets, of which ten are automatically and permanently updated for current meteorological conditions.

Employment   Australia   Egypt
             Canada   United Kingdom

AWDATS display in turret of British 105 mm SP Abbot.

Field artillery digital automatic computer system—'FADAC'

United States of America

FADAC is a first generation field artillery computer system which processes a wide variety of data for tube artillery, guided missiles and free flight rockets. It consists of a computer, test set and programme input unit: a teletypewriter can be coupled to it, and this is used for survey, meteorological data processing and Lance missile fire control procedures. For normal fire control

a digital display of data is used.

FADAC can be used to compute gun-sight data from target co-ordinates for up to five battery positions. It can also resolve survey problems, reduce meteorological information into gun corrections and assist in producing timed fire programmes. It is used to process data from sound-ranging equipment.

Programmes for each different task are kept on tape and fed into the computer through a photo-electric type reader—the 'programme input unit'. No other special equipment is needed so that FADAC can change roles in the field. Individual problems are fed in via a key console. For each role a different input matrix is needed to interpret the keyboard, but the operator can change the matrix himself. Output is by numerical display. The programme for use with guns allows the memory to store data for two calibres or types of guns (rocket and missile programmes are for individual equipments). Data for firing battery positions is stored; the operator selects the battery for which data is required. FADAC is no longer in production and it will be replaced in the US Army by a new battery computer.

Tactical fire direction system 'TACFIRE'

United States of America

The TACFIRE system is designed around the L 3050M computer. It is deployed at both battalion and divisional Fire Direction Centres. It handles the entire fire control process from the direct input of target data by the observer to the display of firing data in the battery command post. It stores gun and ammunition availability states, and the tactical situation expressed as the disposition of enemy and friendly troops. It can handle survey and meteorological calculations.

There are three methods of entry: manual or by fixed or variable format entry devices. Forward observers are equipped with a fixed format message entry device by which target information is codified using 25 key switches. The device transmits this information in digital form over existing radio or wire link communication systems in a 1·3 sec burst transmission. The device is also used to send corrections to adjust the fall of shot. The variable format message entry device is used by survey parties, battery command posts, meteorological observers and other 'out stations' to enter information relevant to their tasks. Direct entry is by keyboard.

At the computer console output is either visual or printed. When visual display on a cathode ray tube is used, a print-out record can also be kept. The usual fire control display which results from an observer's input of target data is in the form of a plan for target engagement based on available fire units which are in range, ammunition states and the scale of response suggested by the type of target. This plan can be accepted or modified before being routed to the relevant battery command posts, where it is displayed numerically as gun sight data.

The main memory unit is part of the divisional Fire Direction Centre equipment. It consists of a Random Access Memory which holds 400,000 words of information and a Bulk Media Memory Unit with a 300,000 word capacity in computer programmes. There is also a Memory Loading Unit by which information stored on tape can be recalled: the tape is used for initial programming and carries 300,000 words.

Development
ATILA (France) will be a comprehensive fire control system on the lines of TACFIRE, but it will go further in that it will include ADP at the battery level. MILIPAC (Canada), TOS (USA) and ARCOS (UK private venture) are light-weight second generation battery level computers.

VIII. Anti-tank Guns and Guided Weapons

The dominating position occupied by the tank in modern land warfare has naturally led to the development of a whole spectrum of anti-tank weapons. At one end there is the tank itself which has developed into a gun-platform for a gun primarily designed to defeat other tanks, and at the other there are a variety of hand-held infantry weapons. There are no clear-cut divisions, but there are, broadly, four classes of weapon.

First there is the true 'gun', a long, powerful, heavy, high-velocity weapon of great accuracy relying on the kinetic energy of the shot to achieve its effect. This is not only the armament of the tank, but also of the tank's close relative, the self-propelled anti-tank gun. The difference between the two lies in the fact that the SP anti-tank gun is primarily a defensive weapon as opposed to an armoured fighting vehicle suited to all phases of combat, and it is accordingly more lightly armoured and not necessarily equipped with a revolving turret. Tanks are so stoutly armoured today that guns of a size able to generate the kinetic energy required to penetrate it using a solid shot or dart are more conveniently carried on a tracked chassis. Towed guns of the size of the 17 pdr and the 100 mm are slow to manhandle in and out of action. The SP gun in addition has obvious advantages as its armoured protection and mobility enables it to take part in a rapidly moving tank battle.

The towed equipments, fitted like the tanks with a high velocity gun, may either be used primarily in the anti-tank role or may also be fitted with a dial sight and clinometer for indirect fire using HE shell. The Russians, who have always favoured guns, consider that their indirect fire guns also have an important secondary role in the whole anti-tank defence lay-out. As regards design, the requirement is not so much a high sustained rate of fire, but the ability to engage successive targets very quickly, so the tendency is towards semi-automatic sliding breech-blocks and fixed ammunition. As the gun has to be deployed well forward and concealed the carriage silhouette is kept low and a generous shield is provided. Some Russian towed guns are fitted with auxiliary propulsion units.

The weight of the larger towed guns reduced their mobility and accordingly the recoilless rifle firing a special armour-piercing HE shell was developed. In the recoilless system a portion of the gas generated by igniting the propellant is vented through the breech to the rear to counteract the recoil. This enables the whole buffer/recuperator system and the trail to be dispensed with and so saves a great deal of weight. The muzzle velocity is low which also makes for a thin walled and lighter piece, but the resultant curved trajectory demands some form of on-carriage range-finding device. The great disadvantage of the recoilless system is that there is a large back-blast which on sandy or dry ground gives away the position of the gun.

The normal sighting system used on anti-tank guns is the rocking bar with the telescope. Range is either judged by eye, or determined by a spotting rifle firing a trace or an indicator round to test the range or, coming increasingly into use, a laser range-finder. The lead to allow for the movement of the target is usually estimated (or guessed) and is applied either by off-setting the telescope, or more usually by aiming off, using graticules which appear in the telescope's field of view. Anti-tank guns require considerable skill in

Figure IX: Principles of the recoilless rifle. *From L. to R.:* 1, 2, round with perforated shell case is loaded. 3. Firing, gases vented to rear. 4 and 5, projectile leaves, shell case ejected. 6, general idea of system, muzzle at bottom of page.

deployment, and brave, well-disciplined, well-trained crews, as once a tank battle starts they attract every form of counter-fire. Only a really skilled layer can be expected to obtain first time hits, which are what count, for the expectation of survival of a gun which has exposed itself by firing and has missed are short. Accordingly attention has turned to the guided missile, which first became prominent in the Vietnam war and later in the Arab–Israeli war of 1973, as its launcher is easy to conceal and the probability of a first-time hit at any point along its effective trajectory high.

Like mortars, anti-tank weapons of all kinds are used by all three arms, but only the long-range, anti-tank guided weapons (LR-ATGW) are considered here, as they can be regarded as a crew-served and, in the case of the British Swingfire, can be fired indirect from behind cover and so are 'artillery'. With the exception of the Soviet Swatter they are all wire-guided; receiving signals through a thin filament which pays out behind during flight. Guidance is of two kinds. 'Command to the Line of Sight' requires the operator to steer the missile on to the target. In a 'Semi-Automatic to the Line of Sight' all the operator has to do is to keep his aiming telescope on the target and its movements are translated into corrections signalled to the missile via the wire.

Missiles are easily deployed and concealed, are versatile (man-handled, vehicle mounted, AFV mounted, or airborne in helicopters); as said, the first time hit probability and lethality are very high, accuracy is not degraded with range, crew-training is short and easy and the exchange ratio in terms of cost between tank and missile is greatly in favour of the missile. There are, as always, compensating disadvantages. There is the question of missile re-supply and the carriage of first-line holdings, as a missile is fragile and bulky compared with an artillery round, the operators of the direct fire variety are very exposed to retaliatory and suppressive fire, and the time of flight is long and the time between engagements also long in consequence. To offset these a large number of missiles and operators must be deployed forward, which was the way the Egyptians obtained their first, surprise effect in Sinai in 1973. The optically controlled wire-guided system has its limitations, but an active or semi-active homing head and a radio link is open to 'spoofing' and electronic counter-measures. Future development is likely to be aimed at the fully automatic weapon which locks on target and homes after launch which can engage out to the limit of target acquisition by day or night and enable a succession of targets to be engaged at intervals of seconds. This of course will inevitably raise complexity and cost.

45 mm anti-tank gun M 1942

Union of Soviet Socialist Republics

Calibre	45 mm
Barrel length	46 calibres
Muzzle brake	Nil
Trail type	Split
Weight	570 kg
Ammunition	HVAP (0·9 kg)
	APHE (1·4 kg)
	HE
Armour penetration	66 mm at 500 m (HVAP)
Rate of fire	25 rds/min
Muzzle velocity	1,070 m/sec (HVAP)
	820 m/sec (APHE)
Maximum range	4,400 m
Maximum effective range	500 m
Elevation limits	−8° + 25°
Traverse on carriage	60°
Detachment	6

The M 1942 is an elderly weapon which is now in very limited service. Its armour penetration is poor; it would be lucky to kill a modern tank, but would be effective against lightly armoured APCs. The unusual calibre of the weapon has precluded any improvement in performance by adopting ammunition developed for more recent weapons.

The vertically sliding breech is semi-automatic, which encourages a high rate of fire. The light weight, fixed ammunition, and good access to the breech give credibility to the claimed rate of fire. In practice, the need to re-lay the gun is probably a limiting factor in achieving this rate. An HE round is available, and indirect sights are fitted, but the maximum range is restricted by the upper elevation limit. The HE shell is too small to be really effective.

The carriage is taken from an earlier gun of the same calibre—the M 1937. The tubular section legs are fitted with fixed spades. A sloping shield whose sides are angled backwards has a folding section which reaches nearly to the ground: it does not overlap the wheels. The hydraulic buffer and spring recuperator are mounted below the barrel.

Employment	Albania
	Bulgaria
	China
	North Korea
	Rumania

45 mm anti-tank gun.

6 pounder anti-tank gun

United Kingdom

Calibre	57 mm
Barrel length	—
Muzzle brake	Single baffle
Trail type	Split
Weight	1,244 kg
Ammunition	APDS
Armour penetration	146 mm at 1,000 m (APOS)
Rate of fire	20 rds/min
Muzzle velocity	900 m/sec
Maximum range	8,990 m
Maximum effective range	500 m
Elevation limits	− 5° + 15°
Traverse on carriage	90°
Detachment	3–6

The 6 pounder was developed at the beginning of World War II to replace the 2 pounder anti-tank gun. Design work started in 1938 and the gun entered service in 1942.

The monobloc barrel has a distinctive spherical muzzle brake and a vertical sliding wedge type breech. The recoil mechanism is mounted below the barrel. The shield is angled back into extensions over the wheels and has a hinged flap to give line of sight to the optical telescopic sights.

The split trail of box section members is of conventional design, but opens wide to allow excellent traverse.

The weapon was produced in America as the 57 mm M 1. It was used in various mounts including tanks and as an SP anti-tank gun on an armoured truck (known as Deacon). It is long since obsolete in the British and American armies.

Employment	Bangladesh	Egypt	Pakistan
	Brazil	India	Spain
	Burma	Israel	Thailand
	Cameroons	Malaysia	

6 pounder Mark IV anti-tank gun.

57 mm anti-tank gun M 1943 (ZIS 2)

Union of Soviet Socialist Republics

Calibre	57 mm
Barrel length	—
Muzzle brake	Double baffle
Trail type	Split
Weight	1,150 kg
Ammunition	HVAP (1·8 kg)
	APHE (3·1 kg)
	HE (2·8 kg)
Armour penetration	140 mm at 500 m (HVAP)
	106 mm at 500 mm (APHE)
Rate of fire	20–25 rds/min
Muzzle velocity	1,270 m/sec (HVAP)
	990 m/sec (APHE)
	706 m/sec (HE)
Maximum range	8,400 m
Maximum effective range	500 m
Elevation limits	−5° + 25°
Traverse on carriage	56°
Detachment	5–7

This equipment is a 57 mm piece mounted on a split trail carriage which it shares with the 76 mm ZIS 3. The appearance of the two guns is very similar, the ZIS 2 having a longer and thinner barrel.

The breech is semi-automatic vertical sliding wedge type, and contributes to the very high rate of fire claimed for this weapon. The performance of the ammunition is good for the age of the weapon, but at a very limited range. Modern recoilless hand held weapons can match this performance without the problems of movement, deployment and concealment associated with a gun of this size. Indirect sights and an HE shell give the gun a secondary role. Range is restricted by the upper elevation limit and the shell is too small to be really effective. An infra-red night-sight can be fitted.

The trail legs are tubular with fixed spades. The top of the square shield folds forward for travelling. As well as being towed it is sometimes carried in the BTR-50P. The barrel has been used in the ASU 57 SP anti-tank gun, and is the basis of the 57 mm auxiliary propelled anti-tank gun. It is known in China as the M 55, but is no longer in the service of the Soviet Army.

Employment:

Albania	East Germany	Rumania
Bulgaria	Haiti	Syria
China	Hungary	Yugoslavia
Cuba	Indonesia	Zaire
Czechoslovakia	North Korea	
Egypt	Poland	

57 mm anti-gun M 1943.

57 mm auxiliary propelled anti-tank gun M 1955

Union of Soviet Socialist Republics

Calibre	57 mm		990 m/sec (APHE)
Barrel length	—		760 m/sec (HE)
Muzzle brake	Double baffle	*Maximum range*	7,000 m
Trail type	Split	*Maximum effective range*	500 m
Weight	1,250 kg	*Elevation limits*	−5° + 15°
Ammunition	HVAP (1·8 kg)	*Traverse on carriage*	56°
	APHE (3·1 kg)	*Detachment*	5–6
	HE (2·8 kg)		
Armour penetration	140 mm at 500 m (HVAP)		
	106 mm at 500 m (APHE)		
Rate of fire	15–20 rds/min		
Muzzle velocity	1,270 m/sec (HVAP)		

This weapon, is a modified ZIS 2 fitted with the M 72 two cylinder 14 horse power petrol engine driving the main carriage wheels. Top speed is 40 kilometres/hour. It is similar to the 85 mm SD 44.

The recoil system is entirely below the barrel. Performance and ammunition options are as for the ZIS 2, except that the drive arrangements limit elevation and therefore range: the reductions in rate of fire and detachment are similar to those noted for the SP version of the SD 44. The ZIS 2 infra-red night sight is available.

The power pack is mounted on the right trail leg. The driver sits in front of it with a steering wheel. A third wheel, mounted at the trail, is steered, and when the gun is in action is folded up to allow the fixed spades to bed in. The steering wheel also folds away. The equipment can be towed conventionally, but the third

wheel must be folded into its firing position. The trail legs also carry removable ammunition lockers. The construction of the legs is changed from tubular (as for ZIS 2) to box section.

Not all users of the ZIS 2 have this modified weapon, which is in service with the Russian airborne forces.

Employment :

Albania	East Germany	Rumania
Cuba	Hungary	USSR
Czechoslovakia		

Auxiliary-propelled version of the 57 mm.

Type 56 recoilless rifle

China

Calibre	75 mm
Barrel length	28 calibres
Muzzle brake	Nil
Trail type	Single support strut
Weight	86 kg
Ammunition	HEAT 80 mm
	HE
Armour penetration	80 mm (HEAT)
Rate of fire	10 rds/min
Muzzle velocity	—
Maximum range	6,600 m
Maximum effective range	500 m
Elevation limits	—
Traverse on carriage	360°
Detachment	4

75 mm Type 56.

The Type 56 recoilless rifle is weapon developed by the Chinese communists from United States' equipment. The original was the M 20 recoilless rifle, and only the general form of the tube and breech remain. The mechanism of the breech is, however, considerably altered. Whilst retaining the conventional long, clean barrel and curved conical breech, the Type 56 is mounted on a distinctive curved tubular axle with a single forward tubular support ending in a transverse towing bar. The tube is connected to the carriage by a single ring clamp with the prominent elevating and traversing screws set at right angles to each other behind and in

front of the ring clamp respectively. The Type 56 or Type 62 sight, mounted on the left above the clamp, permits either direct or indirect fire, using either HEAT or HE rounds, at a rate of up to 10 rounds/minute. It is possible to penetrate some 80 mm of armour. The weapon can be fired without removing the detachable solid-tyred wheels, but is, of course, more accurate and stable without them.

Employment China
Vietnam

17 pounder anti-tank gun

United Kingdom

Calibre	76·2 mm
Barrel length	—
Muzzle brake	Double baffle
Trail type	Split
Weight	3,040 kg
Ammunition	APDS
Armour penetration	222 mm at 1,000 m (APDS)
Rate of fire	20 rds/min
Muzzle velocity	—
Maximum range	10,500 m
Maximum effective range	1,200 m
Elevation limits	−6° + 16·5°
Traverse on carriage	60°
Detachment	4

The 17 pounder entered service in 1942, following the 2 and 6 pounder guns in an attempt to combat the ever increasing weight of tank armour.

The long barrel had a vertical sliding breech block which was very similar in design to the 25 pounder gun/howitzer. The recoil system is below the barrel. Early models were delivered on the 25 pounder box trail, but, the gun is usually associated with its own split trail carriage.

A number of SP versions were developed, and an experimental auxiliary motor version was very similar in concept and looks to the latest 90 mm Rhienmetall gun.

The weapon was superseded in British service by MOBAT.

Employment	Burma	Pakistan
	Egypt	South Africa
	Israel	

The Mark I 17 pounder anti-tank gun.

82 mm recoilless rifle M 59A

Czechoslovakia

Calibre	82 mm	*Maximum range*	7,560 m
Barrel length	46·5 calibres	*Maximum effective range*	1,000 m
Muzzle brake	Nil	*Elevation limits*	−13 + 25°
Trail type	Split	*Traverse on carriage*	360° (see text)
Weight	386 kg	*Detachment*	5
Ammunition	HEAT (6 kg)		
	HE		
Armour penetration	250 mm (HEAT)		
Rate of fire	6 rds/min		
Muzzle velocity	745 m/sec (HEAT)		
	565 m/sec (HE)		

The M 59A has a much greater range than the older and lighter T 21, which is a similar weapon of the same calibre.

A 12·7 mm semi-automatic ZH 59 spotting rifle is mounted above the barrel; no other Warsaw Pact weapon uses this ranging system, although it is common practice in Western armies. Another unusual feature is the provision of an HE round. Despite a limited elevation it has a range of 7,560 m in the field role. It is not clear what fire control arrangements are made but the PB 04K sight is used for direct and indirect laying. Traverse is limited to 60° at full elevation.

The M 59A is normally deployed with motorised rifle regiments as a towed equipment on a light split trail carriage. Manhandling is helped by a bar-like handle at the muzzle. It is towed by its breech behind a jeep-size vehicle, the OAZ 69. It can also be mounted on that vehicle or on the OT 62 APC.

Employment   Czechoslovakia
Egypt

82 mm recoilless rifle M 59A.

82 mm recoilless rifle T 21

Czechoslovakia

Calibre	82 mm
Barrel length	—
Muzzle brake	Nil
Trail type	—
Weight	20 kg
Ammunition	HEAT (2·1 kg)
Armour penetration	230 mm (HEAT)
Rate of fire	5–6 rds/min
Muzzle velocity	250 m/sec
Maximum range	2,600 m
Maximum effective range	300 m
Elevation limits	—
Traverse on carriage	—
Detachment	1–2

The T 21 is a weapon which has a short effective range but an extremely good penetration, made at the Skoda works in Pilsen. It is a very versatile weapon, capable of being fired from its small two-wheeled carriage, from the shoulder or from a fixed mount on the Czech tracked OT 62 armoured personnel carrier, in both direct and indirect roles. Maximum range in the indirect role is 2,600 m. It is a smooth-bore, firing a shaped-charged HEAT fin-stabilised round, which is breech-loaded, and fired electrically—as with the P 27 anti-tank grenade launcher, the trigger action works a magneto. To cope with direct and indirect fire the T 21 is equipped with ordinary 'open' sights graduated in 50 m intervals and also a telescopic sight graduated at 100 m intervals. The 2·1 kilogrammes HEAT round can penetrate up to 230 mm of armour at an effective range of 300 m if the target is moving, and up to 650 m if the target is stationary. Rate of fire is about five rounds/minute, but this could be improved if a spent cartridge extracter were fitted. The breech has to be cleared manually with the aid of an asbestos glove.

The T 21 is usually transported in a truck or armoured personnel carrier, but can be towed for short distances using the long tubular towing handle, normally kept folded over the top of the tube.

Employment   Czechoslovakia
Vietnam

82 mm recoilless rifle T 21.

82 mm recoilless rifle B-10

Union of Soviet Socialist Republics

Calibre	82 mm
Barrel length	20 calibres
Muzzle brake	Nil
Trail type	Tripod
Weight	85 kg
Ammunition	HEAT (7·3 kg)
	HE (8·2 kg)
Armour penetration	300 mm at 400 m (HEAT)
Rate of fire	5–6 rds/min
Muzzle velocity	322 m/sec
Maximum range	4,400 m
Maximum effective range	500 m
Elevation limits	−2° + 35°
Traverse on carriage	360°
Detachment	4

This weapon dates from 1950 and derives from the RPG 82. It is no longer in service with the Soviet Army. Like the B-11 it is a smooth bore equipment, without muzzle brake and towed by its barrel. The projectile is spin stabilised and has the appearance of a mortar bomb. An HE round adds flexibility to the weapon's employment. The PB 02 sighting gear is clamped to the left of the barrel, while a pistol grip and trigger are to the right. The hinged breech opens horizontally.

This weapon is fired from an adjustable height tripod which gives 360° traverse. It travels on a two wheel carriage which can be removed or remain attached in action. A small castor wheel below the muzzle protects the barrel from damage while the weapon is being manhandled. It weighs only 72 kilogrammes in action and is thus within the carrying capacity of its detachment for manoeuvering. It can be mounted on BTR 50 APCs.

Employment:

Bulgaria	Hungary	Syria
China	North Korea	Vietnam
Egypt	Pakistan	
East Germany	Poland	

The 82 mm recoilless rifle B-10 deployed in Sinai.

82 mm recoilless rifle M 60 (BO)

Yugoslavia

Calibre	82 mm
Barrel length	—
Muzzle brake	Nil
Trail type	Pole
Weight	122 kg
Ammunition	HEAT (7·2 kg)
	HE
Armour penetration	220 mm at 500 m (HEAT)
Rate of fire	4–5 rds/min
Muzzle velocity	388 m/sec
Maximum range	4,500 m
Maximum effective range	1,000 m
Elevation limits	−20° + 35°
Traverse on carriage	360°
Detachment	2–5

82 mm recoilless rifle M 60.

This simple weapon consists of a barrel mounted on a two wheel axle with a single steadying leg.

The breech hinges downwards for loading. The PTDM 60 sights are on the left of the barrel, but a foresight is fitted to the right side to enable the detachment commander to indicate targets, and check the lay of the gun.

The standard ammunition is a HEAT round which is notably heavier than that of the Russian B-10 weapon. It is considered effective against static targets up to 1,000 m, but for moving targets 500 m is the practical limit. The armour penetration is sustained over an angle of incidence from 25° to 90°. The rate of fire is not very high for the type of equipment.

A range of 4,500 m for indirect fire is quoted, and the barrel has a generous elevation. However only anti-armour ammunition is provided, nor do there appear to be indirect sights, suggesting that the 'field artillery role' is only theoretical. The supporting leg folds under the breech for travelling, and the weapon is towed by its muzzle. There is no muzzle brake: two handles project horizontally from the towing eye mounting to assist in manhandling. At 122 kg it is an extremely light weapon and can be carried by its detachment over short distances.

Employment   Yugoslavia

85 mm anti-tank gun M 52

Czechoslovakia

Calibre	85 mm
Barrel length	56·2 calibres
Muzzle brake	Double baffle
Trail type	Split
Weight	2,095 kg
Ammunition	APHE (9·3 kg)
	HVAP (5 kg)
	HE (9·5 kg)
Armour penetration	123 mm at 1,000 m (APHE)
	107 mm at 1,000 m (HVAP)
Rate of fire	15 rds/min
Muzzle velocity	1,070 m/sec (HVAP)
	820 m/sec (APHE)
	805 m/sec (HE)

Maximum range	16,200 m
Maximum effective range	1,000 m
Elevation limits	−6° + 38°
Traverse on carriage	60°
Detachment	6

This conventional gun is designed to fire Russian 85 mm M 1945 ammunition: its longer barrel gives a marginally better performance than the Russian gun. The vertical sliding breech block lifts to open and is probably semi-automatic.

The rate of fire is high. The recoil system is mounted under the barrel.

The gun is primarily designed as an anti-tank

weapon. However, it has an HE round and the high muzzle velocity gives an excellent indirect fire performance. The anti-armour penetration of both APHE and HVAP rounds is not good by modern standards.

The design of the carriage provides greater elevation and traverse than its Russian counterpart. The trail legs have fixed spades: the towing eye on the left leg folds inside the leg to clear the spade in action. A stowage box travels on the trail legs and is an important recognition feature. The shield, which has a wavy top, narrows at its base to give a triangular appearance.

Employment Austria
Czechoslovakia
German Peoples' Republic

85 mm anti-tank gun M 1945 (D 44)

Union of Soviet Socialist Republics

Calibre	85 mm
Barrel length	53 calibres
Muzzle brake	Double baffle
Trail type	Split
Weight	1,725 kg
Ammunition	HVAP (5·0 kg)
	APHE (9·3 kg)
	HE (9·5 kg)
Armour penetration	130 mm at 1,000 m (HVAP)
	102 mm at 1,000 m (APHE)
Rate of fire	20 rds/min
Muzzle velocity	1,030 m/sec (HVAP)
	792 m/sec (HE and APHE)
Maximum range	15,650 m
Maximum effective range	1,600 m
Elevation limits	−7° + 42°
Traverse on carriage	54°
Detachment	6

This is a multi purpose weapon which dates from World War II and is designed to be as versatile as the 100 mm M 1955. It is variously known as the 85 mm divisional gun M 1945, and medium anti-tank gun D 44 and D 48. Like the 100 mm, it is used as a tank gun, in this case for the T 34/85. There is an SP version, ASU 85, and a limited mobility type SD 44.

A vertically sliding breech is used and the hydropneumatic recoil system is mounted behind the steeply raked, wavy topped shield.

Armour penetration is not good by modern standards, but the rate of fire is high. It is capable of indirect fire and an HE round is provided. As shown above it has ample range in this role.

The split trail legs are made of tubular members, each of which carries a fixed spade.

Employment	Albania	Guinea	Poland
	Algeria	Hungary	Romania
	Bulgaria	Iran	Sudan
	China	Iraq	Syria
	Cuba	Laos	USSR
	Egypt	Morocco	Vietnam
	East Germany	North Korea	

85 mm anti-tank gun M 1945 (D 44).

85 mm auxiliary propelled gun SD 44

Union of Soviet Socialist Republics

Calibre	85 mm
Barrel length	53 calibres
Muzzle brake	Double baffle
Trail type	Split
Weight	2,256 kg
Ammunition	HVAP (5·0 kg)
	APHE (9·3 kg)
	HE (9·5 kg)
Armour penetration	130 mm at 1,000 m (HVAP)
	102 mm at 1,000 m (APHE)
Rate of fire	15 rds/min
Muzzle velocity	1,030 m/sec (HVAP)
	792 m/sec (HE and APHE)
Maximum range	15,650 m
Maximum effective range	1,600 m
Elevation limits	−7° + 35°
Traverse on carriage	54°
Detachment	5–7

This is an ingenious SP version of the previous entry, the 85 mm M 1945. Performance is unchanged except in a reduction to the rate of fire, due to the mountings of the motor and ammunition bin which restrict the movement of the loaders. The detachment is reduced. The weight is obviously increased but only by a modest 525 kilogrammes.

The M 72 two cylinder engine is mounted on the trail legs and a castor wheel is fitted beneath the spades. The gun runs 'backwards', i.e. away from the line of fire as if it were being towed. The driver sits in front of the power pack behind a conventional steering wheel. The third wheel and steering wheel column fold in action, but the power pack remains on the left trail leg. An ammunition locker is carried on the right trail leg. There is provision for one passenger on the breech, and up to four passengers can be carried. The 14 bhp motor propels the gun up to 7·5 kilometres/hour. Its fuel is carried in the hollow trail legs.

The gun can also be towed behind a vehicle and for this the third wheel is folded between the trail legs, where it is stowed in action.

The weapon is used by Soviet airborne forces.

Employment	Albania	Czechoslovakia	Poland
	Bulgaria	East Germany	Rumania
	Cuba	Hungary	USSR

The 85 mm SD 44 auxiliary propelled gun.

90 mm anti-tank gun

Federal Republic of Germany

Calibre	90 mm
Barrel length	—
Muzzle brake	Double baffle
Trail type	Box
Weight	5,000 kg
Ammunition	HEAT
	HVAP
	Practice
Armour penetration	330 mm at 1,000 m
Rate of fire	12 rds/min
Muzzle velocity	1,181 m/sec
Maximum range	—
Maximum effective range	2,000 m
Elevation limits	−8° + 25°
Traverse on carriage	30°
Detachment	3

This is a self-propelled weapon, which fully exploits the principle of auxiliary propulsion, and which deploys into action as a conventional towed gun. It is in an advanced stage of development. It can be, and for long journeys always is, towed.

The 90 mm gun is taken from the Jagdpanzer Kanone, a fully SP anti-tank weapon. It carries a double baffle muzzle brake and is fitted with a semi-automatic breech. Loading is manual, and firing either electromagnetic or mechanical using a percussion initiation.

Infra-red night sights are fitted as standard equipment.

A box-type trail acts as the vehicle chassis. It carries the recoiling parts, the detachment of three men, and the motor. There is space for 51 rounds of ammunition. The rear wheels (of small diameter) are mounted in a subframe which folds up for firing. The action of folding the subframe emplaces a spade, and is hydraulically powered; hydraulic pressure is produced from a pump driven off the power unit. There is a manual back-up pump fitted. The front suspension is hydraulically locked for firing. One man can, in emergency, deploy and operate the gun! It is possible to fire the gun in the travelling configuration.

The engine is a 1500 cc Porsche which gives a top speed of 20 kilometres/hour; gradients of 50 per cent can be climbed. Manoeuvrability and cross country performance are good: the main drive wheels can be brake steered, and the rear wheels are also steerable.

Employment   Trials only, in West Germany

The gun in action.

With barrel retracted and ready to move off under its own power.

90 mm recoilless rifle PV 1110

Sweden

Calibre	90 mm
Barrel length	36.9 cm
Muzzle brake	Nil
Trail type	Pole
Weight	260 kg
Ammunition	'Hollow charge'
Armour penetration	380 mm at 700 m
Rate of fire	6 rds/min
Muzzle velocity	715 m/sec
Maximum range	—
Maximum effective range	900 m
Elevation limits	−10° + 15°
Traverse on carriage	75°
Detachment	2–3

The PV 1110, made by Bofors, is a smooth bore weapon firing a fin stabilised hollow charge projectile of great penetrating power. The weight of a complete round is 9·6 kilogrammes. The sustained rate of fire is six rounds/minute, and two rounds can be fired in 13 seconds. A 7·62 mm spotting rifle with magazine of 10 rounds is mounted over the barrel. A pistol grip and trigger is fitted below the barrel. The overall weight varies with the mounting, but the gun itself weighs 125 kilogrammes. Traverse also varies with the mounting.

The PV 1110 has three different modes of transport. The normal two-wheel trailer carriage can be replaced by a simple sledge, or the weapon can be vehicle mounted. The trailer consists of a broad sheet steel platform with a two wheel axle and single steady leg by which the weapon is towed. The sledge is a long slender platform on which the piece is mounted so low that the detachment must lie down to operate the weapon: the overall height is only 470 mm. Not only does this give it the lowest profile of any anti-tank weapon of its type, but it obviates the difficulties of digging-in in snowbound country. The SP is mounted on the Volvo 4 × 4 Laplander. The same vehicle, or the Austrian Haflinger, are used as tractors for the towed version.

In each of these the barrel is mounted at its centre of gravity in a tubular member shaped like a question mark.

Employment Sweden

This action photograph demonstrates the extremely low silhouette of the weapon.

90 mm anti-tank gun Model 50

Switzerland

Calibre	90 mm
Barrel length	—
Muzzle brake	—
Trail type	Split
Weight	550 kg
Ammunition	—
Armour penetration	—
Rate of fire	8–10 rds/min
Muzzle velocity	600 m/sec
Maximum range	—
Maximum effective range	500 m
Elevation limits	—
Traverse on carriage	—
Detachment	—

There are two types of 90 mm Swiss anti-tank gun which are very similar. Both have the same downward curved and fragile looking box section trail leg design.

The recoil system is mounted below the barrel. The breech block is an upward opening vertical sliding wedge. No performance figures are available for the ammunition, but its muzzle velocity suggests that it has something in common with the Model 57.

The trail legs of the two weapons end in different types of spade. A simple plank seat is provided for the layer on the left trail leg.

The chief distinguishing feature is the shield. That of the Model 50 is square and is flat in its lateral axis: it bends back at the top and forward to clear the wheels at the bottom.

Employment   Switzerland

90 mm anti-tank gun Model 57

Switzerland

Calibre	90 mm
Barrel length	—
Muzzle brake	Multi-baffle
Trail type	Split
Weight	550 kg
Ammunition	HEAT (3·15 kg)
Armour penetration	250 mm (HEAT)
Rate of fire	8–10 rds/min
Muzzle velocity	600 m/sec
Maximum range	—
Maximum effective range	800–1,000 m
Elevation limits	—
Traverse on carriage	—
Detachment	—

This picture shows the high mounting of the sights, the breech protecting bar and the hooded shield. Note also that the wheels hinge with the trail legs when they are opened in action.

The Model 57 is an improved version of the earlier Model 50. It has the same elegant downward curve to the trail legs, but is easily distinguished by its new shield. It is also known as the Pak 57.

The long barrel is mounted at the centre of gravity, well forward of the breech. The vertically sliding breech block opens downwards. A bar arrangement beneath the breech protects it from damage against ground on recoil at high angles of elevation. The forward mounting of the trunnions and consequently large vertical movements of the breech makes this necessary. The recoil system is mounted under and over the barrel. Access to the breech is good, allowing a high rate of fire.

The sights are mounted in an upward extension of the saddle. The wooden bench seat of the Type 50 is replaced by a shaped seat for the layer.

The wheel axles are fitted to the trail legs and hinge with them on deployment. The shield is well rounded at the top and sweeps back from the front of the recoil system in the form of a hood over the sights.

Employment   Switzerland

Recoilless rifle M 58

Finland

Calibre	95 mm
Barrel length	34·5 calibres
Muzzle brake	Nil
Trail type	—
Weight	140 kg
Ammunition	(10·1 kg)
Armour penetration	300 mm
Rate of fire	6–8 rds/min
Muzzle velocity	615 m/sec
Maximum range	—
Maximum effective range	700 m
Elevation limits	—
Traverse on carriage	—
Detachment	3

This is the only recoilless gun of 95 mm calibre. It is a purely Finnish design. It has two small wheels, but lifting handles are fitted front and rear (forward of the breech) to assist in manhandling. Its detachment of only three can carry it over short distances.

There are two stabilizing legs fitted front and rear.

Used in the heavy weapons companies of infantry battalions.

Employment   Finland

95 mm recoilless rifle with crew at their posts.

---

100 mm field anti-tank gun M 1944 (D 10)

Union of Soviet Socialist Republics

Calibre	100 mm
Barrel length	54 calibres
Muzzle brake	Double baffle
Trail type	Split
Weight	3,460 kg
Ammunition	HVAP (10·2 kg)
	HEAT (12·2)
	APHE (15·9 kg)
	HE (15·7 kg)
Armour penetration	380 mm at 1,000 m (HEAT)
	185 mm at 1,000 m (APHE)
Rate of fire	8–10 rds/min
Muzzle velocity	1,000 m/sec (APHE)
	900 m/sec (HE)
	800 m/sec (HEAT)
Maximum range	21,000 m
Maximum effective range	1,000 m
Elevation limits	−5° + 40°
Traverse on carriage	58°
Detachment	6

100 mm M 1944 in the field role.

The barrel of this equipment was designed for the Russian M 1939 Anti-Aircraft Gun. It appeared as the D 10 at the end of World War II and has since been developed into the M 1955. A D 10T version was

171

mounted in the T 54 tank and SU 100 assault gun. This weapon then is the middle one of three generations of development.

It is essentially an anti-armour weapon despite its name: its ammunition options, low silhouette, limited elevation and high muzzle velocity all indicate this. Fixed ammunition and semi-automatic vertically sliding breech permit a high rate of fire. The ammunition has an excellent armour penetrating performance. The provision of HE ammunition gives the weapon its dual role. Double wheels are fitted to a simple split trail of box section legs. The shield is well angled and mounts useful storage bins under the barrel.

The recoil system is mounted below the barrel.

As is common practice these weapons were passed on to Soviet allies when the M 1955 was introduced. M 1955's have in turn been exported and it is not always clear which country has this gun and which the M 1955.

Employment	Bulgaria	Mongolia	Sudan
	China	Pakistan	USSR
	Congo	Poland	Vietnam
	Egypt	Rumania	Yugoslavia
	India	Somalia	
	North Korea	Syria	

100 mm field-cum-anti-tank gun M 1944 (D 10).

100 mm field anti-tank gun M 1955

Union of Soviet Socialist Republics

Calibre	100 mm
Barrel length	54 calibres
Muzzle brake	Pepper-pot
Trail type	Split
Weight	3,300 kg
Ammunition	HVAP (10·2 kg)
	HEAT (10·2 kg)
	APHE (15·9 kg)
	HE (15·7 kg)
Armour penetration	380 mm at 1,000 m (HEAT)
	185 mm at 1,000 m (APHE)
Rate of fire	10 rds/min
Muzzle velocity	1,000 m/sec (APHE)
	900 m/sec (HE)
	800 m/sec (HEAT)
Maximum range	21,000 m
Maximum effective range	1,000 m

Elevation limits	−5° + 45°
Traverse on carriage	55°
Detachment	8

This long barrelled gun is variously described as an anti-tank and field gun. It is used in both roles, has been mounted in T 54A and T 55 tanks and given a naval mounting. It was especially successful during the Yom Kippur War as an anti-tank gun.

It replaced the M 1944 (D 10) which was similarly a multi-role equipment. The ammunition system is that of the older gun, and shell options centre on an anti-armour capability. The HEAT round is especially effective. Ammunition is fixed and there is no provision for clearing difficult crests either by charge reductions or high angle fire.

The APN 3–5 infra-red sight is fitted; and a new

image intensifying sight is available.

The M 1955 can be distinguished from the earlier D 10 by its single road wheels, castor wheel on the trail and pepper-pot muzzle brake.

The recoil system is fitted above the barrel and behind the shield. It is 700 kilogrammes lighter than the D 10. A modified version with elevation limits of −10° and +20° is known as the T 12.

Employment

Bulgaria	Hungary	Rumania
China	India	Somalia
Czechoslovakia	Iraq	Syria
Egypt	Mongolia	USSR
German Peoples'	North Korea	Vietnam
Republic	Poland	Yugoslavia

100 mm M 1955 field/anti-tank gun.

105 mm recoilless rifle M 65

Yugoslavia

Calibre	105 mm
Barrel length	—
Muzzle brake	Nil
Trail type	Pole
Weight	280 kg
Ammunition	HEAT
Armour penetration	330 mm at 600 m
Rate of fire	6 rds/min
Muzzle velocity	—
Maximum range	6,000 m
Maximum effective range	600 m
Elevation limits	—
Traverse on carriage	—
Detachment	—

Whereas the Soviet Army has now given up large-calibre recoilless guns, Yugoslavia, with its problem of finding effective weapons for use in mountainous terrain, has developed its own large recoilles rifle, in addition to two lighter anti-tank weapons, the RB 57 and the M 60.

Among communist countries' weapons, the M 65 is unusual in that it is fitted with a 12·7 mm spotting machine gun, the UB, used at ranges up to 600 m (the M 65's maximum effective anti-tank range). It employs a 20 round belt, fired either automatic or single shot. The M 65 is a breech-loading weapon with a very long rifled barrel, allowing the gun to fire its HEAT projectiles a distance of 6,000 m. HE rounds have not yet been seen with this weapon. Six rounds can be fired in one minute and the shaped-charge warhead will pierce 330 mm of armour plate.

The gun is mounted on a tripod, the two wheels attaching to the base of the two legs, whilst the third leg extends to the rear and also acts as a towbar. A small, square shield which protects the firer's face from blast is

105 mm recoilless rifle M 65.

fitted in front of the optical sight. This weapon can travel in the normal manner towed by a truck or armoured personnel carrier, or can be broken down for carriage by mule.

Employment Yugoslavia

106 mm recoilless rifle M 40 A1

United States of America

Calibre	106 mm
Barrel length	3,400 mm
Muzzle brake	Nil
Trail type	—
Weight	130 kg
Ammunition	HEAT (7·71 kg)
	HEP-T
Armour penetration	450 mm at 1,000 m (HEAT)
Rate of fire	5 rds/min
Muzzle velocity	503 m/sec (HEAT)
	498 m/sec (HEP-T)
Maximum range	6,876 m
Maximum effective range	700–1,000 m
Elevation limits	−17° + 65°
Traverse on carriage	360°
Detachment	2

This popular weapon dates from 1953. It is a conventional smooth bore, breech loaded weapon, with an interrupted screw type breech. Barrel life is in excess of 2,500 rounds. Percussion firing is used. A ·50 calibre (12·7 mm) spotting rifle is mounted above the barrel. The basic weapon less mounting weighs only 130 kilogrammes.

Elevation varies with the mounting, but is very generous for the trailer mount. At $39\frac{1}{2}°$ elevation the HEP-T round ranges to 6,876 m, giving the weapon a useful secondary role if the necessary fire control arrangements can be made. Armour penetration is formidable. A modified weapon, the M 40AIC has an improved breech mechanism.

A number of mounts have been developed. These are:

M 27: A plain short-legged tripod with a 360° traversing ring.

M 79: Three flat, box-girder legs attached horizontally to a central pedestal with a castor wheel on the forward leg. A large elevating wheel is fitted to the top of the pedestal. This mount is used to fix the weapon into a $\frac{1}{4}$ ton Jeep, which is the most popular configuration.

M 92: A pillar type mount designed to fit the weapon to an open platform mechanical mule for the U.S. Marine Corps.

M 149-E5: A multiple mounting for six rifles fitted to a tracked carrier (ONTOS), which is no longer in service.

The M 40AI is built under licence in Brazil, Israel, Japan (known as Type 60) and Spain. The Austrian M 40AI's are known as Pak 66 and are fitted to a locally designed trailer—giving two barrel positions which give an overall height of 0·63 m or 0·93 m.

Employment

Australia	West Germany	Luxemburg	South Korea
Austria	Greece	Netherlands	Spain
Brazil	India	New Zealand	Switzerland
Cambodia	Iran	Norway	Taiwan
Canada	Israel	Pakistan	Thailand
Chile	Italy	Philippines	Turkey
Denmark	Japan	Portugal	USA
France	Jordan	Singapore	Vietnam

The 106 mm recoilless rifle M 40 A1 mounted on a jeep.

107 mm recoilless rifle B-11

Union of Soviet Socialist Republics

Calibre	107 mm
Barrel length	33 calibres
Muzzle brake	Nil
Trail type	Tripod
Weight	240 kg
Ammunition	HEAT (16·8 kg)
	HE (21·3 kg)
Armour penetration	380 mm at 450m (HEAT)
Rate of fire	5–6 rds/min
Muzzle velocity	410 m/sec
Maximum range	6,650 m
Maximum effective range	450 m
Elevation	$-10° + 45°$
Traverse on carriage	35°
Detachment	5

The B-11 being loaded.

The B-11 consists of the barrel, a simple tripod and a two wheel axle. For firing the wheels can be removed. It weighs only 240 kilogrammes.

It is a smooth bore equipment, firing spin stabilised HE and HEAT ammunition. The heavier HE round can be fired in an indirect fire role to 6,650 m, but in its primary anti-tank role the maximum effective range is 450 m. Armour penetration of 360 mm is at a 90° impact angle. The PBO 4 sights are mounted in a gimbal above the barrel, and are used for direct and indirect laying.

The breech hinges down for loading. The chamber is jacketed with a grill to protect the detachment from the heat generated. It is towed by the barrel.

Traverse is limited, but the weight of gun and size of detachment make manhandling easy.

It is no longer in service in the Soviet Army.

Employment:

Bulgaria	Egypt	Laos
Cambodia	East Germany	North Korea
China	Hungary	Vietnam

B-11s firing.

120 mm MOBAT

United Kingdom

Calibre	120 mm
Barrel length	4,000 mm
Muzzle brake	Nil
Trail type	Box
Weight	764 kg
Ammunition	HESH (12·84 kg)
Armour penetration	—
Rate of fire	—
Muzzle velocity	462 m/sec
Maximum range	800 m
Maximum effective range	800 m
Elevation limits	—
Traverse on carriage	360°
Detachment	3

The first British recoilless anti-tank gun was the L2 BAT (Battalion Anti-Tank gun). The L4 MOBAT is a development of that weapon, but has now been superseded by the L6 WOMBAT.

The rifled barrel is fitted with a large square breech ring. The vertical sliding breech block has an integral venturi and opens downwards. The top of the venturi carries a small loading tray. The complete round with its brass cartridge case weighs 27·2 kilogrammes, a formidable weight to handle and load: hence the provision of a loading tray. The charge is initiated electrically.

A modified 7·62 mm Bren gun is mounted to the left of the barrel as a spotting rifle.

It is a heavy weapon permanently mounted on a two wheel carriage incorporating a steadying box trail. It is towed by its muzzle with the trail clamped beneath the breech.

Employment	Bahrain	Malaysia
	Jordan	New Zealand
	Kenya	UK (reserve only)

Note the loading tray mounted on the venturi which lowers with the breech block.

---

120 mm WOMBAT

United Kingdom

Calibre	120 mm	*Rate of fire*	4 rds/min
Barrel length	4,000 mm	*Muzzle velocity*	462 m/sec
Muzzle brake	Nil	*Maximum range*	—
Trail type	Pole	*Maximum effective range*	1,000 m
Weight	294 kg	*Elevation limits*	—
Ammunition	HESH (12·84 kg)	*Traverse on carriage*	360°
Armour penetration	—	*Detachment*	3

The differences between this weapon and the earlier Mobat are the light small wheel carriage, the smaller and circular breech ring, and the spotting rifle mounted above the barrel.

The WOMBAT was developed from the MOBAT. The chief modifications are to the carriage, sighting and breech. It is only $\frac{1}{3}$ the weight of its predecessor and is more flexible in its mountings.

The new breech hinges to the right. The light weight design contributes considerably to the overall weight saving, but the venturi is retained. The loading tray is no longer available, but is, in any case, unnecessary because of the improved access to the breech. Electrical firing is retained.

The spin stabilised ammunition is the same as for MOBAT; details of its effectiveness have not been released. Range is improved by the better sights, but is effectively limited to 750 m against moving targets. An infra-red night sight is now fitted.

The spotting rifle has been moved to a position above the barrel and is the American 0·50 in calibre (12·7 mm) M 8C.

The basic weapon is mounted on a light and narrow two wheel carriage. The heavy box trail support of the MOBAT is replaced by a single short leg. The weapon is not designed for towing, the wheels being for man-handling and deployment. It is carried porté in a $\frac{3}{4}$ ton Land Rover from which the super-structure has been removed. It can also be fired from the Land Rover. For loading a simple ramp is lowered, and a manual winch is used. Six ready rounds are carried in the vehicle.

An alternative mount is on the roof of AFV 432 APC.

Employment Australia
 U.K.

WOMBAT mounted on the roof decking of an FV 432 APC.

57 mm SP assault gun ASU 57

Union of Soviet Socialist Republics

Calibre	57 mm
Barrel length	—
Muzzle brake	Double or multi-baffle
Ammunition	HVAP (1·8 kg)
	APHE (3·1 kg)
	HE (2·8 kg)
Armour penetration	140 mm at 500 m (HVAP)
	106 mm at 500 m (APHE)
Rate of fire	15–20 rds/min
Muzzle velocity	1,270 m/sec (HVAP)
	990 m/sec (APHE)
	706 m/sec (HE)
Maximum range	8,400
Maximum effective range	500 m
Elevation limits	5° + 15°
Traverse on mounting	12°
Detachment	3–5
Chassis—Type	Individual design
Engine	—
Power	100 bhp
Speed	45 km/hour
Endurance	320 km
Ammunition carried	—

Height × length × width	1·65 × 6·1 × 2·21 m
Weight	5,550 kg

The ASU 57 is the ZIS 2 gun mounted on a light chassis and designed for airborne or air transported operations. It can be air-dropped or lifted by a HOOK helicopter. It was introduced in 1957, but the gun was even then very elderly, and the weapon is now obsolescent. Range and armour penetration are poor by modern standards.

The gun keeps its vertical sliding breech block. It is fitted with the original double baffle muzzle brake or a multi-baffle type. It seems unlikely that the HE shell is used for this SP weapon: its limited ammunition store is more likely to be kept for primary role shell types.

The gun is mounted in an open top casement in which the detachment travels. Elevation and traverse are very limited. The vehicle is powered by a 100 bhp diesel engine. It is very lightly armoured. It has four road wheels with track return rollers between one and two, and two and three.

Employment	Czechoslovakia
	Poland
	USSR

ASU 57s on parade.

76 mm SP anti-tank gun SU 76

Union of Soviet Socialist Republics

Calibre	76·2 mm
Barrel length	42·6 calibres
Muzzle brake	Double baffle
Ammunition	HVAP (3·1 kg)
	APHE (6·5 kg)
	HEAT (4 kg)
	HE (6·2 kg)
Armour penetration	92 mm at 500 m (HVAP)
	69 mm at 500 m (APHE)
	120 mm (HEAT)
Rate of fire	20 rds/min
Muzzle velocity	965 m/sec (HVAP)
	680 m/sec (HE)
	655 m/sec (APHE)
	325 m/sec (HEAT)
Maximum range	13,300 m
Maximum effective range	500 m
Elevation limits	−5° + 34°
Traverse on mounting	30°
Detachment	4
Chassis—Type	T 70
Engine	2 × Otto petrol
Power	2 × 85 bhp
Speed	45 km/hour
Endurance	230 km
Ammunition carried	60

Height × length × width	2·3 × 5·1 × 2·73 m
Weight	11,200 kg

This is the ZIS 3 gun mounted on a lengthened T 70 tank chassis and introduced in 1943. Despite its age it is used extensively outside the Soviet Union. The anti-armour performance is poor by modern standards, but remains effective against APCs.

It is unlikely that the HE round is much used in view of the equipment's primary role as a front-line tank destroyer. However its availability adds flexibility to its deployment. 60 rounds are carried on board—a very good supply.

The PT 70 chassis is powered by two petrol engines each delivering 85 bhp. These give a reasonable 45 kilometres/hour road speed, but the vehicle has a somewhat limited range of action. It is fitted with very narrow tracks running on six road wheels, but the low weight and length of track keep ground pressure down to 0·6 kg/cm². The driver sits in the centre.

Employment	Albania
	China
	North Korea
	Vietnam

76 mm SPs—crews resting.

85 mm SP anti-tank gun ASU 85

Union of Soviet Socialist Republics

Calibre	85 mm
Barrel length	53 calibres
Muzzle brake	Double baffle
Ammunition	HVAP (5 kg)
	APHE (9·3 kg)
	HE (9·5 kg)
Armour penetration	130 mm at 1,000 m
	102 mm at 1,000 m
Rate of fire	4 rds/min
Muzzle velocity	1,030 m/sec (HVAP)
	792 m/sec (HE and APHE)
Maximum range	—
Maximum effective range	1,000 m
Elevation limits	−4° +15°
Traverse on mounting	12°
Detachment	4
Chassis—Type	PT 76
Engine	2 × 6 cylinder Otto
Power	480 bhp
Speed	45 km/hour
Endurance	260 km
Ammunition carried	40
Height × length × width	2·13 × 6·8 × 3·16 m
Weight	16,000 kg

The ASU 85 dates from 1962, but was first shown in 1964 in Poland. It consists of the D 44 gun mounted on the PT-76 light tank chassis.

The gun itself entered service during World War II, but is still widely used in a number of roles including anti-tank and anti-aircraft. The long barrel is fitted with a vertically sliding breech. Armour penetration is poor by modern standards, but more than adequate to defeat armoured personnel carriers or the side armour of tanks.

Like the ASU 57 the ASU 85 is designed primarily for airborne or air-transported operations, although it is too heavy to be air-dropped or carried by helicopter.

The rate of fire is considerably less than that of the towed version because the detachment is smaller and the enclosed fighting compartment constricts movement.

The PT 76 is a popular chassis for hybrid weapons. It is light but roomy and has inherent buoyancy. The two engines give a reasonable road speed, and hydro-jets propel the chassis in water at 10 km/hour.

Employment Poland
            USSR

ASU 85s of an airborne formation marching past.

90 mm SP anti-tank gun JPZ 4-5

Federal Republic of Germany

Calibre	90 mm
Barrel length	—
Muzzle brake	Double baffle
Ammunition	HEAT
	HVAP
	Practice
Armour penetration	330 mm at 1,000 m (HEAT)
Rate of fire	—
Muzzle velocity	1,181 m/sec
Maximum range	12 rds/min
Maximum effective range	2,000 m
Elevation limits	−8° + 15°
Traverse on mountings	30°
Detachment	4
Chassis—Type	Individual
Engine	Daimler Benz 837 Aa
Power	500 bhp
Speed	70 km/hour
Endurance	350 km
Ammunition carried	51
Height × length × width	2·08 × 6·23 (less gun) × 2·98 m
Weight	26,000 kg

Production of 800 of these anti-tank weapons finished in 1967. The 90 mm Bord K L/40·8 gun carries a double baffle muzzle brake and fume extractor. Few details of the gun's performance have been published.

An infra-red target search light, and associated sights, is available, and the driver can be provided with an infra-red viewer. Sighting and laying gear are conventional and range is determined by commander's estimate.

The gun is mounted in the front plates of a low casement which extends the length of the vehicle. The field of fire is good for this type of equipment. There is inboard stowage for 51 rounds.

The chassis runs on five road wheels with three track return rollers. It is powered by a Daimler Benz 837 Aa engine. This is a V8 four stroke diesel producing 500 bhp and, with a power to weight ratio of 19·5 bhp/ton, gives remarkably agile performance. The transmission is the Renk HSWL 123, three speed automatic, fitted with forward and reverse transfer box: performance is therefore the same in both directions.

The weapon is the standard equipment of Panzer-Grenadier Battalions.

Employment   Belgium
                    West Germany

90 mm SP anti-tank gun JPZ 4-5.

90 mm SP gun IKV 103

Sweden

Calibre	90 mm
Barrel length	28 calibres
Muzzle brake	Single baffle
Ammunition	HE (15·5 kg)
	HEAT
Armour penetration	—
Rate of fire	—
Muzzle velocity	607 m/sec
Maximum range	14,600 m
Maximum effective range	—
Elevation limits	—
Traverse on mounting	—
Detachment	4
Chassis—Type	—
Engine	—
Power	145 bhp
Speed	55 km/hour
Endurance	230 km
Ammunition carried	25

Height × length × width	1·84 × 5·85 × 2·23 m
Weight	8,700 kg

The IKV 103 is the 4140 gun mounted on an SP chassis. Despite its age, it is still used in the support of infantry brigades. The gun is mounted in a non-rotating casement, and seems to be a mixture of field gun and anti-tank weapon. The chassis runs on six road wheels with the engine and driving sprockets at the rear: this is much more in accord with a tank destroyer than a field gun.

Ammunition stowage is only 25 rounds. The diesel engine produces 145 bhp only, but the vehicle is not heavy and therefore has a good turn of speed.

The IKV 103 was introduced in 1956 as a development of the older (1952) 75 mm IKV 102.

Employment   Sweden

Few details are known about this gun, which is being introduced in Swedish infantry brigades and the highly mobile 'Norrland' brigades to replace the IKV 103. It appears to have excellent cross country performances and all round traverse.

100 mm SP anti-tank gun SU 100

Union of Soviet Socialist Republics

Calibre	100 mm
Barrel elngth	54 calibres
Muzzle brake	Nil
Ammunition	HVAP
	HEAT
	APHE (15·9 kg)
	HE (15·7 kg)
Armour penetration	380 mm at 1,000 m (HEAT)
	185 mm at 1,000 m (APHE)
Rate of fire	6–8 rds/min
Muzzle velocity	1,000 m/sec (APHE)
	900 m/sec (HE)
Maximum range	—
Maximum effective range	1,000 m
Elevation limits	−4° + 17°
Traverse on mounting	4°
Detachment	4
Chassis—Type	T 34/85
Engine	12 cylinder water cooled petrol
Power	520 bhp
Speed	53 km/hour
Endurance	300 km
Ammunition stowage	52
Height × length × width	2·45 × 9·45 × 3 m
Weight	32,000 kg

This equipment consists of the D 10 gun mounted on the T 34/85 tank chasis.

The SU (Samokhodnaya Ustanovka) series of Soviet SP anti-tank guns are designed to fit any given tank chassis with a heavier gun than is possible in a turret. The penalty is a severe restriction in traverse, so that the tactical handling of these weapons is complementary with its corresponding tank; the SU85 with T-34/76 and this gun with T-34/85.

Only minor modifications have been made to the gun. The detachment is reduced to four, which must have an adverse effect on the rate of fire (8–10 rounds/ minute) which is quoted for the towed gun. An HE round is available for the towed gun which has a re- cognised field role. While the SU 100 will accept this ammunition, it is unlikely that it will be carried in the on-board first line ammunition if the weapon is to be exploited fully as a tank destroyer.

The gun is mounted in a convex mantle to the right of the driver. A conical 'tower' is provided for the commander on the right of the casemate.

The T 34/85 chassis carries 75 mm of frontal armour. Its diesel engine develops 520 bhp and gives a good top speed of 53 kilometres/hour. Ground pressure is 0·8 kg/cm².

Employment:

Algeria	Egypt	Morocco
Bulgaria	East Germany	Romania
China	Iraq	Syria
Cuba	North Korea	North Yemen
Czechoslovakia	Mongolia	Yugoslavia

100 mm SP anti-tank gun SU-100.

105 mm SP anti-tank gun 'K'

Austria

Calibre	105 mm
Barrel length	44 calibres
Muzzle brake	—
Ammunition	HEAT
	APHE
	Smoke
Armour penetration	360 mm at 1,000 m (HEAT)
Rate of fire	12 rds/min
Muzzle velocity	800 m/sec (HEAT)
	700 m/sec (APHE)
Maximum range	2,000 m
Maximum effective range	—
Elevation limits	−6° + 13°
Traverse on mounting	360°
Detachment	3
Chassis—Type	Saurer 4K
Engine	Saurer 4FA
Power	300 bhp
Speed	63 km/hour
Endurance	—
Ammunition carried	17
Height × length × width	1·97 × 5·57 (less gun) × 2·5 m
Weight	17,000 kg

The gun is the French 105 mm D 1504, which is fitted to AMX-13 tank. It fires HEAT and APHE ammunition. Loading is semi-automatic from two six-round magazines in the turret. There is provision for a laser range finder. The X7·5 sight is fitted, together with a dual magnification sight for the commander.

The outstanding feature of this gun is the French FL 12 'oscillating' turret. It consists of a traversing ring which has a pent-roof side elevation, at the apex of which the elevating mass is mounted in trunnions. The result is that the gun is mounted almost level with the top of the turret. A rearward turret extension accommodates recoil and the two magazines. The recoil system is entirely under armour. The turret is power traversed, and will rotate through 360° in 12 seconds.

The chassis is from the Saurer 4K APC, modified to drive the rear sprocket. There are five road wheels and three return rollers. Hydraulic dampers are fitted to the front and rear wheels only. The engine is an in-line six cylinder diesel producing 300 bhp. A manual five-speed gearbox (2F 655) is used. The vehicle wades to one metre unprepared.

Employment   Austria

---

106 mm SP recoilless rifle Type 60

Japan

Calibre	106 mm
Barrel length	3,400 mm
Muzzle brake	Nil
Ammunition	(7·71 kg)
	HEP-T
Armour penetration	450 mm at 1,000 m (HEAT)
Rate of fire	6 rds/min
Muzzle velocity	503 m/sec (HEAT)
	498 m/sec (HEP-T)
Maximum range	6,876 m
Maximum effective range	700–1,000 m
Elevation limits	−5° + 10° (see text)
Traverse on mounting	20° (see text)
Detachment	3
Chassis—Type	Individual
Engine	Komatsu
Power	120 bhp
Speed	48 km/hour
Endurance	130 km
Ammunition carried	—
Height × length × width	1·38 × 4·3 × 2·23 m
Weight	8,020 kg

This weapon entered service in 1960 as the first Japanese post-war AFV. It consists of two recoilless anti-tank rifles mounted on a specially designed tracked chassis. The rifles are the American M 40 A1 weapon made under licence in Japan. The vehicle is similar in concept to the obsolete ONTOS, a US Marine Corps weapon which mounted six rifles.

The smooth bore, breech loaded weapon has an interrupted screw type breech and uses percussion firing. Armour penetration is formidable.

A single ·50 calibre (12·7 mm) spotting machine gun is used to augment the optical sights. No night fighting aids are fitted. A two position mounting gives either an exceptionally low silhouette or, with the guns raised, an increased arc of fire: traverse increases to a total of 60°, and elevation limits are −15° and +25°.

The mount does not have to accept the shock of recoil associated with conventional guns, and a light chassis can be employed. The small six cylinder air cooled diesel engine produces a good turn of speed, while ground pressure is kept down to 0·63 kg/cm². The vehicle wades to 0·8 m.

Employment   Japan

152 mm assault gun JSU 152

Union of Soviet Socialist Republics

Calibre	152 mm
Barrel length	32 calibres
Muzzle brake	Multi-baffle
Ammunition	APHE
	HE
Armour penetration	—
Rate of fire	—
Muzzle velocity	655 m/sec (APHE)
Maximum range	—
Maximum effective range	1,000 m
Elevation limits	−3° + 20°
Traverse on mounting	20°
Detachment	5
Chassis—Type	JS 2
Engine	Diesel
Power	520 bhp
Speed	37 km/hour
Endurance	135 km
Ammunition carried	20
Height × length × width	2·45 × — × 3·04 m
Weight	52,500 kg

During World War II the Russians produced a 152 mm SP assault gun on the KV tank chassis: this was the SU 152, and was superseded after the war by the JSU 152.

This gun appears to be a derivative of the M 1937 (ML 20) howitzer mounted on the JS 2 chassis. It is employed as a heavy anti-tank weapon, assault gun, and SP howitzer, and is thus a very versatile weapon.

The gun projects from a mantelet which is shaped to cover the recoil mechanism mounted below the barrel. There is no turret, the super-structure being built up into a casemate. Traverse is none-the-less generous. Only 20 rounds of ammunition are carried.

The chassis runs on six road wheels. Its endurance is very limited, but auxiliary fuel tanks can be mounted either side of the rear mounted engine's decking.

It is the heaviest and largest SP gun to be produced in Russia. Its smaller relative the JSU 122 is no longer in service, but this 152 mm weapon is still used in a few countries.

Employment	Algeria
	Czechoslovakia
	Egypt
	Iraq

Assault gun JSU 152.

Sagger anti-tank guided weapon

Union of Soviet Socialist Republics

Missile length	880 m
Missile diameter	120 m
Missile weight (before launch)	11·3 kg
Missile wing span	—
Guidance system	Manual command to line of sight
Propulsion	Two stage solid propellant
Velocity	150 m/sec
Range—Maximum	3,300 m
Minimum	550 m
Time of flight to maximum range	22 secs
Warhead	HEAT

Sagger has now replaced Snapper in Soviet equipped Armies. It can be mounted on BMP or BRDM, or it can be manpacked and fired from the ground. In the BMP APC version the missile rail is mounted above the 73 mm smooth bore gun and can be fired from within the vehicle. On the BRDM reconnaissance vehicle six Sagger missiles are mounted on a row of launcher rails which can be elevated to the firing position from inside the vehicle. For manpacked use it has a team of three who can set out up to four missiles connected to a single control sight, with the lid of the carrying case for each missile acting as a launching stand. In the Middle East War of 1973 Sagger achieved fame in the world press as the 'suitcase missile'. The HEAT warhead has a penetration of better than 400 mm of armour plate.

Sagger on BRDM, showing launcher position.

Employment	Algeria	Rumania
	Bulgaria	Syria
	Czechoslovakia	USSR
	Egypt	Vietnam
	East Germany	Yugoslavia
	Hungary	
	Israel	
	Poland	

Sagger mounted on BMP tracked reconnaissance vehicle.

Swatter anti-tank guided weapon

Union of Soviet Socialist Republics

Missile length	1·13 m
Missile diameter	130 mm
Missile weight (before launch)	26·5 kg
Missile wing span	650 mm
Guidance system	Manual command to line of sight
Propulsion	Two stage solid propellant
Velocity	160 m/sec
Range—Maximum	3,500 m
Minimum	600 m
Time of flight to maximum range	20 sec
Warhead	HEAT

Swatter is normally mounted in the BRDM reconnaissance vehicle in a row of four launchers, which can be elevated from its normal travelling position inside the vehicle to the firing position. It is a manual system, but it is the only anti-tank guided weapon to use a radio command link between the tracker sight and the missile. Although this avoids the problem of wire breaks which still occasionally occur in the wire guided system, it does make Swatter vulnerable to electronic counter measures. The HEAT warhead has a delayed action fuze, and it is said to achieve about 500 mm penetration of armour plate.

Employment		
	Czechoslovakia	Poland
	Egypt	Rumania
	East Germany	Syria
	Hungary	USSR

Swatter, mounted on BRDM 1 reconnaissance vehicle.

SS 11 anti-tank guided weapon

France

Missile length	1·21 m
Missile diameter	164 mm
Missile weight (before launch)	29·9 kg
Missile wing span	500 mm
Guidance	Manual command to line of sight
Propulsion	Two stage solid propellant
Velocity	150 m/sec
Range—Maximum	3,000 m
Minimum	500 m
Time of flight to maximum range	20 sec
Warhead	HEAT

SS 11 has twice the range of the earlier SS 10. It is normally fired from a vehicle, but also from a ground launcher. It is manually controlled by a thumbstick, which transmits guidance commands through a wire link to the missile. The missile is automatically gathered into the field of view of the optical sight and is then flown on to the target by the operator. Its HEAT warhead can penetrate 600 mm of armour. The SS 11 is one of the best of the first generation anti-tank guided weapons and it is still widely used in Western Armies, as well as in the Middle East and India. It is gradually being replaced by SS 12, HOT or TOW.

Employment	Argentina	Israel
	Belgium	Italy
	Canada	Kuwait
	Finland	Lebanon
	France	Saudi Arabia
	India	Turkey
	Iran	West Germany

SS 11 on HS 30 at moment of launch.

SS 12 anti-tank guided weapon

France

Missile length	1·87 m
Missile diameter	180 mm
Missile weight (before launch)	75 kg
Missile wing span	650 mm
Guidance system	Semi-automatic command to line of sight
Propulsion	Two stage solid propellant
Velocity	190 m/sec
Range—Maximum	6,000 m
Minimum	400 m
Time of flight to maximum range	32 sec
Warhead	HEAT and anti-personnel

The SS 12 has twice the range of SS 11 and much greater lethality. Like SS 11 it can be fired from a ground launcher or from a vehicle. Its semi-automatic command to line of sight guidance system (*Télécommande Automatique*) is the same as that in Harpon and it is much easier to operate than the earlier manual systems. All the layer has to do is to keep the cross wires of the sight on the centre of the target and the missile will then receive commands automatically through its link to correct its flight on to the target. The guidance equipment follows the layers sight and also tracks the missile using an infra-red device which follows the missile propellant efflux combining this information automatically and sending corrections to bring the missile on to the line of sight. SS 12 is being replaced by HOT.

Employment   France

SS 12 ATGW on trailer.

HOT anti-tank guided weapon

France and the Federal Republic of Germany

Missile length	1·275 m
Missile diameter	136 mm
Missile weight (before launch)	29 kg
Missile wing span	310 mm
Guidance system	Semi-automatic command to line of sight
Propulsion	Two stage solid propellant
Velocity	260 m/sec
Range—Maximum	4,000 m
Minimum	75 m
Time of flight to maximum range	16 sec
Warhead	HEAT

The HOT system (*Haut Subsonique—Optiquement Tele-guide*) is a collaborative venture by France and West Germany. Its guidance system is similar to that of SS 12 and Harpon, but it is launched from a tube on to the line of sight to the target in the same way as a recoilless gun. This enables it to achieve a very short minimum range. It is normally mounted on the AMX 13 or the Jagdpanzer light tank.

Although this system of guidance achieves a fast engagement and a short minimum range, it is not compatible with any lateral separation between the operator and the launcher as in Swingfire, Sagger and Swatter.

Employment   Development, France and West Germany

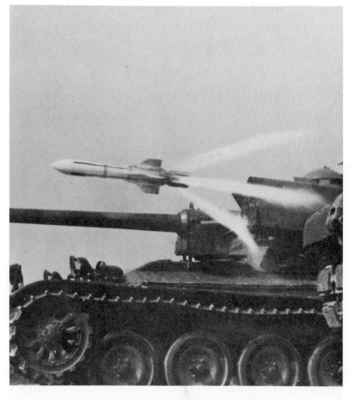

The HOT anti-tank missile after launch from AMX 13 tank.

HOT launched from RJP armoured personnel carrier.

TOW anti-tank guided weapon M 151E2

United States

Missile length	1·285 m
Missile diameter	221 mm
Missile weight (before launch)	24 kg
Missile wing span	—
Guidance system	Semi-automatic command to line of sight
Propulsion	Two stage solid propellant
Velocity	200 m/sec
Range—Maximum	3,000 m
Minimum	65 m
Time of flight to maximum range	15 sec
Warhead	HEAT

The TOW (Tube-launched, Optically-tracked, Wire-guided) system can be mounted on an APC, a ¼ ton jeep or a 'mule' weapon carrier or it can be fired from a tripod on the ground.

The 24 kg missile is fired from a 2·2 m long launching tube which provides initial guidance down the line of sight to the target in the same way as HOT. The semi-automatic guidance system follows the same principles as the HOT, SS 12 and Harpon systems. It is simple to operate since all the operator has to do is to keep the cross wires of the tracker sight on the target. Corrections are transmitted automatically to the missile to bring it on to the line of sight. Again as in HOT fast engagements and a low minimum range are possible, but it has no facility for separation between the operator's sight and the launcher.

Employment	Canada	Luxembourg
	Denmark	Netherlands
	Greece	Norway
	Iran	Oman
	Israel	Turkey
	Italy	USA
	Jordan	West Germany
	Lebanon	

TOW mounted on a 'mule'.

Swingfire

United Kingdom

Missile length	1·06 m
Missile diameter	170 mm
Missile weight (before launch)	26·7 kg
Missile wing span	373 mm
Guidance system	Manual command to line of sight
Propulsion	Single stage solid propellant
Velocity	180 m/secs
Range—Maximum	4,000 m
Minimum	150 m (direct mode), 300 m (separated mode)
Time of flight to maximum range	26 sec
Warhead	Shaped charge

Swingfire is mounted on three vehicles in the British Army, the FV 438, Striker and the FV 712 scout car. In the FV 438 it has two launchers which can be replenished from inside the vehicle, whereas on the FV 712 (four launchers) and Striker (five launchers) the missiles have to be replenished from outside.

Swingfire has a most useful facility in that it can be fired either from the periscopic sight on the vehicle or from a separated sight located up to 100 m horizontally and 23 m vertically away from the launcher. This gives great flexibility in siting the launcher in positions where the operator can have the best field of view, whilst keeping the launcher vehicle concealed from direct counter fire from enemy weapons. When the separated sight is used the missile is automatically programmed to fly into the operator's field of view. He then guides it on to the target by manual command signals with his sight thumbstick transmitted by the wire link to the missile.

Swingfire has a longer minimum range and target engagement time than HOT and TOW, but its separation facility gives its operators better flexibility on the battle field. Also its manual command to line of sight guidance system cannot be 'spoofed' by infra-red decoys offset from the target, which are possible counter measures to the semi-automatic systems.

Employment	Belgium
	Egypt
	UK

Swingfire launched from FV 438.

Swingfire being fired from Striker—its designed mounting adapted
from CVRT.

IX. Anti-aircraft Guns and Surface-to-air Missiles

Land tactics have been dominated for the past thirty years by strike aircraft and, other things being equal, success has invariably gone to the side possessing the advantage in the air. Aircraft have always, for obvious reasons, presented a difficult target, but modern aircraft with their high speeds, capability for low-level flight and robustness have led to research and development of ever more sophisticated weapon systems.

To simplify a complex subject, there were two approaches to the problem. One was an accurate solution of the range-speed equation so as to give the gun the correct lead.

The second was, crudely, to fill the sky with projectiles in the hope that one might register a hit and that at least the sight of tracer and bursts might deter all but the most fanatical pilots from following the correct course for bomb-release. The last was uneconomical both in men and ammunition, while the former became ever more difficult as aircraft speeds went up to the neighbourhood of Mach 1.

Larger guns requiring range/height data and prediction were handicapped by imperfections in locating and target acquisition equipment. Prediction was by mechanically driven analogue computers.

Improvements in radar and the development of the electronic digital computer have completely changed this scene, as have the engineering methods which can now produce automated guns without too great a weight penalty.

A number of countries gave up cannon altogether and concentrated on an exclusively guided missile solution. Others retained only what are virtually multiple machine guns of up to 20 mm for purely low level local protection, but the Russians continue to use guns of all types to supplement their excellent inventory of surface to air missiles (SAMs).

SAMs have their limitations. Their control radars are vulnerable to ECM and also to direct action by land or air, as are the missiles themselves when on the ground. Missile supply in the field has its difficulties and it is easy, as is believed to have happened in 1973, to shoot away the entire holding when under heavy air attack. Guns are much easier to resupply and also more versatile tactically. Given well-trained and spirited detachments, anti-aircraft (AA) guns can still be disturbingly effective as the Viet Cong have shown. Whatever air force men may say, in real action pilots have the very greatest respect even for small weapons which theoretically should not be a threat.

There is one other use for the smaller general purpose automatic weapons. The latest weapon carrier and general tactical vehicle on the battlefield is the helicopter, and for this the lighter AA artillery, especially SPs deployed well forward, are a cost-effective antidote.

There are broadly three methods of deploying air defences. The first is point defence. The vital point to be defended could be a bridge, defile or an HQ; the weapons are deployed so as to intercept the aircraft before the point of bomb (or weapon) release is reached. This becomes increasingly difficult if stand-off missiles are available to the attacker.

The second method is area or 'carpet' defence: this is extremely expensive in the number of weapons used for even small areas of importance.

The third is to distribute light AA weapons organically through combat units so as to provide a spread of immediately available low level defence. Tracked SP armoured AA guns with on-carriage radar and fire-control equipment are admirably suited to accompany tank units which themselves are likely to be priority targets for air attack. Hence the ZSU-23-4, ZSU 57-2, M 42, AMX DCA-30 and smaller hand-held missiles e.g. SA 7, SA 9, Redeye and Blowpipe.

Tactical control presents problems. It is not sufficient to hand out guns and leave the rest to the gunners. In open desert or flat tree-less country (where exercises so often are staged), guns can engage over large fields of fire from almost any position. In most terrain the line of sight of guns, sentries and radars are interrupted by the topography, trees, buildings and also the weather. To find good gun positions the country side will always have to be carefully reconnoitred in advance and deployment controlled so that some weapons are in action and ready to shoot while others are moving to new positions, so ensuring continuous air defence cover.

There is also the question of fire control. Against low level high speed attacks early warning to alert the detachments is essential, and in the stress of battle positive controls must be imposed to ensure the safety of friendly aircraft. In World War II this was also a real problem, but potential more than real, as light air defence was relatively speaking inefficient and was alarming rather than dangerous. Today the hit probability is infinitely higher. The equipments mentioned in this chapter must therefore be seen as only part of a much bigger air defence complex of which guns, SAMs and fighter aircraft are a part, all linked by high speed, sophisticated communications.

The AA gun is a highly specialized weapon which requires elevation to the vertical, all round traverse, a high rate of fire, the ability to fire while the barrel is traversing/elevating and specialised sights. It need not be of a very large calibre, and indeed many are of the machine gun type. In this chapter we are concerned with the heavier equipments which are normally manned by trained artillery personnel.

The problem facing the AA gunner is the small size and great speed of his target. Absolute range is less important than accuracy. The siting of the weapon will be to protect a specific area and since the behaviour of attacking aircraft can be predicted, the individual weapon will be tasked and deployed so as to avoid the random engagement of distant targets.

At short ranges, the gun's zone can be kept within acceptable limits if it is on a suitably stable platform. The choice is invariably a cruciform of legs or girders, an arrangement which requires a four wheel trailer carriage for travelling. The legs can be folded, retracted or hinged and the platform they provide is levelled exactly by jacks. The disadvantages of such equipments are their vulnerability and the time taken to deploy and re-deploy. The alternative for use in the combat zone is the armoured SP gun or multiple gun. However, the SP has its disadvantages; siting must be to give optimum fields of fire, which makes concealment difficult. The smaller, irregularly-shaped, towed gun is easier to deploy and hide. Nor is the need for speedy deployment always paramount. Given that most of the weapons under discussion are not normally associated with the front line, and that they cannot be ubiquitous, the choice of area to defend will probably be of slow moving or static; e.g., 'choke-points' on supply routes, HQ, defiles, dumps and logistic service areas, airfields, on which the nature of aircraft attack plans are predictable.

The second factor affecting accuracy is the sight. The movement of the target and the time of flight of the projectile make it necessary to aim off. The amount of aim-off or "lead" varies with the apparent speed of the aircraft movement. An aircraft flying straight at the gun will have no apparent movement relative to the line of sight, and as the angle of approach changes the apparent crossing speed of the target increases until the maximum is reached at a right angle to the line of sight. The simplest sight consists of a conventional fore-sight and a back-sight made up of concentric rings. Its effectiveness depends almost entirely on the skill of the operator—the third factor of accuracy. Tracer ammunition is used to give a constant indication of the operator's performance. Whatever sighting system is used, it relies on a level platform—hence the universal provision of levelling jacks on the trail legs. The whole area of aiming and operating is open to technological assistance. The earliest aid was a mechanical predictor, used mainly with heavy guns of long range. It fed data to the gun via moving pointers, to which the operator matched the lay of the gun—a form of 'indirect' sighting. Today, the electronics industry has evolved radar and computer control systems of great accuracy, and many of these take over the laying of the gun through servo motors. Eldorado (France), Skyguard (Switzerland) and Fire-Can (USSR) are among the equipments available.

A high rate of fire is essential to increase the probability of a hit. Automatic loading from a hopper or magazine is universal for all but the biggest calibre guns. Sliding breech mechanisms, which are usually associated with automatic fire, are used in all the guns described in this section. The recoil is used to activate the fully automatic guns. In many instances, the description of individual guns gives a slower rate of fire than the cyclic rate which is quoted in the tabulated data. The difference is explained by the effort of manually replenishing the hopper or magazine, but this factor is not significant since the average engagement is probably less than a minute.

The projectile need not be large, as the sophisticated equipment on which modern aircraft depend is vulnerable to the slightest damage. It is this fact which leads to the effectiveness of smaller automatic guns with a high rate of fire. A short time of flight and flat trajectory reduce the problems of laying, so a high muzzle velocity is a universal feature. Barrels are long and the propellant charges relatively big but limited in diameter and length by the loading system.

Popular opinion is that the guided missile provides a better air defence weapon than the gun. Certainly the guidance increases its inherent efficiency, but it is not a perfect answer. It is subject to electronic counter measures, minimum ranges and technical failure, and it is enormously expensive; properly handled guns can also be effective. The efficiency of North Vietnamese 'conventional' AA fire provided a valuable lesson. The answer in the immediate future is a balanced mixture of guns and missiles and, to look at the subject from a wider perspective, a whole spectrum of fire-power ranging from infantry small arms fire, missiles and small automatic cannon handled by non-specialists to guns and major missiles operated by specialist artillery personnel; to which must be added, of course, air-to-air fire-power, all controlled or supported centrally, as far as possible and connected by an elaborate system of surveillance and telecommunications.

Twin 20 mm M3/VDA

France

Calibre	20 mm
Barrel length	2,600 mm
Shell weight	125 g
Cyclic rate of fire	1,050 rds/min
Muzzle velocity	300 m/sec
Maximum horizontal range	2,000 m
Maximum effective slant range	1,500 m
Ceiling	800 m
Detachment	3
Chassis—Type	Panhard M 3/VTT
Engine	1997 cc Panhard 4 HD
Power	90 bhp at 4,700 rev/min
Maximum speed	100 km/hr
Endurance	1,000 km
Ammunition carried	600
Height × length × width	2·1 × 3·79 × 2·0 m
Weight	6,300 kg

The twin 20 mm HSS 820 guns are mounted on a one-man turret on a Panhard M 3 scoutcar. It is a highly mobile weapon system with speeds of up to 100 kph possible over a range of 1,000 km. The EMD X band pulse doppler radar has an acquisition range of 8 km. When a target has been acquired, the bearing and range are automatically fed to the sight by the P 56 Galileo computer. All the gunner has to do is to keep the sight on the target and the computer automatically lays off the correct lead and range, and indicates the moment to open fire. It is thus particularly suitable for short range air defence in support of fast moving operations, although the number of ready to use shells it can carry (600 in two 300 round belts) could be a serious limitation.

Employment France

Twin 20 mm M 3/VDA on Panhard scout car.

Twin 20 mm RH 202 Mk 20

West Germany

Calibre	20 mm
Barrel length	1·84 m
Weight	2,100 kg
Shell weight	HE-IT } linked 250 gm
	APT
Cyclic rate of fire	2,000 rds/min
Muzzle velocity	1,050 m/sec
Maximum horizontal range	3,000 m
Maximum slant range	2,000 m
Ceiling	900 m
Detachment	3

The Rheinmetall 202 Mk 20 is a twin 20 mm gun system mounted on a lightweight two wheeled trailer. The sighting system is a simple optical device, incorporating rigid flight direction lines and a variable prediction line in elevation. It is thus a daylight only weapon. The gunner has to estimate the target speed and range to his intended point of engagement and then to set it on the lead computer. As soon as tracking begins, information is automatically fed into a simple computer, which in turn adjusts the lead marks in the monocular sight. Power for the hydrostatic drives is provided by a petrol driven 8 hp Wankel generator mounted behind the layer's seat. 540 rounds in two belts of 270 are carried on the gun. The gun is towed by a $1\frac{3}{4}$ ton truck and it is operated by three men—a gunner and two ammunition handlers.

Employment   West Germany
Norway

The RH 202 Mk 20 in action.

20 mm Vulcan (M 163)

United States of America

Calibre	20 mm
Barrel length	—
Shell weight	M 50 HE IT-SD
	HE 1
	TP-T
	TP
Cyclic rate of fire	3,000 rds/min
Muzzle velocity	1,088 m/sec
Maximum horizontal range	3,000 m
Maximum effective slant range	2,000 m
Ceiling	900 m
Detachment	4
Chassis—Type	M 113 A 1
Engine	GMC Model 6 V 53 diesel
Power	215 hp
Maximum speed	68 km/hour
Endurance	480 km
Ammunition carried	1,100
Height × length × width	2·74 × 4·87 × 2·81 m
Weight	11,208 kg

This six barrelled 20 mm gatling gun is mounted on the M 113A1 APC chassis. Its ammunition feed system does not have links, which reduces the chance of stoppages in its very high rate of fire guns. The X band pulse-doppler radar acquires targets out to 5,000 m, but it only indicates range and bearing, target tracking being visual through a lead-computing sight. Although the six barrels have an excellent rate of fire the number of

The Vulcan gun on M 113 chassis.

ready to use rounds carried is a severe limitation and it means that each gun must be accompanied by its own ammunition limber vehicle. In the US Army local warning is passed to Vulcan by the Forward Area Alerting Radar (FAAR) system.

The M 167 is a much lighter wheeled trailer version (1,360 kg) of Vulcan which can be towed by a 1¼ ton truck. Both versions have a detachment of four men—commander, layer, ammunition number and driver.

Employment   Israel
                  USA

The Vulcan gun M 167, trailer mounted.

23 mm SP anti-aircraft gun ZSU-23-4

Union of Soviet Socialist Republics

Calibre	23 mm
Barrel length	—
Shell weight	HE 183 g
	AP 190 g
Cyclic rate of fire	1,000 rev/min/gun
Muzzle velocity	930 m/sec
Maximum horizontal	
range	3,000 m
Maximum effective slant	
range	2,000 m
Ceiling	1,000 m
Detachment	4
Chassis—Type	PT 76/ASU-85
Engine	V-6, 6 cylinder diesel
Power	240 hp at 1,800 rev/min
Maximum	
speed	44 km/hour
Endurance	260 km
Ammunition carried	2,000 plus 3,000 in limber
	vehicle
Height × length × width	2·25 × 6·10 × 2·80 m
Weight	1,400 kg

Twin 23 mm on 626 trailer.

This gun was first introduced into the Soviet Army in 1965 using the PT 76/ASU-85 chassis. It has four 23 mm guns each able to fire at 1,000 rounds per minute. The upper mounting has 360° traverse and allows the guns to elevate to 85°. Fire control is either by optical sights, which are housed on the turret behind the guns, or by the 'Gundish' radar which has an acquisition range of 8,000 m. This was the most effective gun in the October 1973 war, accounting for a high percentage of Israeli aircraft losses. With the SA-9 missile system it provides a comprehensive very low/low level air defence of forward areas. Many Soviet-equipped countries have a twin 23 mm version of the same gun mounted on a trailer.

Employment	Bulgaria	Finland	Poland
	Czechoslovakia	Hungary	Syria
	Egypt	India	USSR
	East Germany	Iran	

23 mm AA gun ZSU-23-4.

30 mm SP anti-aircraft gun 'Falcon'

United Kingdom

Calibre	30 mm
Barrel length	—
Shell weight	0·36 kg
Cyclic rate of fire	650 rds/barrel/min
Muzzle velocity	1,080 m/sec
Maximum horizontal range	10,000 m
Maximum effective slant range	3,000 m
Ceiling	1,000 m
Detachment	3
Chassis—Type	Abbot SP gun
Engine	Rolls Royce K60
Power	211 bhp
Speed	48 km/hour
Endurance	370 km
Ammunition stowage	620 rds
Height × length × width	2·51 × 5·7 × 2·6 m
Weight	15,850 kg

The Falcon has been developed by Vickers Ltd. and consists of two HO 831-SLM 30 mm cannon mounted in a turret on the Abbot chassis. Both components have been described elsewhere but can be summarised as follows.

The chassis is that of the Abbot SP gun and is based on the FV 430 series Armoured Personnel Carrier. It runs on five road wheels with engine and driver at the front. The Rolls Royce engine is a six cylinder horizontally opposed two-stroke turbo-charged diesel. The transmission is by Alison automatic gear box and Cletrac steering unit. The chassis has an excellent and proven cross-country performance.

The guns are made by Oerlikon-Buhrle in Switzerland. Their basic design allows a number of ammunition feed options, and in this application the open link belt is used feeding from the inboard side of each gun. The barrels are bayonet fitted to the body for quick changing.

The mounting is in a new purpose-built turret which is armour-plated against small arms fire and shell splinters. The commander's and gunner's seats are adjustable; access to them is through the roof. The fighting compartment is sealed from the guns to avoid fumes fouling the atmosphere, and to reduce noise when firing. The guns are cocked and fired (single shot or automatic) electrically.

The boxed ammunition (HE, AP or practice) is stored in the chassis in a compartment sealed from the turret. The ammunition belts feed to the turret by chutes. Spent cartridges and belt links are ejected sideways through the elevation trunnion bearings.

Elevation and traverse are electrically powered and controlled by a joystick. The commander has his own control which overrides the gunner's. The guns are stabilised for firing on the move by a rate gyro system. This system, made by GEC-AEI (Electronics) Ltd., is based on that used in the Chieftain tank.

The fire control system is optical, supported by a small predictor computer. The gun is invulnerable to electronic counter measures, cheap to build and easy to maintain because it has no radar. The gunner's periscopic sight has a 50° field of view with a circular aiming mark displayed in the viewer. The aiming display is computer controlled to provide automatic compensation for target movement. The range is set manually, and is used by the computer to determine the optimum lead by reference to the rate of tracking.

A ×6 magnification periscopic sight is also provided for use against ground targets.

Employment   Development only in UK.

Falcon gun on Abbot chassis.

Twin 30 mm anti-aircraft gun M 53

Czechoslovakia

Calibre	30 mm
Barrel length	70 calibres
Weight	2,100 kg
Shell weight	0·45 kg
Cyclic rate of fire	500 rds/min/barrel
Muzzle velocity	1,000 m/sec
Maximum horizontal range	10,000 m
Maximum effective slant range	3,000 m
Ceiling	1,000 m
Detachment	4

This twin barrelled gun was first seen in 1958, and remains in service with the Czech divisional anti-aircraft regiments. The very long barrels with their multi-baffle muzzle brakes are fitted in quick-change mountings. Ammunition in 10 round clips, is loaded into a horizontal feed on the left of the gun. This system limits the rate of fire to 100 rounds/minute/barrel, although the cyclic rate for fire is much higher.

There are two types of ammunition: HE and AP. Both weigh 0·45 kilogrammes, and give the same performance. The AP round will penetrate 60 mm of armour at 500 m. The gun has a modest range, and relies on optical laying using a cart wheel sight. Traverse and elevation are hydraulically powered.

The guns are mounted on a light, four-wheel trailer without any protective armour. The weapon fires on its wheels with screw-type firing jacks beneath each axle. An SP version, the M 53/59 is described separately.

Employment	Cuba	Iraq
	Czechoslovakia	Uganda
	India	

Twin 30 mm M 53.

30 mm Type 661 anti-aircraft cannon

Switzerland

Calibre	30 mm
Barrel length	—
Weight	1,550 kg
Shell weight	0·36 kg
Cyclic rate of fire	600–650 rds/min
Muzzle velocity	1,080 m/sec
Maximum horizontal range	—
Maximum effective slant range	3,000 m
Ceiling	1,000 m
Detachment	1

30 mm HO 661 in action.

The Type 661 consists of the HO 831 SLM automatic cannon on a simple trailer mounting, and is highly mobile. It has a small, circular platform, with four outrigger stabilizers which fold for travelling. The wheels are removed for firing.

The gun is operated and fired by one man using a joystick to operate hydraulic control in elevation and azimuth, and a Type P 36 Galileo mechanical fire control computer sight. The layer sits behind the gun astride the rear mounting, and has some body protection from a contoured shield. Hydraulic power is supplied from a pump driven by a small Wankel engine.

For this mounting, the magazine loading system, feeding from the left is used.

Employment Switzerland

30 mm automatic cannon HO 831-SLM

Switzerland

Calibre	30 mm
Barrel length	—
Weight	N/A
Shell weight	0·36 kg
Cyclic rate of fire	600–650 rds/min
Muzzle velocity	1,080 m/sec
Maximum horizontal range	—
Maximum effective slant range	3,000 m
Ceiling	1,000 m
Detachment	3

This gun was developed by Hispano-Suiza and was known as the HSS 831: Oerlikon-Buhrle have now taken over the Hispano-Suiza Company and the prefix HSS has been changed to HO. The HO 831-SLM gun was developed from the 831-A, the most important change being the reductions of shell weight from 0·42 kilogrammes to 0·36 kilogrammes. The barrel is attached by a bayonet-joint to the breech assembly for ease of maintenance and rapid changing in action. It is a versatile gun, and the basis of a number of weapon systems built outside Switzerland for land and shipborne use.

The breech is designed to be fed from left or right, and two feed systems are available: an open link belt, or an offset magazine of eight five-round clips. A British variant, developed for naval use has magazines of 140 rounds with feed chutes hold a further 20 rounds. These loading and feeding options give great freedom to the designer of the mounting, hence the popularity of this gun in a number of weapon systems.

Ammunition available includes HE and practice shells with or without tracer and an AP incendiary shell.

Performance varies with the mounting sights and fire control equipment used.

Employment Switzerland

Twin 30 mm SP anti-aircraft gun M 53/59

Czechoslovakia

Calibre	30 mm
Barrel length	70 calibres
Shell weight	0·45 kg
Cyclic rate of fire	500 rds/min/barrel
Muzzle velocity	1,000 m/sec
Maximum horizontal range	10,000 m
Maximum effective slant range	3,000 m
Ceiling	1,000 m
Detachment	5
Chassis—Type	PRAGA V3S 6 × 6
Engine	—
Power	—
Maximum speed	—
Endurance	—
Ammunition carried	—
Height × length × width	—

Weight   9,500 kg

This is the SP version of the M 53 with twin guns in a partially enclosed mounting installed on the armoured version of the PRAGA V3S 6 × 6. The multi-baffle muzzle brake and hydraulic control system are identical with the M 53 but the loading system is altered to a magazine using a vertical feed. The rectangular curved magazine holds 50 rounds and aids the recognition of this version. Two spare magazines are carried on the gun tray of the vehicle.

This weapon is in service with divisional anti-aircraft regiments and the anti-aircraft companies of the armoured regiments of the Czech Army.

Employment   Cuba
Czechoslovakia
Yugoslavia

The SP M 53/59 on parade.

30 mm twin SP AMX-DCA 30

France

Calibre	30 mm
Barrel length	—
Shell weight	0·36 kg
Cyclic rate of fire	600 rds/min
Muzzle velocity	1,080 m/sec
Maximum horizontal	
range	10,000 m
Maximum effective	
slant range	3,000 m
Ceiling	1,000 m
Detachment	4
Chassis—Type	AMX 30
Engine	
Hispano Suiza HS110	
Power	720 bhp
Maximum	
speed	65 km/hour
Endurance	
Ammunition carried	—
Height × length × width	3 × 6·8 × 3·1 m
Weight	3,600 kg

This is the HO-831 gun, twin mounted in the SAMM S40 1A turret on an AMX 30 tank chassis. The turret and guns were introduced in 1964 mounted on the lighter AMX 13 tank chassis. The new chassis, which is now coming into service, carries more ammunition, and has an electric power supply which is independent of the main engine. With this mounting and the introduction of an integral fire control radar (the Oeil Noir) the weapon becomes self-contained. In order to be most effective it must have early warning from an area radar system, but the guns can then lock to the on-board radar data, using computer control for the calculation of essential lead angles. The optical sights are for emergency use only.

The AMX 30 is a large vehicle: the SAMM turret adds 0·71 m to its height even when the radar dish is folded flat for travelling. Despite its weight (about 36,000 kilogrammes) the flat 12 cylinder multi-fuel super-charged engine gives 20 bhp/ton, and gives a good performance.

Employment France

The SP AMX-DCA 30 with guns elevated and radar dish (*behind*) erect for action.

35 mm SP anti-aircraft gun 'Gepard'

Federal Republic of Germany

Calibre	35 mm
Barrel length	90 calibres
Shell weight	0·55 kg
Cyclic rate of fire	550 rds/min/barrel
Muzzle velocity	1·175 m/sec
Maximum horizontal range	12,000 m
Maximum effective range	4,000 m
Ceiling	1,200 m
Detachment	3
Chassis—Type	Leopard main Battle tank
Engine	Daimler-Benz
Power	830 bhp
Maximum speed	65 km/hour
Endurance	600 km
Ammunition stowage	238
Height × length × width	— × 6·94 × 3·25 m
Weight	—

The Gepard, or Flakpanzer 1, has been designed to support forward combat teams. It consists of two Oerlikon 35 mm cannon mounted in a fully enclosed turret on the Leopard main battle tank chassis. The vehicle incorporates tracking and search radar, and provides its own electrical power. It is therefore a fully independent weapon system. The first prototype was completed in 1968.

The guns are those of the Swiss K 63, but are modified to belt feed. The cyclic rate of fire is not therefore limited by the need for manual loading of clips as it is with the original equipment. However the on-board ammunition supply is very limited. It is probable that the radar and fire control equipment take up much of the space in the fighting compartment—but these very arrangements allow best use to be made of ammunition in short, accurate engagements.

Both HE and AP rounds are available. Lethality is claimed to equal the 40 mm Bofors shell, and the AP round penetrates 44 mm of armour at 1,000 m.

The guns are mounted either side of the turret, the tracking radar head between them at the front, and the search radar antenna above and to the rear. The search radar is the Siemans MPDR-12. It is a pulse doppler

35 mm SP AA gun—Gepard. The acquisition radar is mounted above the turret and the tracking radar between and below the guns.

type, incorporates IFF and is fitted with an automatic alarm. Transfer to the tracking radar is automatic on the operators command. The mounting of the tracking radar allows targets in a 200° arc to be accepted without slewing the turret. It is a monopulse doppler type made by Siemans-Albis. Target data for the fire control computer which calculates the optimum point of aim is augmented by muzzle velocity data from the guns: the distinctive measuring devices fitted to the muzzles are the same as those used on the K 63.

All electronics include a self test facility. The fire control computer is covered by a small emergency computer, and the whole automatic system is backed-up by an optical system. This system is periscopic for best crew protection, and allows for visual target acquisition, battlefield surveillance and gun sighting against ground and air targets. To allow for firing on the move the sights are gyro stabilised.

The Leopard chassis dates from 1965. It has good battlefield mobility which stems from a power to weight ratio of 21 bhp/ton. The powerful engine is a super-charged, compression ignition, multifuel V 10. Drive is

transmitted through a four speed automatic gearbox. The vehicle is fully proofed against nuclear radiation and chemical attack, and wades to a depth of 1·2 m without special preparation. In the Gepard version a 90 bhp diesel engine powers a 60 kilowatt generator.

Although the Gepard is generally credited as a German equipment, it is in fact the result of an international project. The guns and fire control computer were Swiss (Oerlikon/Contraves); the chassis and tracking radar German (Kraus-Maffei and Siemans-Albis); and the search radar Dutch (Hollandse Signaals-apparaten). The German production version uses Seimans search radar. A second development, for the Netherlands Armed Forces retains the German firm's IFF, but is otherwise fitted with Hollandse Signaals-apparraten radars.

Employment   Belgium
               Federal Republic of Germany
               Italy
               Netherlands

Twin 35 mm anti-aircraft gun K 63

Switzerland

Calibre	35 mm
Barrel length	90 calibres
Weight	6,400 kg
Shell weight	0·55 kg
Cyclic rate of fire	550 rds/min/barrel
Muzzle velocity	1,175 m/sec
Maximum horizontal range	—
Maximum effective slant range	4,000 m
Ceiling	1,200 m
Detachment	4

This Oerlikon gun is used in both this, land based mounting or as a ship-borne anti-aircraft gun. It is known in Austria as the M 65 and has also been built under licence in Japan. The high cyclic rate of fire cannot be sustained in practice because of the manual feed system using six round clips. Both HE and AP ammunition is available: the AP round penetrates 44 mm of armour at 1,000 m.

The gun is constructed so that the barrels and their feed systems are interchangeable between left and right mounting.

The four road wheels are swung clear of the ground for firing but remain on their axles. Two outriggers make up a cruciform platform with hydraulic jacks at each end of the chassis, and on each outrigger: time into action—1½ minutes.

Three modes of operation are provided: fully auto-

The K 63 in action with the road wheels folded on their axles over the carriage, the outriggers deployed and the whole weapon supported on hydraulic jacks. Note the muzzle velocity measuring device between the barrels.

mated electrical control linked to Super Fledermaus radar: by column control with optical sights: by mechanical hand wheels. The weapon is fitted with a device which constantly monitors muzzle velocity. The very high laying speeds achieved by the electrical motors are a feature of the design: 360° traverse is achieved in three seconds.

Employment   Austria   South Africa
               Finland   Switzerland
               Japan

37 mm anti-aircraft gun M 1939

Union of Soviet Socialist Republics

Calibre	37 mm
Barrel length	70 calibres
Weight	2,050 kg
Shell weight	0·74 kg (HE)
	0·77 kg (AP)
	0·62 kg (HVAP)
Cyclic rate of fire	180 rds/min
Muzzle velocity	960 m/sec (HVAP)
	880 m/sec (HE and AP)
Maximum horizontal range	8,000 m
Maximum effective slant range	3,000 m
Ceiling	1,000 m
Detachment	8

This gun is very similar to the Bofors L/60 from which it derives. The conical flash eliminator is one detail which is retained from the original design. Loading is manual: clips of five rounds are loaded into a hopper with gravity feed to the vertically opening sliding breech. Extraction of spent cartridges is automatic down a chute beneath the breech. The cylic rate of fire is only 160 rounds/minute which compares un-favourably with the rate of the 40 mm Bofors gun L/70. The manual loading arrangements further reduce the rate in practice to about 80 rounds/minute. The armour penetration of the AP shell is 46 mm at 500 m.

Sighting is optical. Split functions laying is used and is manual.

The gun is mounted on a four-wheel carriage. For action the wheels are removed, and a screw type jack supports each axle. Two swinging outriggers are deployed to complete a cruciform firing platform. A shield is sometimes fitted.

The M 1939s of the Soviet Army have been relegated to the reserve. The Chinese guns of this type are known as M 55.

Employment:

Afghanistan	Czechoslovakia	Pakistan
Albania	Egypt	Somalia
Algeria	East Germany	Sudan
Bulgaria	Laos	Tanzania
Cambodia	Mongolia	USSR
China	Morocco	Vietnam
Congo	North Korea	Yugoslavia
Cuba	North Yemen	Zaire

Left: Bringing the gun into action.

Below: The gun action, legs extended, jacks lowered and ammunition hopper in position.

40 mm anti-aircraft gun L/60

Sweden

Calibre	40 mm
Barrel length	60 calibres
Weight	1,750 kg
Shell weight	0·96 kg
Cyclic rate of fire	120 rds/min
Muzzle velocity	850 m/sec
Maximum horizontal range	8,700 m
Maximum effective slant range	3,000 m
Ceiling	1,000 m
Detachment	7

This pre-World War II equipment has been produced in a number of versions with many different control and sighting systems. It is mounted on a four wheel carriage, and may be fired from its wheels, although the wheels are normally removed for firing and stability is obtained by using two girder outriggers and four jacks. Ammunition is hand loaded in clips of four rounds to a hopper with a vertical feed. There is automatic extraction of the empty case through a chute mounted below the gun. There is a flat shield to provide protection to the crew, and this together with the distinctive conical flash eliminator form useful recognition features. AP rounds are available, in addition to HE, to give the gun a surface-to-surface capability. Armour penetration is 55 mm at 500 m.

40 mm Bofors L/60 AA gun.

Employment

Argentina	Austria	Brazil

Burma	Indonesia	Norway
Cambodia	Israel	Pakistan
Cyprus	Ivory Coast	Sudan
Ecuador	Jordan	Taiwan
Egypt	Lebanon	Thailand
Eire	Libya	Tunisia
Finland	Malaysia	Turkey
Greece	Nepal	Yugoslavia
India	Nigeria	Zaire

40 mm automatic gun L/70

Sweden

Calibre	40 mm
Barrel length	70 calibres
Weight	5,150 kg
Shell weight	1 kg
Cyclic rate of fire	240 rds/min
Muzzle velocity	1,000 m/sec
Maximum horizontal range	12,500 m
Maximum effective slant range	3,000 m
Ceiling	1,200 m
Detachment	7

This gun was developed as a successor to the L/60 and takes its title from the calibre length of the barrel. It first came into service in 1951 and has become widely used since that time. Over 5,000 have been built.

Ammunition in clips of four rounds is hand fed by two loading numbers to a hopper with a vertical feed. It is possible to stack up to 16 rounds in the hopper for ready use, and a further 48 rounds are carried at the rear of the platform. HE, AP and APDS ammunition is available. The HE round is fitted with a percussion fuze, and a self-destruct fuze set for 8·5 seconds after firing. A new and reputedly highly effective pre-fragmented round, with proximity fuze has been developed.

The gun is mounted on a four wheel trailer and has a good cross-country capability; for firing the wheels are normally removed and two swinging outriggers provide a cruciform for stability, the gun being levelled by means of four jacks. The gun is usually seen with a wrap-round armoured shield, and its principal recognition feature is the long slender barrel with a conical flash eliminator. Some models have built-in power units, but the weapon usually relies on an external power source.

Control is normally by a single layer using a control column and an electro-hydraulic elevating and traversing system, but provision is made for hand control using two hand wheels and mechanical drive. Provision is also made for remote control from any of the associated fire control radars using a cable link. A number of radar control systems are used; the principle types are:

Eldorado-Mirado (France)   Super Fledermaus

L/45 (Netherlands)   (Switzerland)
PS O4R (Sweden)   FCE 7 (UK)

An Italian version of this gun is known as the Breda/Bofors. It can be fitted with an automatic feed working from a 144 round magazine.

Employment	Australia	Iran	Norway
	Austria	Israel	Spain
	Canada	Italy	Sweden
	France	Japan	UK
	India	Netherlands	

FCE 7 fire control radar, used teamed with L/70.

40 mm Bofors L/70 AA gun.

Bofors 40 mm 75

Sweden

Calibre	40 mm
Barrel length	70 calibre
Weight	5,150 kg
Shell weight	Prefragmented proximity fuzed (875 g)
	HE tracer (960 g)
	AP tracer (930 g)
Cyclic rate of fire	300 rds/min
Muzzle velocity	1,035 m/secs
Maximum horizontal range	12,500 m
	4,000 m
Maximum effective slant range	3,500 m
Ceiling	1,250 m
Detachment	5

The Bofors gun system 75 is a modification of the L 40/70, and it incorporates the same 40 mm gun. However it represents a considerable improvement over the L 40/70, and Bofors claim that it is about ten times more effective. It has a miniaturised fire control system and a power supply unit mounted on it, and thus it only requires one towing vehicle.

The fire control system, called BOFI (Bofors Optronic Fire-control Instrument), consists of a day and night sight, a range finding laser and a computer which automatically calculates the aim-off position. The optical target indicator enables the commander standing to the side of the gun, to give an automatic indication of an enemy aircraft to the layer. A petrol-driven four stroke generator is mounted at the rear of the lower carriage and provides the necessary power to the electrohydraulic laying mechanism and to the fire control equipment. In addition to the new proximity-fuzed prefragmented ammunition, the 40/75 can fire conventional high explosive, armour-piercing or practice rounds. A total of 122 ready-to-use shells can be carried on the gun—26 in the hopper and 96 in the racks. It is towed by an 8 tonne truck or equivalent and it has a detachment of five—commander, layer, two loaders and ammunition handler/driver.

Employment Sweden

The Bofors 40 mm 75 AA gun.

40 mm twin SP M 42

United States of America

Calibre	40 mm
Barrel length	60 calibres
Shell weight	0·96 kg
Cyclic rate of fire	120 rds/min/barrel
Muzzle velocity	850 m/sec
Maximum horizontal range	8,700 m
Maximum effective slant range	3,200 m
Ceiling	1,000 m
Detachment	4
Chassis—Type	—
Engine	—
Power	—
Maximum speed	72 km/hour
Endurance	160 km
Ammunition carried	—
Height × length × width	2·84 × 6·35 × 3·2 m
Weight	22,500 kg

This is a fully tracked armoured chassis mounting twin L/60 Bofors guns and has been in service since 1953. The guns are mounted in a cylindrical open-topped turret which is operated under power control (although hand operation is possible). As with the L/60 the gun is hand loaded with clips of four rounds to hoppers providing vertical feed. The sighting system incorporates a computer for the calculation of aim off but there is no radar capability and visual aim is required which limits the range and operational effectiveness. Although the M 42 is heavy it does not afford much protection to its crew, and due to its lack of radar it does not meet the modern requirement very well. It is being replaced by Vulcan and Chaparral in the US Army.

Employment   Austria
Italy
West Germany
USA

40 mm twin SP M 42 AA gun.

57 mm anti-aircraft gun

Czechoslovakia

Calibre	57 mm
Barrel length	60 calibres
Weight	5,150 kg
Shell weight	2.5 kg
Cyclic rate of fire	100 rds/min
Muzzle velocity	1,000 m/sec
Maximum horizontal range	12,000 m
Maximum effective slant range	4,000 m
Ceiling	2,000 m
Detachment	7

This gun was produced in the Skoda works in very limited numbers, and is similar to the Russian S 60 which eventually replaced it. The gun is slightly heavier than the S 60 and has a lower muzzle velocity. It is mounted on a four wheel carriage which is lowered to bring the gun to the firing position, but the wheels are not removed. Laying is manual power assisted.

These guns were sold by the Czechs when they accepted S 60 into service.

Employment   Cuba
                Guinea
                Mali

57 mm AA gun—similar to D-60.

57 mm anti-aircraft gun M 54

Sweden

Calibre	57 mm
Barrel length	60 calibres
Weight	8,100 kg
Shell weight	2·6 kg
Cyclic rate of fire	160 rds/min
Muzzle velocity	920 m/sec
Maximum horizontal range	14,500 m
Maximum effective slant range	4,000 m
Ceiling	2,000 m
Detachment	6 +

The M 54 is closely related to the Bofors 40 mm weapon. The layout and operation of the gun follows the pattern of the L/70, and the typically Bofors conical flash eliminator is fitted. The cyclic rate of fire is high for the calibre of the weapon, but this rate cannot be maintained in practice because of the problem of handling the ammunition. The ready use ammunition racks used on the L/70 are retained.

The gun is mounted on a four-wheel carriage. In action it is supported on four jacks, which serve to level the equipment. Two of the screw-type jacks lift the wheels clear from the ground, the other two are mounted on swinging outriggers which make up a cruciform. The large shield at the front and sides of the gun is an important recognition feature.

Employment   Belgium
                Sweden

The gun, its firing position and detachment at their posts.

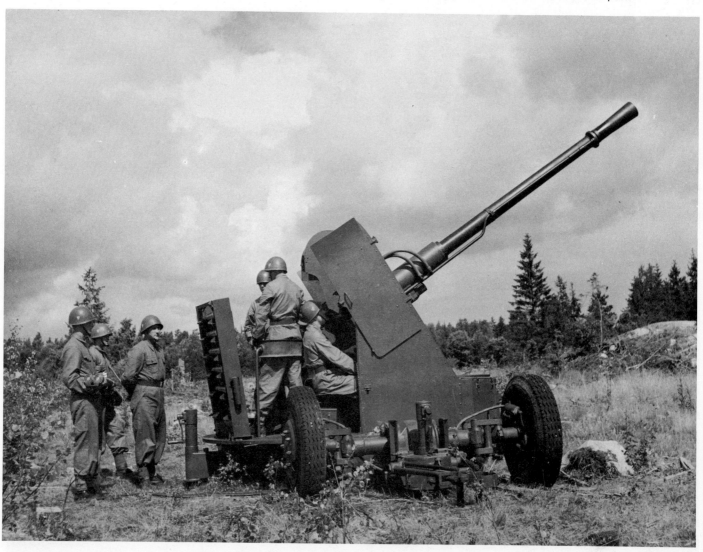

57 mm anti-aircraft gun M 1950 (S 60)

Union of Soviet Socialist Republics

Calibre	57 mm
Barrel length	70 calibres
Weight	4,500 kg
Shell weight	2·81 kg (HE)
	2·83 kg (AP)
Cyclic rate of fire	100–120 rds/min
Muzzle velocity	1,000 m/sec
Maximum horizontal	
range	12,000 m
Maximum effective	
slant range	4,000 m
Ceiling	2,000 m
Detachment	8

This equipment, which was first seen in 1950, uses the same gun as the ZSU 57-2 SP anti-aircraft equipment, and the ASU 57, M 1943 and M 1955 anti-tank guns. It was developed by the Russians from a captured German gun which was in its final development stages.

Ammunition is loaded into a slide feeding mechanism in clips of four rounds: this handling process reduces the rate of fire to 70 rounds/minute. A proximity fuze is used. The APHE round penetrates 106 mm of armour at 500 m. The gun is mounted on a four wheel carriage. It can fire on its wheels, but to an effective slant range of only 4,000 m, Normally, two swinging outriggers are deployed in action, and the carriage is supported on four levelling jacks. The wheels are not removed in action: they are fixed to trailing-arm suspension members, which, when raised to the horizontal, lift the wheels clean off the ground. For travelling the suspension arms are at a distinctive 45° angle. The pepper-pot muzzle brake is an equally distinctive recognition feature.

Three fire control options are available: a computing sight is fitted to the weapon, the SON 9 radar in conjunction with the PUAZO 6/60 director, and the FIRECAN S-band radar fire control system. The SON 9 is being replaced by SON 9A mounted on the URAL 375, and known as FLAPWHEEL.

Employment:

Afghanistan	East Germany	Poland
Albania	Indonesia	Romania
Bulgaria	Iran	Syria
Cambodia	Iraq	Vietnam
China	Libya	South Yemen
Congo	Mongolia	Yugoslavia
Czechoslovakia	North Korea	
Egypt	Pakistan	

Guns and tractors on parade.

57 mm SP ZSU 57-2

Union of Soviet Socialist Republics

Calibre	57 mm
Barrel length	70 calibres
Shell weight	2·8 kg (HE)
	3·1 kg (AP)
Cyclic rate of fire	210–240 rds/min/barrel
Muzzle velocity	1,000 m/sec
Maximum horizontal range	12,000 m
Maximum effective slant range	4,000 m
Ceiling	2,000 m
Detachment	6
Chassis—Type	Individual
Engine	V-2-54
Power	520 bhp
Maximum speed	48 km/hour
Endurance	400 km

Height × length × width 2·75 × 8·53 × 3·27 m
Weight 27, 550 kg

This is the SP version of the S 60 mounting two guns in a distinctive square turret above a flat topped tracked chassis with a drivers compartment in the extreme left front corner. The recognition features in addition to the distinctive turret shape are the pepperpot muzzle brakes. The turret is open topped which limits the protection offered to the detachment.

Optical sights are fitted and night vision aids are available.

Employment	Czechoslovakia	Iran	USSR
	Egypt	North Korea	Vietnam
	Finland	Poland	Yugoslavia
	Hungary		

The 57 mm SP ZSU 57-2.

85 mm anti-aircraft gun M 1944 (KS 18)

Union of Soviet Socialist Republics

Calibre	85 mm
Barrel length	50 calibres
Weight	4,500 kg
Shell weight	9·5 kg (HE)
	9·3 kg (APHE)
	5·0 kg (HVAP)
Cyclic rate of fire	15–20 rds/min
Muzzle velocity	1,030 m/sec (HVAP)
	972 m/sec (HE and APHE)
Maximum horizontal range	15,500 m
Maximum effective slant range	6,000 m
Ceiling	3,000 m
Detachment	7

The KS 18 is a development of the pre-World War II KS 12, which is now obsolete. The gun is also used as an anti-tank and tank gun.

The KS 18 does not have an automatic loading system. The rate of fire is therefore poor by anti-aircraft standards, but is helped by a semi-automatic vertically sliding breech, and fixed ammunition. The hydro-pneumatic recoil gear is mounted under and over the barrel. A singular conical multi-baffle muzzle brake is fitted.

The gun is pedestal mounted on a circular platform on a four wheel carriage. Two swinging outriggers make-up a cruciform mounting in action: the wheels are removed.

Both anti-aircraft and anti-tank optical sights are fitted, giving the gun an important dual capability. Fire control by SON 9 Radar and PUAZO 6/12 director is also available, and S 60 Firecan radar control is compatible with this gun.

The Czech Army is equipped with a similar gun manufactured by themselves which is usually known as the M 53 (not to be confused with the 30 mm M 53). This gun is identical in almost all respects, differences being a T-shaped muzzle brake and minor modifications to the shield and travelling platform.

Employment:

Afghanistan	Egypt	Sudan
Albania	East Germany	South Yemen
Bulgaria	Hungary	Syria
Cambodia	Iran	Vietnam
China	Iraq	Yugoslavia
Cuba	North Korea	
Czechoslovakia	Poland	

A section of 85 mm AA M 1944 KS (18) on the march.

3·7 inch anti-aircraft gun Mk 3A

United Kingdom

Calibre	3·7 inches (94 mm)
Barrel length	185 inches (470 mm)
Weight	20,541 lb (8,392 kg)
Shell weight	28 lb (12·6 kg)
Cyclic rate of fire	20 rev/min
Muzzle velocity	792 m/sec
Maximum horizontal range	18,800 m
Maximum effective slant range	12,000 m
Ceiling	9,000 m
Detachment	7

The 3·7 inch anti-aircraft gun saw action in British and Commonwealth armies throughout World War II. It was used to great effect in the ground role in Burma in 1944/45. The gun has undergone several improvements, and the final modification of the mobile version is still in service in five countries. It is towed by a 10 ton equivalent truck on a transporting carriage, which is normally removed when the gun is brought into action. The Mk 3A version is fitted with an automatic fuse setting, loading and firing mechanism, which enables its high rate of fire.

Employment	Burma	Pakistan
	India	South Africa
	Malaysia	

3·7 inch AA guns firing at practice.

100 mm heavy anti-aircraft gun M 49 (KS 19)

Union of Soviet Socialist Republics

Calibre	100 mm
Barrel length	54 calibres
Weight	11,000 kg
Shell weight	15·7 kg (HE)
	15·9 kg (APHE)
Cyclic rate of fire	15–20 rds/min
Muzzle velocity	900 m/sec (HE)
	1,000 m/sec (APHE)
Maximum horizontal	
range	21,000 m
Maximum effective	
slant range	7,000 m
Ceiling	3,500 m
Detachment	7

This is the same 100 mm gun which has been used for two anti-tank guns, a tank gun and an assault gun. In this anti-aircraft mounting, a multi-baffle muzzle brake is fitted and horizontal sliding semi-automatic breech block is used on conjunction with a power rammer. An automatic fuze setter is built in. Ammunition is loaded from the left into a vertical feed from a cylindrical loading tray. The result of these arrangements is that the rate of fire is as good as the smaller 85 mm KS 18. The recoil gear is mounted over and under the barrel.

The gun's rectangular platform mounting is carried on four road wheels which are removed in action.

Fire control arrangements are the same as for the KS 18: the SON 9, or SON 9A is used in conjunction with PUAZO 6/19 director, or the S-band radar FIRECAN is used.

This equipment entered service in 1949 to replace the 85 mm KS 12 and has now been replaced in the Soviet armed forces by SAM systems.

Employment:

Afghanistan	Cuba	Morocco
Algeria	Egypt	Poland
Bulgaria	East Germany	Rumania
Cambodia	Hungary	Vietnam
China	Iraq	

A 100 mm gun in a pit: detachments running to their posts.

130 mm heavy anti-aircraft gun M 55 (KS 30)

Union of Soviet Socialist Republics

Calibre	130 mm
Barrel length	54 calibres
Weight	30,000 kg
Shell weight	34 kg
Cyclic rate of fire	12 rds/min
Muzzle velocity	950 m/sec
Maximum horizontal range	29,000 m
Maximum effective slant range	10,000 m
Ceiling	6,000 m
Detachment	8

130 mm heavy AA gun M 58 (KS 30).

Like most Russian guns, the 130 mm has many applications. This anti-aircraft weapon has a semi-automatic horizontal sliding breech, an automatic fuze setter, and power ramming. Something of the guns multi-role background is reflected in the use of separate ammunition: a design, or perhaps logistic, compromise which must reduce the high rate of fire desirable in an anti-aircraft gun. The breech and loading arrangement are based on the 100 mm KS 19 design.

This equipment is very similar to an obsolete American 120 mm air defence weapon. It is mounted on a heavy platform with four twin wheels which are removed prior to firing to enable the folding front of the platform to be lowered. Box section outriggers are used for stabilisation and these fold upwards for travelling. The gun is not provided with a shield. The gun is towed by the URAL 375 using a single tubular draw bar.

Fire control is by SON 9, or SON 9A radar and PUAZO-30 director. Its primary role in defence of static potential targets has been taken over by guided weapons in Soviet and Warsaw Pact Countries.

Employment
Vietnam

Redeye

United States of America

Missile diameter	70 mm
Missile length	1·22 m
Missile weight	13 kg
Guidance system	Infra-red homing
Propulsion	Two stage solid propellant
Maximum effective altitude	900 m
Maximum effective slant range	3,000 m
Warhead	HE
Fire control	none

Redeye has been in service for over five years. It is designed to provide very low/low level self-defence to forward troops against attacking aircraft. It is robust and simple to operate. Like SA-7 the operator aims the weapon at the attacking aircraft until a buzzer indicates that the infra-red seeking head has locked on to the target's heat source. He then fires it and the missile automatically homes on to the exhaust jets of the aircraft. Redeye was originally intended to be an all-arms weapon but because of problems of fire control it has become a specialist operated weapon as part of the artillery family of air defence weapons.

Employment   Australia   Sweden
                   Denmark   USA

Redeye—missile container.

Redeye launcher—rear to the right.

SA-7 (NATO code—GRAIL)

Union of Soviet Socialist Republics

Missile diameter	70 mm
Missile length	1·3 m
Missile weight	9·2 kg
Guidance system	Infra-red homing
Propulsion	Three stage solid propellant
Maximum effective altitude	900 m
Maximum effective slant range	3,000 m
Warhead	HE blast
Fire control	none

The SA-7 is a very low/low level hand held surface to air missile system for self defence against attacking aircraft. It is robust and simple to operate. As with Redeye, the operator only has to aim it at the attacker, until the missile head is receiving a sufficient level of infra-red radiation, and fire it. The missile will then home automatically on to the hot exhaust jets of the enemy aircraft as it recedes. SA-7 first saw active service in Vietnam, and many thousands were fired in the October 1973 War. Its drawbacks are that, being a tail-chaser, it is normally only effective after an attack has been delivered, and it has only a small warhead whose effect can be negated by armour plate over the aircraft's jet pipe.

Employment	Bulgaria	Poland
	Czechoslovakia	Rumania
	Egypt	Syria
	East Germany	USSR
	Hungary	Vietnam
	Iraq	South Yemen

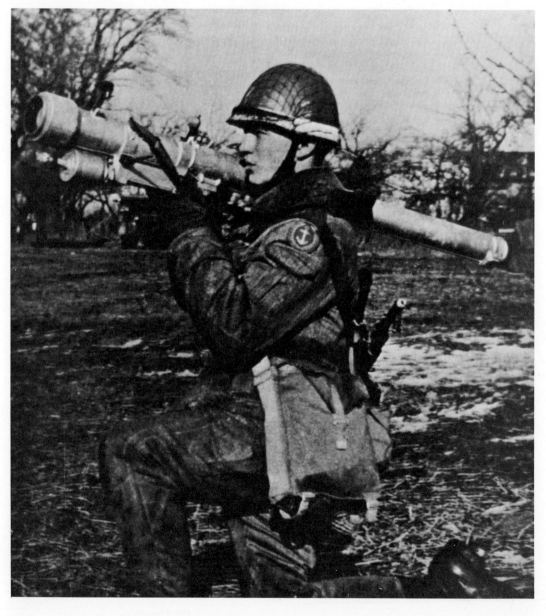

SA-7 and operator.

Blowpipe

United Kingdom

Missile diameter	76 mm
Missile length	1·4 m
Missile weight	14 kg (in canister)
Guidance system	Radio command with optical tracking
Propulsion	Two stage solid propellant
Maximum effective altitude	1,500 m
Maximum effective slant range	3,000 m
Warhead	He with proximity fuse
Fire control	none

Blowpipe is the only man-portable low/very low air defence missile in service with a true forward-hitting capability. It consists of an aiming unit, which with its IFF facility weighs 7 kg, and a launch canister. The total weight of the system on the operators shoulder is 21 kg. After an engagement has been completed, the empty canister is discarded, and the aiming unit is clipped to a new missile canister in a few seconds. The aiming unit has a sensor which automatically gathers the missile into the line of sight to the target after launch. The operator then flies the missile on to the target by a joystick control with his thumb. This automatically transmits radio guidance commands to the missile. Blowpipe was originally intended to be an all Arms self-defence weapon, but, because of the problems of control, it is now operated by artillery air defence batteries. Blowpipe can also be used in an anti-APC role in emergencies.

Employment   Canada
United Kingdom

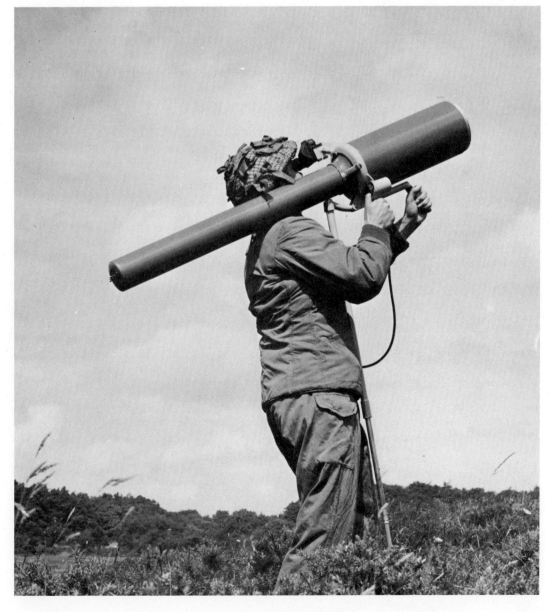

Blowpipe: UK low level SAM.

Stinger

United States of America

Missile diameter	70 mm
Missile length	1·52 m
Missile weight	13·4 kg
Guidance system	Infra-red homing
Propulsion	Two stage solid propellant
Maximum effective altitude	Estimated 1,500 m
Maximum effective slant range	Estimated 4,000 m
Warhead	HE
Fire control	none

Stinger is being developed as a replacement for Redeye—the very low/low level self-defence role. Although it also uses passive infra-red homing to guide it to the target, it has a much more sensitive homing head than Redeye and it is claimed that this will give it some degree of forward-hitting capacity against the attacking aircraft's plume signature. The US also have a competing man-portable system under development called the Stinger Alternate, which is believed to be a laser beam-rider like RBS-70, and this will certainly be able to engage approaching aircraft successfully. It is understood that no US decision has yet been made as to which of these two will replace Redeye in the US Army.

Employment   Trials only in USA

Stinger and operators.

RBS 70

Sweden and Switzerland

Missile diameter	106 mm
Missile length	1·32 m
Missile weight	23·5 kg
Guidance system	Optical laser beam-rider
Propulsion	Two stage solid propellant
Maximum effective altitude	3,000 m
Maximum effective slant range	5,000 m
Warhead	Prefragmented proximity fused
Fire control	PS-70/R radar

RBS 70 is being developed by Sweden in collaboration with Switzerland as a very low/low level self-defence weapon. The sight generates a laser guidance beam which coincides with the line of sight to the attacking aircraft. The missile remains in the centre of the beam after launch until it hits the aircraft—all the operator has to do is to keep the sight accurately on the target. The sight (35 kg) clips on to the missile container, which is then attached to a lightweight tripod stand (22 kg). This provides a seat and a steady aiming position for the operator. Like Blowpipe, the RBS 70 is a true self-defence weapon, in that it can engage approaching aircraft before they have reached the point of weapon release. A further advantage it has over the tail-chasers, like Redeye and SA-7, is that there are no practical counter-measures at present to the laser beam guidance it uses.

Employment   Sweden
Switzerland

RBS 70 showing tripod support.

SA-9 (NATO code—Gaskin)

Union of Soviet Socialist Republics

Missile diameter	70 mm
Missile length	1·3 m
Missile weight	9·2 kg
Guidance system	Infra-red homing
Propulsion	Three stage solid propellant
Maximum effective altitude	900 m
Maximum effective slant range	3,000 m
Warhead	HE blast
Fire control	By Gundish radar on ZSU-23-4

SA-9 is a mobile very low/low level missile system, which

is being introduced in the Soviet Army to complement the ZSU-23-4 gun for forward area defence. When in position it uses the ZSU-23-4's Gundish radar for local warning and fire control. Four missiles are mounted on a modified BRDM-2 with twin elevating launchers either side of the operator's sight. The turret has a 360° traverse. The missile appears to be an improved version of the SA-7 and it probably uses the same infra-red homing head.

Employment	Egypt
	Syria
	USSR

SA-9—'Gaskin'.

SA-8

Union of Soviet Socialist Republics

Missile diameter	210 mm
Missile length	3·20 m
Missile weight	About 200 kg
Guidance system	Probably semi-automatic command to line of sight
Propulsion	Probably two stage solid propellant
Maximum effective altitude	Estimated 3,500 m
Maximum effective slant range	Estimated 6,500 m
Warhead	HE with proximity fuze
Fire control	Radar

SA-8 is a low level air defence system designed to bridge the gap between the very low/low level SA-7 and SA-9 and the low/medium level SA-6. It first appeared in public in the November 1975 parade in Moscow, and it is now entering service in the Soviet Army. The entire system, consisting of four missiles, search and tracking radars, and a fire control unit, is mounted on one six-wheeled vehicle. The positioning of the radar dishes and antennae indicates that its guidance system is probably semi-automatic command to line of sight similar to those of Roland and Rapier and its performance is likely to be much the same. The SA-8 appears to have an all-weather 24 hour capability, and it will be a useful addition to the already powerful Soviet air defence inventory. It could be the same missile as the naval SA-N-4.

Employment   USSR

SA-8 low level air defence system, on parade.

Chaparral

United States of America

Missile diameter	130 mm
Missile length	2·91 m
Missile weight	85 kg
Guidance system	Infra-red homing
Propulsion	Solid propellant
Maximum effective altitude	2,000 m
Maximum effective slant range	4,000 m
Warhead	HE
Fire control	Forward Area Alerting Radar system

Chaparral is designed for low/very low level air defence and in the US Army it is used in conjunction with the Vulcan gun system. Four missiles are mounted on rotating launches turret on the M-730 self-propelled tracked vehicle. The missile is basically the supersonic air-to-air Sidewinder IC, modified for ground-to-air use and it is stored and handled as an assembled round of ammunition. It is a tail-chaser, which is aimed by the gunner through an optical sight until the infra-red homing head has locked onto the heat source of the target's jet efflux. After launch it automatically homes onto its target.

The M-730 can be made amphibious in a short time by adding a simple swimming kit. It carries a five man detachment and can travel at 40 mph on a road. In the US Army the Forward Area Alerting Radar system provides local warning for Chaparral and Vulcan.

Employment   Israel
                 USA

The Chaparral system in action.

Tigercat

United Kingdom

Missile diameter	190 mm
Missile length	1·48 m
Missile weight	63 kg
Guidance system	Command to line of sight
Propulsion	Two stage solid propellant
Maximum effective altitude	3,000 m
Maximum effective slant slant range	4,800 m
Warhead	HE
Fire control	Radar

Tigercat is a trailer mounted version of Seacat for battlefield low level air defence. The system consists of a launcher, which has three missiles, and a tracker/director. The operator guides the missile to the target with a thumb stick with radio commands being automatically passed to the missile. Tigercat can be given a 24 hour capability by the addition of the Marconi ST 850 radar which is also mounted on a trailer. Rapier is to replace Tigercat in British service.

Employment	Argentina	Qatar
	India	South Africa
	Iran	UK
	Israel	

Tigercat, test firing.

Rapier

United Kingdom

Missile diameter	127 mm	*Maximum effective altitude*	3,500 m
Missile length	2·24 m	*Maximum effective slant range*	6,500 m
Missile weight	65 kg	*Warhead*	HE
Guidance system	Semi-automatic command to line of sight	*Fire control*	Radar
Propulsion	Two stage solid propellant		

Rapier air defence system—tracker and operators in foreground.

Rapier is a lightweight low level air defence system. In the British Army it is mounted on a trailer towed by a $\frac{3}{4}$-ton landrover, and there is a second landrover in the firing unit towing a trailer containing additional missiles. The Rapier system consists of a launcher, which mounts four missiles two each side of the search and acquisition radar dome, an optical tracker and a small generator. These three components are connected together by cables. The detachment has five men, but once the system is in action the engagement sequence is controlled entirely by one tracker operator. Once the search radar has acquired a target and recognised it as hostile, it automatically alerts the tracker operator and directs the optical tracker until the aircraft can be seen in sight. All the operator then has to do is to keep the tracker's crosswires on the target with a joystick control and to fire a missile, when the computer indicates that the target is within range for effective engagement. The semi-automatic command to line of sight guidance is achieved by a television camera, which tracks the missile's flare, collimated with the optical tracker. The guidance commands to bring the missile onto the line of sight to the target are automatically computed and transmitted to the missile.

A blindfire radar for Rapier, known as DN 181, is being developed as an addition to the optical system, and this will provide a full 24 hour capability. It will be mounted on a similar trailer to that of the launcher, towed by a $\frac{3}{4}$-ton truck.

One of the features of the Rapier system is the revolutionary test and repair vehicles, which have been developed to permit maintenance and repair in the forward areas. These use computerised test facilities mounted in a landrover (the Forward Repair and Test Vehicle) and in 4-ton trucks at battery level, one for electronic and electrical repairs and one for optics and hydraulics.

Employment Iran   United Kingdom

Roland

France

Missile diameter	160 mm
Missile length	2·40 m
Missile weight	63 kg
Guidance system	Semi-automatic command to line of sight
Propulsion	Two stage solid propellant
Maximum effective altitude	3,500 m
Maximum effective slant range	6,500 m
Warhead	He with proximity fuze
Fire control	Radar

Roland is an antonomous low-level air defence system. It will be mounted on the Marder or AMX 30 chassis in the West German and French Armies, and the US Army intends to mount it on the wheeled GOER for rear areas and on their future infantry APC for support of forward troops. The pulse doppler surveillance radar detects and identifies the target for the operator to fire and track the missile through his optical sight. The missile is automatically guided on to the line of sight to the target by an infra-red guidance system similar to that used for the HOT anti-tank guided weapon. Roland I will be introduced first, as a daylight only system. Roland II will be a 24 hours blindfire system, with a radar tracker being used in the place of the optical sight.

Employment   Development in France
West Germany
USA

Roland low level air defence system.

Crotale

France

Missile diameter	150 mm
Missile length	2·89 m
Missile weight	80 kg
Guidance system	Radar Command
Propulsion	Single stage solid propellant
Maximum effective altitude	3,000 m
Maximum effective slant range	6,000 m
Warhead	HE with proximity fuze
Fire control	Radar

Crotale has been developed by France as a low-level air defence system. The French Army has preferred Roland for this role, but South Africa has a version of Crotale in service called Cactus. Four missiles and a command guidance radar are mounted on a rotating launcher on a lightly armoured wheeled vehicle. A similar vehicle mounts a Thompson pulse-doppler S band surveillance radar, which has an automatic target evaluation system. Data is passed from the surveillance radar to the launcher by cable for distances up to 400 m, or by radio up to 5,000 m.

Employment   Libya
South Africa
Saudi Arabia

Crotale low level air defence system.

Indigo

Italy

Missile diameter	195 mm
Missile length	3·076 m
Missile weight	120 kg
Guidance system	Radio command/beam-riding
Propulsion	Single stage solid propellant
Maximum effective altitude	3,500 m ⎫ (estimated)
Maximum slant range	6,500 m ⎭
Warhead	HE fragmentation with proximity fuse
Fire control	Superfledermaus

Italy is developing Indigo as a trailer-mounted low-level air defence system. The system consists of one or more launchers, each with six missiles, a modified Superfledermaus fire control system and a pulse-doppler search radar, all connected by cable. The primary method of guidance is beam-riding on the line of sight to the target, but radio command guidance with infra-red tracking is provided as a back up, if for some reason the beam-riding fails or is effectively countered. The three basic trailers of the system are towed by a 4-ton truck. It is understood that a tracked self-propelled version of Indigo is also under development.

Employment   Development in Italy

SA-3 (NATO code—Goa)

Union of Soviet Socialist Republics

Missile diameter	450 mm
Missile length	6·7 m
Missile weight	950 kg
Guidance system	Radar command guidance
Propulsion	Two stage solid propellant
Maximum effective altitude	20,000 m ⎫ (estimated)
Maximum effective slant range	25,000 m ⎭
Warhead	70 kg HE blast
Fire control	Low Blow

The SA-3 is a low/medium level system with a pair of missiles on a six-wheeled ZIL 157 truck. Fire control is provided by the NATO code Low Blow radar in association with a further surveillance radar. It provides low/medium level cover at divisional level and is the link between the SA-2 and SA-4 and the forward area SA-6. SA-3 has been in service since about 1960. There is Naval version of SA-3.

Employment		
	Bulgaria	Libya
	Czechoslovakia	Poland
	Egypt	Rumania
	East Germany	Syria
	Hungary	USSR
	Iraq	Vietnam

Foreground, two missiles on launcher (the tip of a third missile from another SA-3 launcher in the background appears between them).

Hawk

United States of America

Missile diameter	350 mm
Missile length	5·12 m
Missile weight	580 kg
Guidance system	Semi-active homing
Propulsion	Two stage solid propellant
Maximum effective altitude	15,000 m ⎫ (estimated)
Maximum effective slant range	20,000 m ⎭
Warhead	HE blast fragmentation
Fire control	Pulse and continuous wave acquisition radar

Hawk (Homing All the Way Killer) is a highly mobile low/medium level air defence system, which can engage supersonic aircraft between 100 m and 15,000 m. Three missiles are mounted either on a two-wheeled trailer or on the self-propelled tracked XM-727. Ground support equipment in a Hawk battery consists of a pulse acquisition radar, a continuous wave acquisition radar, a range-only radar, two illuminating radars, six three-missile launchers, a tracked missile loader-transporter and the command post. When the acquisition radars have detected a target, it is illuminated by one of the continuous wave illuminating radars. After launch the missile tracks the electromagnetic energy which is reflected from the illuminated target, in a similar way to Thunderbird II.

A later version known as Improved Hawk will have a new guidance package, a larger warhead and a better propellant. Solid state components will reduce the maintenance load in the field.

Employment

Belgium	Israel	Saudi-Arabia
Brazil	Italy	Spain
Denmark	Kuwait	Sweden
France	Japan	Taiwan
West Germany	South Korea	Thailand
Greece	Laos	USA
Iran	Netherlands	

Hawk mounted on XM 727.

SA-2 (NATO code—Guideline)

Union of Soviet Socialist Republics

Missile diameter	500 mm
Missile length	10·6 m
Missile weight	2,300 kg
Guidance system	Radio command guided
Propulsion	Liquid propellant with solid fuel boosters
Maximum effective altitude	20,000 m ⎫ (estimated)
Maximum effective slant range	35,000 m ⎭
Warhead	130 kg HE blast
Fire control	NATO Code-Fan Song radar

SA-2 is a medium/high level surface-to-air missile mounted on an articulated trailer, towed by a ZIL 157 truck. It has been in service since the 1950's and there are already several versions of it, possibly with terminal guidance, in the Soviet Army. It has poor cross-country ability and would not be expected to be deployed in forward areas.

Employment

Afghanistan	Hungary	Poland
Albania	India	Rumania
Bulgaria	Iraq	Syria
Cuba	Libya	USSR
Czechoslovakia	Mongolia	Vietnam
Egypt	North Korea	Yugoslavia
East Germany		

SA-2—Guideline.

SA-6 (NATO code—Gainful)

Union of Soviet Socialist Republics

Missile diameter	335 mm
Missile length	6 m
Missile weight	550 kg
Guidance system	Semi-active radar
Propulsion	Ramjet with solid fuel booster
Maximum effective altitude	15,000 m ⎫ (estimated)
Maximum effective slant range	25,000 m ⎭
Warhead	80 kg HE blast with proximity fuze
Fire control	NATO code-Straight Flush radar system

The SA-6 is a low/medium level surface-to-air missile mounted on a tracked launcher vehicle. It is used to provide comprehensive air defence cover of forward areas, together with the very low/low level SA-7 and 9, and the S-60 and ZSU-23-4 gun systems. Fire control is provided by the Straight Flush radar and a separate surveillance radar and height finder. The SA-6 was the most successful air defence missile in the October 1973 war. It is equivalent to the US HAWK.

Employment	Bulgaria	Libya
	Czechoslovakia	Poland
	East Germany	Rumania
	Egypt	Syria
	Hungary	USSR
	Iraq	

Foreground, Straight-flush radar—SA 6 in background.

SA-4 (NATO code—Ganef)

Union of Soviet Socialist Republics

Missile diameter	800 mm
Missile length	9 m
Missile weight	2,000 kg
Guidance system	Radar command guidance
Propulsion	Ramjet with 4 solid fuel boosters
Maximum effective altitude	30,000 m
Maximum effective slant range	40,000 m
Warhead	HE blast
Fire control	NATO code—Pat Hand

(estimated) for altitude and slant range.

The SA-4 is a medium/high level surface-to-air missile system with two missiles mounted in tandem on a heavy tracked launcher vehicle. It is easily distinguishable by its four wrap-round boosters, which are similar in appearance to those on Thunderbird II and Bloodhound. Its C-band Pat Hand radar provides fire control in association with surveillance and height-finding radars. All its radars are mounted on heavy tracked vehicles. Despite its impressive size SA-4 appears to have good cross-country mobility and could on occasions be deployed at brigade/regimental level. It is equivalent to US Nike Hercules.

Employment USSR

SA 4—Ganef.

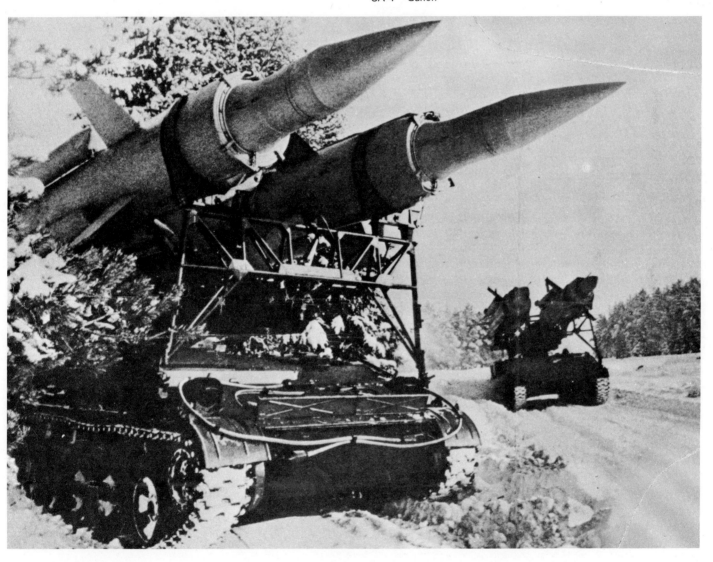

Thunderbird II

United Kingdom

Missile diameter	540 mm
Missile length	6·40 m
Missile weight	2,250 kg
Guidance system	Semi-active radar homing
Propulsion	Solid propellant with four solid fuel boosters
Maximum effective altitude	over 30,000 m
Maximum effective slant range	over 40,000 m } (estimated)
Warhead	HE proximity fuzed
Fire control	Target illuminating radar

Thunderbird II is a mobile medium level surface to air missile system. A missile firing troop has three launchers, a target illuminating radar and a launch control post. The firing of three troops is controlled by a battery command post which has a tactical control radar and a height finding radar. At regimental level there is a long-range surveillance radar to provide early warning. Target data is passed by digital link direct to the launch control posts for the target illuminating radars to begin tracking their targets. All equipment in the regiment is mounted on wheeled vehicles or trailers.

Employment UK

Thunderbird II.

Bloodhound II

United Kingdom

Missile	550 m
Missile length	7·75 m
Missile weight	2,454 kg
Guidance system	Semi-active homing
Propulsion	Ramjet with four solid propellant boosters
Maximum effective altitude	Estimated 30,000 m
Maximum effective slant range	Estimated 40,000 m
Warhead	HE with proximity fuze
Fire control	Target illuminating radar

Bloodhound II replaced the earlier version in the mid 1960s as a medium/high level air defence system. The semi-active homing system requires the target aircraft to be illuminated by an X band continuous wave-doppler radar during the missile's flight. It is primarily a static weapon system for asset defence with the long range Type 87 target illuminating radar, but there is also a trailer mounted version with a mobile Type 86 Indigo Corkscrew radar, which is the same as the British Army Radar No 10 used with Thunderbird II. Each launcher has one missile. One target illuminating radar, with its associated computers in a command post, can control up to four missiles.

Employment Australia Switzerland
Singapore UK
Sweden

Bloodhound II.

Nike Hercules

United States of America

Missile diameter	800 mm
Missile length	12·5 m
Missile weight	4,500 kg
Guidance system	Command
Propulsion	Two stage solid propellant
Maximum effective altitude	35,000 m
Maximum effective slant range	70,000 m $\Big\}$ (estimated)
Warhead	HE or nuclear
Fire control	Radar

Nike Hercules is the principal NATO medium/high level air defence system. Like its predecessor Nike Ajax, many Nike Hercules are in fixed sites defending cities and military installations, but those which provide cover for the field army have road mobility. A Nike Hercules battery's ground equipment consists of a high and a low power acquisition radar, a target tracking radar, a missile tracking radar, data processing computers, a number of remotely controlled launchers and electronic counter measures equipment. The target is first detected by the acquisition radar and then pinpointed for interception by the target tracker. The missile is guided to the target by the interplay of data from the target and missile tracking radars. Nike Hercules was first introduced at the end of the 1950s and Sam-D is being developed as its successor.

Employment	Belgium	Japan	Spain
	Denmark	South Korea	Taiwan
	West Germany	Netherlands	Turkey
	Greece	Norway	USA
	Italy		

Nike Hercules: left foreground.

Sam-D

United States of America

Missile diameter	400 mm
Missile length	5·2 m
Missile weight	—
Guidance system	Command with semi-active homing
Propulsion	Single stage solid propellant
Maximum effective altitude	40,000 m ⎫
Maximum effective slant range	⎬ (estimated)
	60,000 m ⎭
Warhead	HE or nuclear
Fire control	Radar

Sam-D is being developed as a medium/high level air defence system to replace Nike Hercules and Hawk. The launcher and its ground-support equipment will be mounted on tracked vehicles and so it will be much more mobile than Nike. The prototype has six missiles on a launcher and a possible organisation would provide eight launchers per battery. One phased-array radar is used for surveillance, target acquisition and target tracking. This one radar performs the tasks which require five radars in a Nike battery and four radars in a Hawk battery.

Miniaturization and advances in the art of solid-state components have made possible an extremely compact organisation of a Sam-D battery with only a dozen or so vehicles involved in the firing sequence, and a far better reliability in the field.

Employment Development in USA

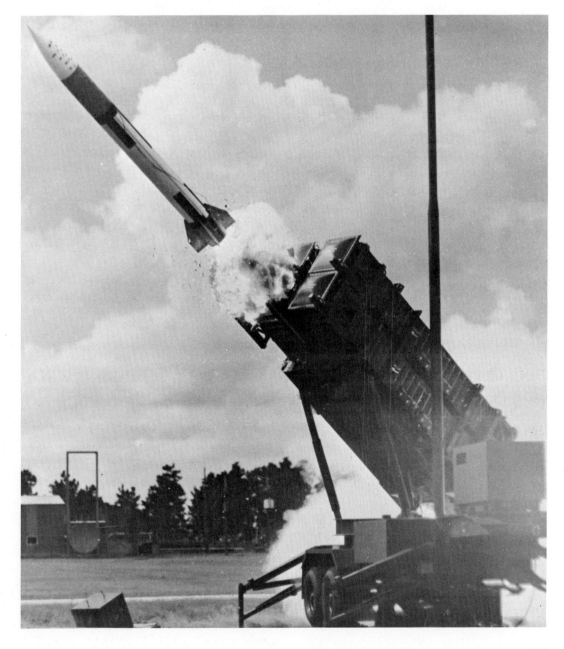

Sam-D—a test firing.

X. Air Defence Ancillary Equipment

All but the smallest air defence weapons operate at a range which is too great for accurate visual control. Furthermore, the weapon must be able to react to the modern aircraft's all-weather day and night capability and its speed which brings it into range too fast for visual target acquisition.

A number of tactical radars are available with both a search and tracking capability. In this section, only radars which are used for gun and smaller missile control are included. The many similar systems, which are an integral part of the larger missile systems, have already been described with the missile concerned.

Eldorado (TH-D-1229)

France

Eldorado is a one man operated, trailer-mounted air defence fire control system. The trailer, with roof-mounted radar antenna and its own power pack, is self-sufficient, but weighs only 1,600 kg. An optical system works in parallel with the radar, and both systems are displayed simultaneously to the operator. The equipment has an inbuilt target acquisition capability, but is designed to operate with Mirador, a specialist acquisition radar, whose circuitry is built into Eldorado, and whose antenna and tripod fit into the Eldorado trailer.

Eldorado trailer.

Mirador II

France

General. This S-band coherent pulse radar is primarily a target acquisition system for use with guns or missiles. It has high resistance to electronic counter-measures. It can be used in a tracking mode while scanning.

Capabilities. Mirador II is effective against low and very low targets. It produces a 360° search pattern, the radar head rotating at one revolution per second. Maximum detection range is 18 km. It resolves range to 400 m, or 200 m when tracking, and is accurate to 0·75° in azimuth.

Operation. An audible alarm system indicates the presence of a target. Target data can be passed to several fire positions. A plan position indicator presents the operator with radial speed and range information to enable a speedy threat evaluation.

Mirador aerial and tripod.

L 4/5 weapon control system
Netherlands

General. The L 4/5 is a system which dates from the early 1960's and is designed for gun or missile control. The complete system is mounted on a four-wheel trailer from which a canvas extension is deployed in action. There are three antennae, two for search and one for tracking. IFF is fitted, together with numerous anti-jamming features. The complete system weighs 6,000 kg, and is operated by two or three men.

Capabilities. Each L 4/5 can control up to three guns or missiles simultaneously. The two search antennae are mounted back to back and search the medium/low, and very low height bands respectively. The search antennae can continue to operate while the tracking radar is in use. A back-up optical sight is fitted. Maximum range is 30 km, and the system can handle target speeds up to 500 m/sec.

Operation. The rapid 360° spiral search pattern of the search radar produces a continuous plan position indicator display in the control cabin. Sector or continuous search can be selected. Targets are picked up for tracking automatically, or manually.

The L 4/5 system deployed for action.

VL 4/41 fire control system—'Flycatcher'
Netherlands

General. Flycatcher is a new X-band radar equipment which is adapted from the fire control system fitted to the Gepard. It can control up to three guns, or two guns and one missile. It is housed in a container with the antennae normally carried internally but mounted on the roof in action. A television camera can be mounted with the tracking antenna.

Capabilities. The range is 30 km. Target speed limitations are 500 m/sec horizontally, and 300 m/sec vertically. The computer produces firing data, which includes ballistic corrections for the gun's performance.

Operation. The appearance of a target in the search pattern triggers an alarm. Targets are automatically interrogated by IFF.

Flycatcher, showing entrance to cabin and generator.

Ericsson/Arenco radar system

Sweden

General. L. M. Ericsson have produced several X-band air defence fire control radars. The PE-48/T is used in conjunction with an Arenco computer.

Capabilities. The system is a tracking radar which produces firing data for two 40 mm or 57 mm guns. It can also be used in the search mode.

PE-452/T radar system

Sweden

General. This is an elderly radar/optical system. The PE-452/T works in conjunction with a Contraves optical tracker: the X-band radar measures range, while the optical system produces angular measurements. A com-puter combines both inputs into gun firing data.

Capabilities. Being partly optical, this system is not suited to all-weather day and night operation. Two 40 mm guns can be controlled.

Skyguard fire control system

Switzerland

General. Skyguard can be used to control both guns and missiles. The system consists of a search radar, tracking radar, and television tracking. A Contraves Core II M digital computer is used. Both radars are of the pulse-doppler type, and operate independently. A generator is built into the trailer which contains the system.

Capabilities. The pulse-doppler search radar features high clutter suppression, high resistance to electronic counter-measures, and automatic target transfer to the tracking radar. A target alarm is fitted. The computer is used to assess the threat, produce target data for the guns and missiles, test the operation of the equipment and produce electronic training signals. There is provision for IFF. Range is 20 km and range accuracy is 160 m.

Operation. The plan position indicator can be used to present target displays from 0·3 to 20 km in range. One or two operators are needed depending on the tactical situation.

Skyguard low-level radar and fire-control system.

Superfledermaus fire control system

Switzerland

General. Superfledermaus is designed to control three missiles or three guns of 35–40 mm calibre. It has X-band acquisition and tracking radars, and a back-up telescopic sight for the latter. It is mounted on a four-wheel trailer, weighs 5,000 kg, and has been sold to over twenty countries. Data production is computerised and a constant muzzle velocity measurement facility at each gun is included in the fire control system.

Capabilities. Using a helical or sector scan, targets can be acquired up to 50 km. Autotrack is effective to 40 km. The computerised data production incorporates correction for gun parallax, wind speed and air density as well as muzzle velocity.

Operation. There is autotransfer from acquisition to tracking radars with a plan position indicator and range/height indicator to present the maximum tactical information to the operator.

Side view showing detail of the trailer.

'Fire Can' fire control radar

Union of Soviet Socialist Republics

General. Fire Can is an elderly S-band radar with a search and tracking capability. It is trailer mounted, and has a single 1,500 mm dish antenna. The dish is perforated to reduce weight.

Capabilities. Fire Can can acquire targets to a range of 80 km. The maximum tracking range is 35 km and accuracy in the order of 15 m is probable.

Operation. In the search mode all targets are indicated on a plan position indicator. Target selection, and transfer to the tracking mode is manual. This radar is used to control 57 mm and 85 mm guns.

XI. Coast Artillery

Coast artillery as a specialised branch fell into disuse after World War II. Fortresses with fixed armaments from 6 inch to 15 inch in concrete emplacements designed to protect naval bases and anchorages proved only too vulnerable to land attack and aerial bombing. Equally the supporting fire of naval craft and aerial bombardment effectively neutralised coastal fortifications sited to cover beaches and landing places suitable for invasion. While it was realised that coast artillery was to some extent a deterrent it locked up men and equipment in fixed defences which in the event seldom if ever fired a shot. Further, the advance of weapon technology in the shape of airpower and surface-to-surface guided missiles specially designed for attacking ships provided a far more flexible and effective counter both to invasion and to long-range ship-to-shore bombardment.

It is always difficult to draw boundaries between weapon systems but the anti-ship missiles are essentially automatically piloted aircraft designed to fly at altitudes as low as two metres above the sea level and are not, as far as is known, normally handled by artillery personnel although all are potentially shore-to-ship weapons and two, the Matra and Oto Melara OTOMAT (France and Italy) and the Swedish Saab RB-08, can be used in this role. Similarly any naval gun system can be adapted for shore-to-ship role without major modification. None of these weapons is included in this chapter.

Nevertheless guns, especially if sited in commanding positions, are still an economical method of providing close-in defence of harbour and anchorages against surprise attack or fast, small raiding craft and also for the control of straits and approaches through shoals or shallows where shipping must follow a predetermined course. 'Classical' coast systems were very effective. The range was discovered by continuously solving the triangle formed by the height of the gun above sea-level and the angle of sight from the gun to the target and range and bearing data was passed electronically to the split function layers by the 'follow-the-pointer' system. Even with manually operated breech mechanisms laying direct and estimating the lead, the chance of a hit in two or three rounds was good. Some of these antiquated but still servicable systems of fire control may still be in service for harbour defence. Their disadvantage is that they are all optical and depend on good visibility, and the director operators and layers have to be skilled, intelligent and regularly practised.

Anti-aircraft guns, if they can be modified to shoot with angle of sights of depression with their radars and fire-control instruments are effective all-weather coast defence artillery. The German 88 mm Flak 36 is used in this role in Yugoslavia. Reportedly such coast batteries as are known are adaptations from other roles. Only the Swedish firm of Bofors has designed guns specifically for coast defence; the 75 mm described here and a 120 mm.

According to *The Military Balance 1975–1976* (published by the International Institute for Strategic Studies, London) The Soviet Union, Norway, Sweden, Yugoslavia and Cuba have coast artillery units which are naval manned. The most complete, as might be expected, are the Soviet Union's, covering all naval bases and major ports as well as providing full visual and radar cover along the coast line. Cuba is equipped with the Samlet missile. In Finland, Portugal and Spain the coast artillery is manned by the army. Albania and Egypt may also maintain some coast defence units.

75 mm coast defence gun L/60

Sweden

Calibre	75 mm
Barrel length	60 calibres
Muzzle brake	Nil
Weight	—
Ammunition	HE (5·52 kg)
	AP (5·73 kg)
Rate of fire	25 rds/min
Muzzle velocity	870 m/sec
Maximum range	12,000 m
Elevation limits	−5° +20°
Traverse on carriage	360°
Detachment	5

The Swedish coast defence system is controlled by the Navy. It consists of 20 batteries equipped with guns, and RB 08 and SS 11 missiles. This gun is made by Bofors and mounted in fixed emplacements which have an armoured dome type turret built over a bunker which houses ammunition.

The monobloc barrel is fitted with a fume extractor but no muzzle brake. The vertically sliding breech block opens downwards, a design feature which helps to reduce the height of the turret to a minimum. The barrel is mounted into a 'cradle' structure which extends rearwards and houses the automatic loading device and recoil system, and also counter balances the elevating mass. Thus only the barrel projects from the turret.

Loading is fully automatic, operated partly by recoil action, and partly by electric power. The fixed ammunition is stored in a magazine chamber beneath the turret.

An electrically operated rod-type hoist moves the cartridges up one step for each movement of the hoist driving mechanism which consists of a worm and bevel gear driven via a connecting rod linkage. The movement of the hoist is controlled by cam-actuated microswitches, which control the entire functioning of the hoist. In an emergency the hoist can be operated manually.

The cartridges, which are transported in the hoist in an upright position, are transferred to the loading channel by means of a loading tube. During the hoisting procedure, the loading tube is hooked up vertically over the hoist drum, and when a cartridge has been hoisted up into the loading tube, the tube is automatically

Turret and cupola—L/60 system. Note fume-extractor on barrel.

released and manually turned in to the loading channel in front of the rammer. The loading tube is supported on a pendulum which moves around the elevation trunnion centre. Raising the pendulum and loading tube with cartridge is effected by means of a torsion spring which is cocked by the recoil movement. The gun has a spring-operated rammer, which is also cocked by the recoil. The rammer is released automatically when the loading tube is swung up to the loading channel.

Split function, manual laying is used. For indirect laying, 'follow-the-pointers' are used. For direct aiming there is a periscopic sight with dual eyepieces, one for the elevation layer and one for the traversing layer. The tangent elevation is set manually by means of a hand-wheel, which actuates scales in the focus of the object lens of the periscopic sight. The gun is fired mechanically by means of a pedal located at the traversing layer's position.

The entire installation weighs 17,500 kg, which includes the 5,250 kg turret dome with its 70 mm of armour. The rate of fire is very high, but is limited by the speed of operation of the ammunition hoist: when operated manually only 15 of the 11·5 kg rounds can be lifted per minute.

Employment Sweden

Sectional view of the L/60 system, showing ammunition hoist and operators' positions just below turret.

88 mm coast defence gun Flak 36
Germany

Calibre	88 mm
Barrel length	56 calibres
Muzzle brake	Nil
Weight	5,100 kg
Ammunition	HE (44 kg)
	AP
	HVAP
Rate of fire	15–20 rds/min
Muzzle velocity	820 m/sec
Maximum range	14,860 m
Elevation limits	—
Traverse on carriage	—
Detachment	—

This is the famous Krupp anti-aircraft gun of World War II, now relegated to a coast defence role, and that only by Yugoslavia. It is fitted with a semi-automatic loading device which produces the high rate of fire. This feature, together with the 'follow-the-pointers' sights, is retained from the original anti-aircraft mounting and makes the gun especially effective against moving targets.

The guns are mounted in permanent fixed emplacements along the Adriatic coast.

Employment   Yugoslavia

---

130 mm coast defence gun
Union of Soviet Socialist Republics

Calibre	130 mm
Barrel length	55 calibres
Muzzle brake	Pepperpot
Weight	19,000 kg
Ammunition	HE (33·4 kg)
	APHE (33·6 kg)
Rate of fire	5–10 rds/min
Muzzle velocity	930 m/sec
Maximum range	27,000 m
Elevation limits	−5° +45°
Traverse on carriage	360°
Height on wheels	2·8 m
Detachment	—

This gun is thought to be the M 1936 naval gun mounted on a World War II German carriage. The gun's ancestry, muzzle velocity and shell weight are common to the M 1946 field gun, but the range quoted differs. It is also related to the 130 mm anti-aircraft gun M 55.

The elderly carriage of this coast defence version consists of a turntable platform mounted on four double road wheels; the wheels, axles, and tow bar are removed in action; these parts alone weigh 3,000 kg. The barrel, with the recoil mechanism beneath it, is mounted high on the carriage in a massive cradle. A large curved shield is fitted.

The quoted rate of fire is high for the size of the gun and suggests that loading may be automated or mechanically assisted. The loading system used for the 130 mm anti-aircraft gun would seem suitable.

Employment   Egypt
USSR

130 mm coast defence gun in its travelling position.

Glossary of artillery terms

This is intended as a guide to the non-specialist reader. The precision of many once exact terms has been eroded by popular usage; e.g. 'barrage' and 'shrapnel', while others have dropped out of use in an era in which elaborate fire-plans prepared in advance for attack or defence have become unfashionable; e.g. the true 'barrage' and 'counter-preparation'. American and English usages differ and may cause confusion; e.g. what the US artillery calls 'time fire' the British call 'air burst' (i.e. burst in the air with a time or VT fuze) and the British 'time, or timed, programme' is a schedule of fire coordinating the engagement of targets with the projected operations of other troops, usually in the attack, although there are, especially in the Soviet Army, elaborate defensive fire plans. Artillery tactics and design are technical subjects and naturally a technical jargon has grown up to describe them. Only those terms which will assist the ordinary reader to understand the art and in recognition of equipments have been included here.

Accuracy　Defined by size of zone or *CEP*. See also *Consistency*.

Adjust　Adjusting fire. See *Ranging*.

Aiming Circle (US)　See *Director*.

Aiming Point, Aiming Post　Natural reference point from which angles in azimuth of lines of fire are measured by dial sight. Aiming posts carried as part of gun stores are stuck in ground as an alternative method.

Ammunition　See under special headings: *Round* of, *Fixed, Semi-fixed, Separate, Shot, Shell*, etc.

Angle of Sight (US *Site*)　Angle line joining gun to target makes with horizontal.

Angular Measure　Sights graduated in the familiar degrees and minutes are now to be found only on obsolescent British equipments such as the 25 pdr. The artillery measure is the *Mil*, of which there are, confusingly, two sorts. The British and the Americans count 6,400 mils as equivalent to 360°. As well there is the 'Continental' mil which is used by the USSR and the WTO artilleries counting 6,000 mils to 360°. Mils are used not only for sight data but compass bearings and all survey and other calculations.

Armour Piercing (AP)　High explosive or kinetic energy solid shot. See under *HEAT, HESH, Discarding Sabot*.

Assault Gun　Hybrid weapon, tracked and armoured, and used as indirect fire weapons, anti-tank weapons or direct fire artillery weapons. They fall into the class of armoured fighting vehicle (AFV) as well as 'artillery'.

Auxiliary Propulsion Unit　Fitted on carriage to some tractor drawn equipments to facilitate movement without having to call up bulky tractor.

Balancing Springs　Used to restore balance of barrel and recoil gear assembly when trunnions cannot be placed at the centre of gravity.

Ballistics　Science of; concerned with events in bore of gun and also trajectory of *projectile* and its behaviour in flight.

Ballistic—for projectile in free flight as opposed to guided.

Barrage　Colloquially synonym for 'bombardment'. Originally standing belt of fire (see *Defensive Fire*) to halt attack. Now moving or rolling belt of fire used to cover advance or assault.

Barrel　Of gun, also '*piece*' (trad., but in British use) and '*tube*' (US).

Base Ejection　Of 'carrier' shells used, e.g. for delivering smoke canisters, in which a small charge blows off the base and ejects the filling.

Base Plate　Steel disc used to support breech end of mortar.

Battalion　Artillery unit formed by grouping batteries together (but in British usage this is a 'regiment').

Battery　Group of 4 or 6 guns with command post, signal communications etc. calibrated to shoot as one weapon.

Bearing Picket　Post or picket marking position from which survey can be initiated, from bearings to natural reference points and grid location provided.

Bomb　Projectile fired from mortar, from its shape, resembling aerial bomb.

Bomblet　Sub-munitions carried in warhead of shell or missile to obtain scattered effect (see *minelet*).

Breech-Loading　Also in British usage synonym for self-sealing.

Breech-Mechanism　If breech loading (BL), made up of cylindrical block with interrupted screw-threads to engage breech, gears or linkage and lever to open and shut it, lock containing firing mechanism, and means of obturation, or sealing breech to prevent escape of propellant gases. If quick-firing (QF) or cartridge-sealed may have block sliding vertically or horizontally in mortice cut in breech. Semi-automatic QF breeches open on recoil ejecting the spent cartridge case and so facilitate rapid reloading.

Buffer　See *Recoil gear*. Absorbs shock of discharge of gun slowly and so relieves strain on carriage and reduces violent backward recoil.

Burst rate of fire　Of field artillery. As opposed to sustained rate of fire. A very high rate of fire for a brief period whose aim is to inflict casualties before the target can move, disperse or go to cover.

Calibration　Determination of muzzle velocity of gun, which varies due to wear of bore from constant firing and other factors. Used to make guns 'shoot together' and in conformity with the map range.

Calibrating Sight Type of sight on which muzzle velocity is set on scales and applies an automatic correction to range.

Calibre Diameter of bore. The length of the barrel is sometimes expressed in multiples of the calibre.

Cannon Archaic, but sometimes still used as generic term for all 'tube' artillery.

Carriage The wheels, trail, axle, recoil gear etc. on which the 'piece', or barrel is mounted, in a tractor drawn equipment; see also *Self-propelled*.

Cartridge Made up of charge or charges of propellant explosive contained in bags for self-sealing breech mechanisms or in fixed or semi-fixed metal cartridge cases.

Case Shot Sometimes 'canister'. Cylindrical container of bullets which opens at muzzle. Used to obtain close range lethal effect against personnel. Obsolete, but a modern version containing steel flechettes has been considered for close defence of gun positions against infantry attack.

Circular Error, Probable (CEP) Area in which 50 per cent of projectiles fired are likely to fall. It should be noted that the flatter the trajectory the more this area becomes not circular but elliptical, see *Zone*.

Clinometer Used for measuring angles in vertical plane to lay for elevation.

Concentration Artillery concentration, concentration of fire. Fire of two or more batteries and on occasion of all batteries in range, brought down on one single target. Very short, intense bursts of fire from the maximum of guns appropriate to the target are the basis of current artillery tactics in the age of highly fluid armoured land warfare, and all technical development in *location, survey, calibration prediction, calibration meteor* and *communications* is directed to this end to make it as accurate as possible and with the shortest possible response time.

Consistency Cognate with *accuracy*. Degree and regularity with which gun performs as compared with its predicted ballistic characteristics.

Counter-Battery, -Bombardment Branch of gunnery concerned with suppression of hostile artillery fire.

Correction of the moment See *Meteor*.

Covering Fire Used to suppress or 'neutralise' fire of hostile weapons during attack.

Crew Of gun. The British use 'detachment'; comprising gun commander (NCO) layer or layers, loaders, fuze-setters, ammunition handlers.

Cross Observation Means of locating and engaging targets by observation from two or more surveyed posts. See *Flash-spotting*.

Defilade Concealed by lie of land from enemy observation to the front, but able to fire freely at targets to a flank. Usually of anti-tank guns.

Defensive Fire Belt of fire or concentration of fire, usually predicted, placed in path of attack.

Dial Sight Used to measure angles in azimuth for *indirect fire*.

Direct Fire, Laying Used when the target is visible from the gun position.

Director Also (US) *aiming circle*. Angle measuring instrument resembling theodolite used for laying out lines of fire and for artillery survey.

Discarding Sabot (APDS) Composite super high velocity anti-tank shot made up of sub-calibre dart or arrow of tungsten carbide or other very hard alloy and light annular metal segments—'sabots'—of size to fit bore which are discarded on emerging from muzzle.

Driving Band Soft metal (usually copper) fitted circumferentially to projectile to engage in *rifling* and so impart spin.

Drone Originally pilotless aircraft used as target for air defence artillery. Flies a pre-set course and is equipped with camera or sensors used for surveillance and target acquisition. A remotely piloted vehicle (RPV) has a similar role but is controlled throughout its flight.

Doppler Effect Apparent variation in frequency of electromagnetic radiation emitted or reflected from a moving object as measured by a stationary observer. Used to detect movement and for the measurement of muzzle velocities. (The same phenomena occurs acoustically; the pitch of the noise of an approaching vehicle being apparently higher and becoming lower as it recedes.)

Electronic Counter Measures (ECM) Also—Electronic Counter-Counter Measures (ECCM). Interference with the radar and radio-communications of weapons, creation of false targets etc. A complex, highly technical, highly classified activity. The general reader only requires to note that in principle any system which relies on transmissions in the electro-magnetic spectrum is vulnerable.

Elevation Angular movement of barrel in vertical plane to vary trajectory and so range. (Technical terms are 'quadrant' elevation, being sum of tangent elevation, the measure of range, and the angle of sight, being the elevation at which the gun is actually laid. The 'angle of projection' is the angle at which the projectile actually departs after aberrations due to 'jump', due to the shock of firing, and 'droop', the angular girder sag of the barrel from its point of support.)

Equilibrator Device fitted to restore balance to 'elevating mass' (i.e. barrel and recoil gear) when trunnions are not placed at centre of gravity.

Equipment (British usage) The whole weapon—gun, carriage, sights and associated gun stores such as ropes, tools etc.

Fin Stabilised Projectiles whose point-first flight attitude is determined by fins—fixed, as in mortar-bombs, or deploying immediately leaving the bore, as for some projectiles fired from smooth-bore guns. As opposed to spin imparted by rifling in the bore. (Note that some guns can fire unrotating fin-stabilised projectiles from a rifled bore, e.g. the Soviet 122 mm using a slipping driving band.)

Fire Plan Pre-planned use of artillery fire, usually based on a timed programme, if for an attack, coordinating all artillery fire with phases of an operation. (As opposed to engagement of targets of opportunity acquired by forward observers or surveillance devices.)

Fixed Ammunition In which the metal cartridge case is fixed to the shell or shot for ease of loading, hence 'quickfiring' for this type of gun.

Flash Spotting   Method of locating guns by cross observation on flash of discharge.

Fragmentation   Breaking up of the wall of an HE shell to provide fragments or splinters travelling at lethal speeds (colloquially but inaccurately 'shrapnel').

Fuze   Device fitted to shell to explode HE filling on impact, or after delay so as to explode inside armour or concrete or earth emplacement, or operating by time or electronically at chosen point on trajectory.

'Grid'   Arbitrary rectangular coordinate markings on map usually at 1 km spacing orientated north–south and east–west used for describing locations. See *Survey.* Basic firing data can be calculated rapidly from the grid positions of guns and targets.

Gun   Used as generic term for all 'tube' artillery, also for actual *tube*, or *barrel*, or '*piece*'. Specifically and technically a long, high velocity weapon, as compared with a *howitzer*.

Gun-howitzer   (Obsolete term) Weapon combining the characteristics of gun and howitzer, i.e. long range and high velocity at top charge and ability to vary charges and trajectories so as to obtain steep angles of projection and descent. In this sense most modern field artillery equipments are 'gun-hows'.

Guidance   In the artillery field guided missiles include a wide variety of systems from large long range missiles used to deliver battlefield nuclear warheads to air defence missiles and anti-tank missiles. They can be divided broadly into missiles which fly and require a continuous flow of corrections and those which follow a free or ballistic trajectory receiving a *mid-course* correction, or which become fully guided in the vicinity of the target: 'Terminal Guidance'. Missiles can also be distinguished by the system employed, and the degree of automatic control. In some the correctional data are provided by an outside agency which 'tells' the missile where to go; in others the system is carried on board. (A fully automated on-board system, of course, destroys a set of expensive apparatus for every firing.) Some missiles combine two systems, e.g. using command guidance or inertial guidance to approach the target's vicinity and then changing to a homing system.

Beam rider   Target is followed by a beam, e.g. laser and guidance system measures deviation of missile course from signal received.

Command guidance   An outside source using a radar and computer monitors target and missile course and transmits course corrections.

Inertial guidance   Based on accelerometers, as used in navigational devices. Immune to ECM.

Active Homing   On-board system transmits radiation and homes on reflection from target.

Semi-Active Homer   External transmitter radiates and missile homes on reflections.

Passive Homer   Homes on natural radiation from the target, e.g. infra-red from hot jet efflux.

Laser Guidance   Same as semi-active, but the narrow coherent laser beam can be used to pick out a specific target.

Electro-Optical   Not used so far for artillery but basically observes image of the target and persists in course which keeps target picture or pattern in view.

Semi-Automatic Command to the Line of Sight   Used in anti-tank guided weapons, e.g. TOW, and means that operator has only to keep sight on target and course corrections will automatically follow (as distinct from 'command guidance', in which the operator steers the missile so as to hit the target).

'Fire and Forget'   Colloquial term for active or passive homing all-the-way device.

'Wire Guided'   Not a guidance system but method of transferring a course correction to missile; e.g. TOW, HOT, Swingfire. The missile reels out a wire for the transmission of correctional signals which remains connected to the tracker sight.

Harassing Fire   Used to interrupt movement, HQ or administrative area arrangements in rear areas, or to lower morale.

Handspikes   Long, wooden, usually iron-shod levers used either fitted into sockets on trail to enable several men to lift it, or under trail to move trail laterally for big switches.

HEAT   High explosive anti-tank shell, with hollow-charge HE filling.

HESH   High explosive squash head anti-tank shell: Designed to open on impact placing flattened HE filling against armour plate and detonate, the subsequent shock-wave blowing off lethal fragments from inside of the armour.

High Angle Fire   Using angles of projection between 45°–80°.

High Explosive   (As opposed to relatively slow burning propellant explosives which can be harnessed to provide thrust for a projectile in bore of gun, or for rocket.) So called *brisant* compounds producing violent shock waves capable of shattering shell walls, damaging structures, etc. based on e.g. picric acid, tri-nitro-toluene mixed with additives.

Hollow Charge   Or 'shaped' charge, usually cylindrical with concave end which on detonation focuses the explosive effect, driving jet of hot gas of great penetrating power through armour or concrete.

Howitzer   Specifically a short, large calibre weapon firing a heavy shell (as compared with a gun of the same order or size) at muzzle velocities varied by increasing or decreasing the propellant charge and so at varying trajectories suited to the terrain and mission with usually steep angles of projection and of descent.

Indirect Fire   From concealed gun whose layers cannot see the target; by applying firing data on the orders of a remotely sited observer or, if 'predicted', calculated in the command post.

Infra-Red   Radiation from part of electromagnetic spectrum below the visible red band used for tracking some anti-tank-guided missiles, for some night vision and surveillance devices and for passive homing by some missiles.

Interdiction Loose term used to describe fire (see also harassing fire) to deny or inhibit use of area, e.g. route or defile, to enemy, or to take toll of echelons following leading assault troops.

Jacks Fitted to some field artillery carriages so as to raise wheels off the ground to promote stability and in air defence equipments also to level the carriage for firing.

Kinetic Energy Of e.g. shot or fragments, striking force due to motion, measured by multiplying mass by square of velocity at impact.

Laser Acronym from *Light Amplification by Stimulated Emission of Radiation*. Intense parallel beams of light or infra-red radiation of coherent wave-length obtained by applying energy to device called 'laser' used for guidance, range-finding. (Reputedly under development is use of laser beams to attack targets directly, but the technical obstacles are formidable.)

Laying Artillery term for aiming, having applied all data to sights. Direct laying is by sighting telescope. Indirect laying is, in azimuth, by a periscopic optical sight graduated for angular measure using an agreed aiming point or reference object and in elevation by reference to the horizontal plane supplied by spirit levels set along the line of sight and at right angles to it.

Lead Angular correction applied to sights required to hit moving target.

Limber (US 'Caisson') Two-wheeled vehicle with hook to take eye on trail and so convert gun carriage to 4-wheeled vehicle, with 'perch' and with eye to connect with hook on tractor. (Obsolete.) Carried some ready-use ammunition and gun-stores.

Location, -ing Branch of surveillance concerned with locating targets especially guns and mortars with sufficient accuracy to enable fire to be applied.

Lock Firing device, incorporated in breech mechanism. May be percussion mechanism manually operated to set off primer in metal cartridge case or tube, or electrical.

Mean Point of Impact (**MPI**) Centre of *zone* or *CEP*.

'Meteor' Abbr. of 'meteorological correction of the moment'. Data essential for predicted fire, e.g. air temperature and wind speeds and directions at various altitudes, barometric pressure.

Mil See *Angular Measure*.

Minelet Anti-tank, or anti-personnel delivered by shell or missile war-head. Also 'remotely delivered mines' (RDM).

Missile Used loosely for both free-flight or 'ballistic' rockets, i.e. those following a ballistic path, and also for guided weapons. E.g. SAM for surface-to-air missile, but (British) anti-tank guided weapon (ATGW) or surface-to-air guided weapon (SAGW).

Mortar Usually muzzle-loading smooth bore artillery equipment using high angle fire only. (Note: Usually mobile, light or medium equipments and simple to operate, but some are heavy and may have rifling and breech loading.)

Muzzle Brake Device using energy of gas from propellant explosion to check or mitigate recoil.

Muzzle Velocity Knowledge of essential for correct adjustment of sights to enable guns to shoot true to map and in harmony with other guns. Ascertained by measurement of wear in bore, number of equivalent full charges fired, observation of fall of shot on measured range, firing through timing screens, by photographing shell in flight and in the most modern method by electronic devices using *doppler* principle giving instant automatic read-out.

Observed Fire Indirect fire controlled by eye from a forward observation post and corrected by the fall of shot by ranging or adjusting. Given well-trained, tactically alert observers with delegated powers (so that they do not have to refer back for permission to shoot) still the most effective system for emergencies and fluid operations. It is simple and remains standard for mortar fire control.

Obturator, -ion Part of breech mechanism which prevents the escape of gas to the rear. In QF, or cartridge-sealed guns, the metal cartridge acts as an obturator. In self-sealing guns an asbestos pad is squeezed by the propellant gases to expand round the circumference of the breech face and so seals it.

Piece Archaic, but still in British use; pedantically, for 'barrel' or 'gun'.

Platform Generally, levelled or level site on which equipment is deployed in firing position. Specifically, circular metal platform on which road wheels of a towed field equipment can be placed to facilitate rapid traverse; the carriage being anchored to the platform by tie-rods and so obviating the use of trail-spades which have to be dug out laboriously once embedded if a large switch is ordered.

Predicted Fire Fire brought down by calculation without preliminary ranging. If predicted fire can be brought down accurately and quickly it has great advantages over observed adjusted fire because of its surprise effect; it is also economical of artillery ammunition. It is therefore becoming increasingly the normal method of engagement, and sophisticated equipment for range-finding, survey, meteor and computerised calculation and data storage to accomplish it is in service or under development.

Projectile Term embracing all shot or shell fired from a gun.

Propellant Relatively slow burning explosive, usually cordite, used to propel shell and some solid fuel rockets. In some missiles a solid propellant is used but in some of the more sophisticated and larger ones liquid propellants, which are combinations of fuels and oxidising agents.

Ranging To ascertain range and bearing of target by observing trial shots, after obtaining rough data from map. See *Adjust, Register*.

Recoil Gear Spring, but more usually air/hydraulic, made up of *buffer* to absorb recoil and *recuperator* to run gun barrel out to correct firing position.

Recoilless Guns whose recoil is exactly counteracted by releasing proportion of propellant gases rearwards through vents in specially designed breech.

Recuperator Part of recoil gear which stores energy of recoil and runs barrel out to firing position ready for next round.

Register To check firing data to targets by trials shots or by survey methods in preparation for opening fire later.

Rifling Spiral grooves cut in bore of gun to grip driving band of shell and impart rotation.

Rocket, -Propulsion, -Assisted Propulsion achieved by the reaction from propellant gases vented from the rear of a missile. The propellant may be either solid or liquid. Some mortar-bombs and shells are rocket assisted; i.e. initiated from a gun and then boosted in flight by a rocket. Range can thus be extended without the need for a longer and heavier equipment, but at the cost of a rather more costly and complicated projectile, with a reduced explosive filling.

Rocking Bar Basic sighting system by which the sight bracket is tilted forward by the desired elevation and brought back to the horizontal by elevating the gun-barrel which then has the correct quadrant elevation.

Round Of ammunition, comprising projectile, cart-ridge and fuze, which last may be ready fixed in shell or provided separately so as to permit fuze appropriate to mission to be fitted before loading.

Saddle Part of gun carriage, on which barrel/recoil assembly rests and in turn rests on trail axle assembly.

Self-propelled Weapon system usually mounted on tracked, armoured carriage, often resembling tank but distinguished from it by virtue of the fact that it is not primarily designed for close combat or offensive use, except SP anti-tank guns. See *Assault guns.*

Shell Hollow cylindrical projectile with ogival pointed nose—container for HE, smoke canisters, minelets, bomblets or smoke producing or toxic chemicals.

Shield Steel plate fitted on the lighter towed equip-ments to protect crew from small arms fire and shell-fragments from front.

Shot Solid projectile for armour piercing. Either shell-shaped or a very thin lance or dart shape; made of toughened steel or very hard alloy.

Shrapnel Obsolete anti-personnel weapon consisting of lead bullets released by air-burst shell. Colloquially, lethal fragments from case of HE shell. Modern technical term is 'pre-formed, fragmented' (PFF) designed for use against either armour or personnel.

Soft-Recoil Experimental device by which recoil forces are absorbed by coinciding firing with run-out.

Sound Ranging Method of locating guns by recording time intervals of arrival of sound waves from shock of discharge at an array of special microphones in surveyed positions.

Spade, Trail-spade Fitted at end of trail to embed on recoil of carriage and prevent further rearward movement. See *Platform,* which also grips soil and prevents rearward movement of carriage in firing but leaves trail free to move in azimuth.

Split Function Laying In some equipments the task of laying for azimuth or 'line' and for elevation are divided between two layers.

Spotting Rifle Small calibre rifle fitted to some anti-tank equipments to obtain correct range inconspicuously.

Surveillance Used generally of devices or agencies whose role is to scan hostile territory and provide tactical and target information. See *Location.*

Survey Process of relating guns, observation posts and targets to the map grid, essential for predicted fire or for concentrating fire of separated batteries. (Note that a preliminary fix by ordinary map-reading methods by eye and compass provides an instant rough fix enabling observed fire to open from the moment of deployment.)

Switch To alter the line of fire in azimuth.

Target Acquisition Self-explanatory jargon term usually applied to detection, selection and engagement of targets; originally in air defence, now generally.

Trajectory Ballistic path of projectile. In a vacuum a parabola; in practice due to air resistance and loss of velocity it is asymmetrical, with the angle of descent much steeper than the angle of projection. (Note: the height of the vertex of the trajectory in feet is four times the square of the time of flight so that even with a field howitzer at a moderate range and a time of flight of 30 seconds this can be 3,600 feet; which emphasises the need for correct meteor data at all altitudes of ballistic interest, and also the risk to low-flying aircraft.)

Trail Long member by which gun-carriage is towed when moving. In action rests on ground forming three point base with road wheels.

Pole trail Single hollow metal tube.

Box trail Two long and two short members enabling the breech to be depressed at high elevation between the two long members.

Split trail Double trail each with spade hinged forward to open out on deployment, so enabling the gun barrel a wide angle of traverse without the need to break out the spades and move the trail and carriage.

Note: Some equipments, e.g. air defence, and the Soviet 122 mm, have instead of trails, members which on deployment provide a cruciform or other shaped base, levelled by jacks, which permit all-round traverse.

Traverse To move or 'switch' the gun relative to the carriage in azimuth—'top traverse'—or movement of the whole carriage in azimuth.

Traversing lever Metal extension at end of trail to facilitate traverse.

Trunnions Horizontal cylindrical projections from the barrel/recoil gear assembly riding in trunnion bearings permitting elevation.

Tube Synonym for piece, gun or barrel (US); tubular lining of gun permitting worn rifling to be easily changed in action; tube with firing compound used in lock of breech loading guns to initiate explosion of propellant charge.

Weapon System A comprehensive term meaning more than mere 'weapon'. The system comprises the gun, or launcher, the missile or the technical fire control system, the command system and the communications linking the various parts.

Zone Of gun. See 'CEP'. Pattern described by large number of successive shots from gun.

Artillery weapons in service in each country

(Brackets denote equipment shortly to be in service)

| COUNTRY | FIELD GUNS AND HOWITZERS | | | MORTARS | SURFACE-TO-SURFACE MISSILES |
	LIGHT	MEDIUM	HEAVY		
Afghanistan	76 mm M 1942	122 mm M 1937 152 mm ML 20		120 mm M 1943 160 mm M 43	122 mm BM 21
Albania	76 mm M 1942	122 mm M 1937/8 152 mm ML 20 and D 1	203 mm M 1955	120 mm M 1943 160 mm M 43	
Algeria	85 mm M 52	122 mm M 1937/8 152 mm ML 20		120 mm M 1943 240 mm M 53	140 mm BM 14 240 mm BM 24 400 mm FROG 4
Argentina	105 mm M 18/40 105 mm Pack How 105 mm M 101 A1	155 mm M 2 155 mm M 114 A1 155 mm SP Mk 3		120 mm MO-120-60	
Australia	25 pdr 105 mm Pack How 105 mm M 101 A1	5·5 inch			
Austria	85 mm M 52 105 mm M 18/40 105 mm Pack How 105 mm M 101 A1	155 mm M 2 155 mm M 114 A1 155 mm M 109		107 mm M 30 120 mm M 1943	128 mm M 51
Bangladesh	105 mm Pack How 105 mm M 101 A1 25 pdr			120 mm M 1938	
Belgium	105 mm Pack How 105 mm M 101 A1 105 mm SP M 108	155 mm M 114 A1 155 mm M 44 155 mm M 109	8 inch M 115 8 inch SP M 110		762 mm Honest John 557 mm Lance
Bolivia	75 mm M 116 105 mm M 101 A1			107 mm M 30	
Brazil	75 mm M 116 105 mm M 101 A1 105 mm SP M 52	155 mm M 114 A1			80 mm 108-R 114 mm
Bulgaria	76 mm M 1942	122 mm M 1937/8 122 mm D 74 130 mm M 1946 152 mm ML 20	203 mm M 1955	120 mm M 1943 240 mm M 53	128 mm M 51 600 mm FROG 7 850 mm SCUD-A
Burma	76 mm M 48 B1 25 pdr	5·5 inch		120 mm UBM 52	
Canada	105 mm Pack How 105 mm M 101 A1	155 mm M 109			

ANTI-TANK			AIR DEFENCE	
GUNS	**RECOILLESS RIFLES**	**GUIDED WEAPONS**	**GUNS**	**MISSILES**
100 mm M 1944			37 mm M 1939 57 mm M 1950 85 mm M 1944 100 mm KS 19	SA-2 (Air Force)
45 mm M 1942 57 mm M 1943 and 1955 85 mm M 1945 85 mm SD 44 SU 76			37 mm M 1939 57 mm M 1950 85 mm M 1944	SA-2 (Air Force)
85 mm M 1945 SU 100 JSU 152		Sagger	37 mm M 1939 100 mm KS 19	
	106 mm M 40 A1	SS 11	30 mm (unidentified) 40 mm L 60	Tigercat
	106 mm M 40 A1 120 mm Wombat		40 mm L 70	Redeye Bloodhound 2 (Air Force)
85 mm M 52 105 mm K	106 mm M 40 A1		20 mm GA 1–BO 1 Twin 35 mm K 63 40 mm L 60 40 mm L 70 Twin 40 mm SP M 42	
6 pdr				
90 mm JPZ 4-5		Swingfire SS-11	Twin 35 mm Gepard 57 mm M 54	Hawk Nike Hercules (Air Force)
6 pdr	106 mm M 40 A1		40 mm L 60	Hawk
45 mm M 1942 57 mm M 1943 85 mm M 1945 85 mm SD44 100 mm M 1944 and 1955 SU 100	82 mm B 10 107 mm B11	Sagger	ZSU 23-4 37 mm M 1939 57 mm M 1950 85 mm M 1944 100 mm KS 19	SA-7 SA-2 (Air Force) SA-3 (Air Force) SA-6 (Air Force)
6 pdr 17 pdr			40 mm L 60 3·7 inch	
	106 mm M 40 A1	SS-11 Tow	40 mm L 70	Blowpipe

Artillery weapons in service in each country

| COUNTRY | FIELD GUNS AND HOWITZERS | | | MORTARS | SURFACE-TO-SURFACE MISSILES |
	LIGHT	MEDIUM	HEAVY		
Chile	105 mm Pack How 105 mm M 18/40 105 mm M 101 A1				
China	75 mm Type 94 75 mm M 116 76 mm M 1942 85 mm Type 56	122 mm M 1938 (Type 54) 122 mm D 74 130 mm M 1946 152 mm ML 20 and D 1	203 mm M 1955	107 mm M 1938 120 mm M 1943 160 mm M 43 160 mm M 53	107 mm (Type 63) 128 mm M 51 140 mm BM 14
Colombia	105 mm M 101 A1				
Congo	75 mm M 116	122 mm M 1937		120 mm M 1943	
Cuba	75 mm M 116 76 mm M 1942 105 mm M 101 A1	122 mm M 1937/38 122 mm D 74 and D 30 130 mm M 1946 152 mm ML 20 and D 20			400 mm FROG 4
Czechoslovakia	76 mm M 1942 85 mm M 52 105 mm M 18/40	122 mm M 1938 122 mm D 30 152 mm M 18/46 152 mm ML 20	203 mm M 1955	120 mm M 1943 160 mm M 43	122 mm BM 21 (M 1972) 128 mm M 51 140 mm BM 14 600 mm FROG 7 850 mm SCUD-A
Denmark	105 mm M 101 A1	155 mm M 2 155 mm M 114 A1 155 mm M 109	8 inch M 115		762 mm Honest John
Equador	105 mm M 101 A1	155 mm SP M 44			
Egypt	76 mm M 1942 25 pdr	122 mm M 1937/8 122 mm D 74 and D 30 130 mm M 1946 152 mm ML 20 and D 1	203 mm M 1955	120 mm M 1943 160 mm M 43 160 mm M 53	122 mm BM 21 128 mm M 51 140 mm BM 14 240 mm BM 24 600 mm FROG 7 850 mm SCUD-A
Eire	25 pdr 105 mm Pack How			120 mm M 41 C	
Ethiopia	75 mm M 116 105 mm M 101 A	155 mm M 2		107 mm M 1938 4·2 inch	
Finland	105 mm M 61/37	122 mm Tampella M 60 122 mm M 1938 122 mm D 30 130 mm M 1946 152 mm M 10 155 mm M 68		120 mm M 65 120 mm Light Tampella 160 mm Tampella	

ANTI-TANK			AIR DEFENCE	
GUNS	**RECOILLESS RIFLES**	**GUIDED WEAPONS**	**GUNS**	**MISSILES**
	106 mm M 40 A1			
45 mm M 1942 57 mm M 1943 75 mm Type 56 85 mm M 1945 100 mm M 1944 and 1955 SU 76 SU 100	82 mm B 10 107 mm B 11		37 mm M 1939 57 mm M 1950 85 mm M 1944 100 mm KS 19	
57 mm M 1943 100 mm M 1944			37 mm M 1939 57 mm M 1950	
57 mm M 1943 and 1955 85 mm M 1945 85 mm SD 44 SU 100			30 mm M 53/59 37 mm M 1939 57 mm M 57 85 mm M 1944 100 mm KS 19	SA-2 (Air Force)
57 mm M 1943 and 1955 85 mm M 52 85 mm SD 44 100 mm M 1955 ASU 57 SU 100 JSU 152	82 mm M 59 A 82 mm T 21	Sagger Swatter	ZSU 23-4 30 mm M 53/59 37 mm M 1939 57 mm M 1950 85 mm M 1944 ZSU 57-2	SA-7 SA-2 (Air Force) SA-3 (Air Force) SA-6 (Air Force)
	106 mm M 40 A1	Tow		Redeye Hawk (Air Force) Nike Hercules (Air Force)
			40 mm L 60	
6 pdr 57 mm M 1943 17 pdr 85 mm M 1945 100 mm M 1944 and 1955 SU 100 JSU 152	82 mm M 59 A 82 mm B 10 107 mm B 11	Sagger Swatter	Twin 23 mm ZSU 23-4 ZSU 57-2 37 mm M 1939 40 mm L 60 57 mm M 1950 85 mm M 1944 100 mm KS 19	SA-7 SA-9 SA-2 SA-3 SA-6
	90 mm PV 1110		40 mm L 60	
	95 mm M 58	SS-11	ZSU 23-4 ZSU 57-2 Twin 35 mm K 63 40 mm L 60	

COUNTRY	FIELD GUNS AND HOWITZERS			MORTARS	SURFACE-TO-SURFACE MISSILES
	LIGHT	MEDIUM	HEAVY		

France	105 mm Pack How
	105 mm Light Gun
	105 mm M 101 A1
	105 mm SPAMX
	  105/50
		155 mm SP Mk 3
		155 mm SPGCT
		155 mm M 50
				120 mm MO-120-
				  AM 50
				120 mm MO-120-
				  60
				120 mm MO-120-
				  M 65
				120 mm MO-120-
				  RT-61
					762 mm Honest
					  John
					650 mm Pluton
					(140 mm RAP 14)
					(145 mm
					  RAFALE)

East Germany	76 mm M 1942	122 mm M 1938
		122 mm D 74 and
		  D 30
		130 mm M 1946
		152 mm D 1 and
		  D 20
			203 mm M 1955	107 mm M 1938
				120 mm M 1943
				160 mm M 43
					122 mm BM 21
					140 mm BM 14
					240 mm BM 24
					600 mm FROG 7
					850 mm SCUD-A
					  and -B

West Germany	105 mm (L)
	105 mm Pack How
	105 mm M 101 A1
		155 mm M 114 A1
		155 mm M 109 G
		(155 mm FH 70)
		(155 mm SP 70)
			175 mm SP
			  M 107
			8 inch SP
			  M 110
				120 mm M 65	110 mm Lars
					762 mm Honest
					  John
					557 mm Lance
					790 mm Sergeant
					1,000 mm
					  Pershing (Air
					  Force)

Greece	25 pdr 105 mm M 101 A1	155 mm M 2 155 mm M 114 A1	175 mm SP M 107 8 inch M 115		762 mm Honest John
Hungary	76 mm M 1942	122 mm M 1937/8 122 mm D 74 and D 30	203 mm M 1955	120 mm M 53 160 mm M 53	122 mm BM 21 140 mm BM 14 600 mm FROG 7 850 mm SCUD-A
India	75 mm M 116 76 mm M 1942 25 pdr 105 mm Pack How 105 mm Abbot	130 mm M 1946 5·5 inch 152 mm D 20	8 inch M 115	107 mm M 1938 120 mm M 43 160 mm M 53	
Indonesia	76 mm M 1942 25 pdr 105 mm M 101 A1	122 mm M 1937			
Iran	75 mm M 116 105 mm M 101 A1	130 mm M 1946 155 mm M 114 A1 155 mm M 109	175 mm SP M 107 8 inch M 115 8 inch SP M 110		122 mm BM 21
Iraq	75 mm M 1942	122 mm M 1938 130 mm M 1946 5·5 inch		120 mm M 1943 160 mm M 53	600 mm FROG 7 850 mm SCUD-A

ANTI-TANK			AIR DEFENCE	
GUNS	RECOILLESS RIFLES	GUIDED WEAPONS	GUNS	MISSILES

	106 mm M 40 A1	SS-11
		SS-12
		(Hot)
			Twin 20 mm SP
			  M 3/VDA
			Twin 30 mm
			  SP AMX DCA-30
			40 mm L 70
				(Roland)
				Hawk

57 mm M 1943 and 1955 ASU 85 85 mm M 52 85 mm M 1945 and SD 44 100 mm M 1955 SU 100	82 mm B 10 107 mm B 11	Sagger Swatter	Twin 23 mm 37 mm M 1939 57 mm M 1950 85 mm M 1944 100 mm KS 19 ZSU 23-4	SA-7 SA-2 (Air Force) SA-3 (Air Force) SA-6 (Air Force)
90 mm SP 90 mm JPZ 4-5	106 mm M 40 A1	SS-11 Tow	20 mm RH 202 Twin 35 mm Gepard Twin 40 mm SP M 42	(Roland) Hawk (Air Force) Nike Hercules (Air Force)
	106 mm M 40 A1	Tow	40 mm L 60	Hawk Nike Hercules
57 mm M 1943 and 1955 85 mm M 1945 85 mm SD 44	82 mm B 10 107 mm B 11	Sagger Swatter	ZSU 23-4 57 mm M 1950 ZSU 57-2 85 mm M 1944 100 mm KS 19	SA-7 SA-2 (Air Force) SA-3 (Air Force) SA-6 (Air Force)
6 pdr 100 mm M 1944 and 1955	106 mm M 40 A1	SS-11	ZSU 23-4 30 mm M 53 40 mm L 60 40 mm L 70 3·7 inch	Tigercat SA-2 (Air Force)
57 mm M 1943			Twin 23 mm 40 mm L 60 57 mm M 1950	
85 mm M 1945	106 mm M 40 A1	Tow SS-11	ZSU 23-4 40 mm L 70 57 mm M 1950 ZSU 57-2 85 mm M 1944	Hawk (Air Force) Rapier (Air Force) Tigercat (Air Force)
85 mm M 1945 100 mm M 1955 SU 100 JSU 152			Twin 23 mm 30 mm M 53 57 mm M 1950 85 mm M 1944 100 mm KS 19	SA-7 (Air Force) SA-2 (Air Force) SA-3 (Air Force) SA-6 (Air Force)

Artillery weapons in service in each country

| COUNTRY | FIELD GUNS AND HOWITZERS | | | MORTARS | SURFACE-TO-SURFACE MISSILES |
	LIGHT	MEDIUM	HEAVY		
Israel	105 mm M 101 A1 25 pdr	122 mm D 74 and D 30 130 mm M 1946 155 mm M 114 A1 and M 68 155 mm L 33 155 mm SP M 109	175 mm SP M 107 8 inch SP M 110	120 mm M 65 120 mm Light Tampella 160 mm Tampella	240 mm BM 24 Wolf 557 mm Lance MD 660
Italy	105 mm Pack How 105 mm M 101 A1	155 mm M 2 155 mm M 114 A1 (155 mm FH 70) 155 mm SP M 109 (155 mm SP 70)	175 mm SP M 107 8 inch M 115 8 inch SP M 110	107 mm M 30	557 mm Lance 76 mm Samurai 82 mm Attila 2 108 mm Mira 158 mm BR 51 GS
Japan	75 mm M 116 105 mm M 101 A1 105 mm SP M 52	155 mm M 2 155 mm M 114 A1 155 mm M 44	8 inch M 115	107 mm M 30	194 mm Bora
Jordan	25 pdr 105 mm M 101 A1 105 mm SP M 52	155 mm M 2 155 mm M 114 A1	8 inch M 115	107 mm M 1938 120 mm M 1938	
North Korea	76 mm M 1942	122 mm M 1937/8 130 mm M 1946 152 mm ML 20		107 mm M 1938 120 mm M 1943 160 mm M 43 200 mm BMD 20	600 mm FROG 7
South Korea	105 mm M 101 A1	155 mm M 2 155 mm M 114 A1	8 inch M 115	107 mm M 30	762 mm Honest John
Kuwait	25 pdr	155 mm M 2			
Laos	75 mm M 1897 75 mm M 116 105 mm M 101 A1	155 mm M 114 A1		4·2 inch	
Lebanon	75 mm M 116	122 mm M 1937 155 mm M 114 A1		120 mm M 1938	
Libya	105 mm M 101 A1 105 mm SP Abbot	122 mm M 1937 155 mm M 114 A1 155 mm SP M 109			
Malaysia	25 pdr 105 mm Pack How	5·5 inch		4·2 inch	
Mexico	75 mm M 1897 105 mm M 101 A1				
Mongolia		130 mm M 1946 152 mm ML 20			
Morocco	75 mm M 1897 105 mm AMX 105/50 76 mm M 116 105 mm M 101 A1			120 mm M 1938	

ANTI-TANK			AIR DEFENCE	
GUNS	**RECOILLESS RIFLES**	**GUIDED WEAPONS**	**GUNS**	**MISSILES**
6 pdr 17 pdr	106 mm M 40 A1	Tow SS-11 Sagger (Hot)	20 mm Vulcan 30 mm (unidentified) 40 mm L 60	Redeye Chaparral Hawk
	106 mm M 40 A1	SS-11 Tow	30 mm (unidentified) 40 mm L 70 40 mm SP M 42	(Indigo) Hawk Nike Hercules (Air Force)
	106 mm M 40 A1 106 mm SP Type 60		Twin 35 mm K 63 40 mm L 70	Hawk Nike Hercules (Air Force)
	106 mm M 40 A1 120 mm Mobat	Tow	40 mm L 60	
45 mm M 1942 57 mm M 1943 85 mm M 1945 100 mm M 1944 and 1955 SU 76 SU 100	82 mm B 10 107 mm B 11		37 mm M 1939 57 mm M 1950 ZSU 57-2 85 mm M 1944	SA-2
	106 mm M 40 A1			Hawk Nike Hercules
		SS-11		Hawk (Air Force)
85 mm M 1945	107 mm B 11		37 mm M 1939	
		SS-11 Tow	20 mm (unidentified) 30 mm M 53 40 mm L 60 Twin 40 mm SP M 42	
			Twin 23 mm 57 mm M 1950 40 mm L 60	Crotale SA-2 (Air Force) SA-3 (Air Force) SA-6 (Air Force)
6 pdr	120 mm Mobat		40 mm L 60 3·7 inch	
100 mm M 1944 and 1955 SU 100			37 mm M 1939 57 mm M 1950	SA-2 (Air Force)
85 mm M 1945 SU 100	106 mm M 40 A1		37 mm M 1939 100 mm KS 19	

| COUNTRY | FIELD GUNS AND HOWITZERS | | | MORTARS | SURFACE-TO-SURFACE MISSILES |
	LIGHT	MEDIUM	HEAVY		
Nepal	75 mm M 116			4·2 inch	

Netherlands	105 mm M 101 A1
	105 mm SP
	  AMX 105/50
		155 mm M 114 A1
		155 mm M 2
		155 mm SP M 109
			175 mm SP
			  M 107
			8 inch M 115
			8 inch SP M 110
				107 mm M 1938	762 mm Honest
					  John
					537 mm Lance

New Zealand	25 pdr 105 mm Pack How	5·5 inch			
Nigeria	76 mm M 1942 25 pdr 105 mm Pack How	122 mm D 74 and D 30 130 mm M 1946			
Norway	105 mm M 18/39 105 mm M 101 A1	155 mm SP M 109			
Oman	75 mm M 116 25 pdr	5·5 inch			
Pakistan	75 mm M 116 25 pdr 105 mm Pack How 105 mm M 101 A1	122 mm M 1937 130 mm M 1946 5·5 inch 155 mm M 2 155 mm M 114 A1		107 mm M 1938 120 mm M 1943	
Paraguay	75 mm M 116 105 mm M 101 A1				
Peru	105 mm M 101 A1	122 mm M 1937 152 mm ML 20 155 mm M 114 A1			
Philippines	105 mm M 101 A1	155 mm M 114 A1		107 mm M 30	

Poland	76 mm M 1942	122 mm M 1937/8
		122 mm D 74 and
		  D 30
		130 mm M 1946
		152 mm ML 20,
		  D 1 and D 20
			203 mm M 1955	107 mm M 1938	122 mm BM 21
					140 mm BM 14
					240 mm BM 24
					600 mm FROG 7
					850 mm SCUD-A

Portugal	25 pdr 105 mm M 18/40 105 mm M 101 A1	5·5 inch 155 mm M 114 A1			
Rumania	76 mm M 1942	122 mm M 1937/8 122 mm D 74 152 mm D 20	203 mm M 1955	120 mm M 1943	128 mm M 51 140 mm BM 14 600 mm FROG 7 850 mm SCUD-A
Saudia Arabia	105 mm Pack How 105 mm M 102				

| ANTI-TANK | | | AIR DEFENCE | |
GUNS	RECOILLESS RIFLES	GUIDED WEAPONS	GUNS	MISSILES
			40 mm L 60	
	106 mm M 40 A1	Tow	40 mm L 70 Twin 35 mm Gepard	Hawk (Air Force) Nike Hercules (Air Force)
	106 mm M 40 A1 120 mm Mobat			
			20 mm (unidentified) 40 mm L 60	
	106 mm M 40 A1	Tow	20 mm RH 202 40 mm L 60 40 mm L 70 (Air Force)	Nike Hercules (Air Force) (Roland)
		Tow		(Rapier) (Air Force)
6 pdr 17 pdr 100 mm M 1944	82 mm B 10 106 mm M 40 A1		Twin 23 mm 30 mm (unidentified) 37 mm M 1939 40 mm L 60 57 mm M 1950 3·7 inch	
	106 mm M 40 A1			
57 mm M 1943 85 mm M 1945 85 mm SD 44 100 mm M 1944 and 1955 ASU 57 SU 100 JSU 122 ASU 85	82 mm B 10	Sagger Swatter	ZSU 23-4 57 mm M 1950 85 mm M 1944 100 mm KS 19 ZSU 57-2	SA-7 SA-2 (Air Force) SA-3 (Air Force) SA-6 (Air Force)
	106 mm M 40 A1		40 mm (unidentified)	
45 mm M 1942 57 mm M 1943 and 1955 85 mm M 1945 85 mm SD 44 100 mm M 1944 and 1955 SU 100 JSU 122		Sagger Swatter	30 mm (unidentified) 37 mm M 1939 57 mm M 1950 100 mm KS 19	SA-7 SA-2 (Air Force) SA-3 (Air Force) SA-6 (Air Force)
		SS-11	Twin 40 mm SP M 42	Crotale Hawk (Rapier)

| COUNTRY | FIELD GUNS AND HOWITZERS | | | MORTARS | SURFACE-TO-SURFACE MISSILES |
	LIGHT	MEDIUM	HEAVY		
Singapore	25 pdr 25 pdr SP Sexton	155 mm M 114 A1		120 mm Light Tampella	
Somalia	76 mm M 1942	122 mm M 1937			
South Africa	25 pdr	5·5 inch			
Spain	105 mm Pack How 105 mm 105/26 105 mm M 101 A1 105 mm SP M 52 105 mm SP M 108	122 mm 122/46 122 mm M 1937 155 mm M 2 155 mm M 114 A1 155 mm M 44 105 mm SP M 109	175 mm SP M 107 8 inch M 115	105 mm EC1 A 105 L 120 mm SL	108 mm R-6-B-2 110 mm T Type 216 mm E 3 300 mm D-3 381 mm G-3
Sri Lanka	76 mm M 48 B1 25 pdr 105 mm M 101 A1				
Sudan	25 pdr 105 mm Pack How	122 mm M 1937		120 mm M 1938	
Sweden	105 mm M 18/39 105 mm M/40 105 mm 4140	155 mm Model F 155 mm FH 77 155 mm SP VK 155 L/50		120 mm M 41c	
Switzerland	105 mm 4140 105 mm M 35 105 mm M 46 105 mm SP AMX 105 B	155 mm SP M 109 U		120 mm MW 41	81 mm DIRA
Syria		122 mm M 1937 122 mm D 30 130 mm M 1946 152 mm ML 20 and D 1		120 mm M 1943 160 mm M 43 160 mm M 53	122 mm BM 21 140 mm BM 14 240 mm BM 24 600 mm FROG 7 850 mm SCUD-A
Taiwan	75 mm M 116 105 mm M 101 A1	155 mm M 114 A1			762 mm Honest John
Tanzania	76 mm M 1942	122 mm M 1937		120 mm M 1938	
Thailand	75 mm M 116 105 mm M 101 A1	155 mm M 114 A1			
Tunisia	105 mm SP M 52	155 mm M 114 A1			
Turkey	75 mm M 116 105 mm M 101 A1 105 mm SP M 108	155 mm M 2 155 mm M 114 A1	8 inch M 115	4·2 inch	762 mm Honest John

ANTI-TANK			AIR DEFENCE	
GUNS	**RECOILLESS RIFLES**	**GUIDED WEAPONS**	**GUNS**	**MISSILES**
	106 mm M 40 A1			Bloodhound 2
100 mm M 1944 and 1955			37 mm M 1939 57 mm M 1950 100 mm KS 19	
17 pdr 90 mm M 41			20 mm (unidentified) Twin 35 mm K 63 40 mm L 70 3·7 inch	Cactus (Crotale) Tigercat
6 pdr	106 mm M 40 A1		20 mm (unidentified) 40 mm L 70	Hawk Nike Hercules
85 mm M 1945 100 mm M 1944			37 mm M 1939 40 mm L 60 85 mm M 1944	
90 mm IKV 103	90 mm PV 1110	SS-11	20 mm M 40-70 40 mm L 75 40 mm L 70 57 mm M 54	Redeye (RBS-70) Hawk Bloodhound 2 (Air Force)
90 mm Model 50 90 mm Model 57	106 mm M 40 A1		Twin 20 mm GA1-DO1 30 mm Type 661 30 mm HO 831-SLM Twin 35 mm K 63	(RBS-70) Bloodhound 3 (Air Force)
57 mm M 1943 85 mm M 1945 100 mm M 1944 and 1955 SU 100	82 mm B 10	Sagger Swatter	ZSU 23-4 37 mm M 1939 57 mm M 1950 85 mm M 1944 100 mm KS 19	SA-7 SA-9 SA-2 SA-3 SA-6
	106 mm M 40 A1		40 mm L 60	Hawk Nike Hercules
			37 mm M 1939	
	6 pdr 106 mm M 40 A1		40 mm L 60	Hawk
			40 mm L 60	
	106 mm M 40 A1	SS-11 Tow	20 mm (unidentified) 40 mm L 60	Nike Hercules (Air Force)

COUNTRY	FIELD GUNS AND HOWITZERS			MORTARS	SURFACE-TO-SURFACE MISSILES
	LIGHT	MEDIUM	HEAVY		
USSR	76 mm M 1942	122 mm M 1938 122 mm D 74 and D 30 130 mm M 1946 152 mm ML 70, D 20 and M 19	203 mm M 1955	107 mm M 1938 120 mm M 1943 240 mm M 53	122 mm BM 21 140 mm M 1965 140 mm BM 14 240 mm BM 24 250 mm BMD 25 600 mm FROG 1-7 850 mm SCUD-A and -B 850 mm Scaleboard
UK	105 mm Pack How 105 mm Light Gun 105 mm SP Abbot	5·5 inch 155 mm SP M 109 (155 mm FH 70) (155 mm SP 70)	175 mm SP M 107 8 inch SP M 110		762 mm Honest John 557 mm Lance
USA	105 mm M 101 A1 105 mm M 102 (105 mm XM 204) 105 mm SP M 108 105 mm SP M 52	155 mm M 115 A1 155 mm SP M 44 (155 mm XM 198) 155 mm SP M 109 A1	175 mm SP M 107 8 inch SP M 110 8 inch M 115	107 mm M 30	762 mm Honest John 557 mm Lance 790 mm Sergeant 1,000 mm Pershing
Venezuela	105 mm M 101 A1	155 mm SP Mk 3			
Vietnam (equipment of the former army of South Vietnam which is almost entirely from USA has not been included)	75 mm Type 94 75 mm M 116 76 mm M 1942	122 mm M 1937/8 122 mm D 74 130 mm M 1946 152 mm ML 20, D 1 and D 20		107 mm M 1938 120 mm M 1943 160 mm M 43	122 mm BM 21 140 mm BM 14
North Yemen	76 mm M 1942	122 mm M 1937		120 mm M 1943	
South Yemen	25 pdr 105 mm Pack How	122 mm M 1937		120 mm M 1943	
Yugoslavia	76 mm M 1942 76 mm M 48 B1 105 mm M 18 105 mm M 56	122 mm M 1938 130 mm M 1946 152 mm ML 20 155 mm M 114 A1		120 mm M 1943 120 mm UBM 52	128 mm M 51
Zaire	75 mm M 116	122 mm M 1937		107 mm M 30	
Zambia	105 mm Pack How				

ANTI-TANK			AIR DEFENCE	
GUNS	**RECOILLESS RIFLES**	**GUIDED WEAPONS**	**GUNS**	**MISSILES**
57 mm M 1955 85 mm M 1946 85 mm SD 44 100 mm M 1944 and 1955 ASU 57 ASU 85 JSU 122		Sagger Swatter	Twin 23 ZSU 23-4 37 mm M 1939 57 mm M 1950 ZSU 57-2 85 mm M 1944 100 mm KS 19 130 mm M 1955	SA-7 SA-9 SA-8 SA-2 SA-3 SA-4 SA-6
	120 mm Mobat 120 mm Wombat	Swingfire	40 mm L 70 (Twin 30 mm SP Falcon)	Blowpipe Rapier Tigercat Thunderbird 2 Bloodhound 2 (Air Force)
	106 mm M 40 A1	Tow	20 mm Vulcan 40 mm SP M 42	Redeye (Stinger) Chaparral (Roland) Hawk Nike Hercules (Sam-D)
			40 mm L 60	
75 mm Type 56 85 mm M 1945 SU 76	82 mm T 21 82 mm B 10 107 mm B 11	Sagger	Twin 23 mm 37 mm M 1939 57 mm M 1950 ZSU 57-2 85 mm M 1944 100 mm KS 19 130 mm KS 30	SA-7 SA-2 SA-3
SU 100			37 mm M 1939	
			Twin 23 mm 37 mm M 1939 57 mm M 1950 85 mm M 1944	SA-7
57 mm M 1943 100 mm 1944 and 1955 SU 100	82 mm M 60 105 mm M 65	Sagger	20 mm (unidentified) Twin 30 mm M 53/59 37 mm M 1939 40 mm L 60 57 mm M 1950 ZSU 57-2 85 mm M 1944 88 mm Flak 36	SA-2 (Air Force)
57 mm M 1943			20 mm (unidentified) 37 mm M 1939 40 mm L 60	
			20 mm (unidentified)	

Index of Weapons

The reader experienced in weaponry who wishes to refer to the characteristics of a weapon of known identity, or whose function or approximate size he knows, can most conveniently trace its particulars by using the contents list and the table showing weapons in service in each country. He can then consult the appropriate section in the text bearing in mind that the weapons are arranged in ascending order of calibre or missile diameter: e.g., all towed 57 mm anti-tank guns are together, the earlier marks preceding the later. If only the code-name e.g., Gainful; acronym, e.g. Amets, or initials, e.g. TOW is known, these are in alphabetical order in the first part of the index. Weapons and equipments described by calibre, mark or date, e.g. 152 mm howitzer M 1938 (M10) are under sections of the index corresponding to the sections in the text and in the same order as the contents list; not alphabetical. E.g. 105 mm SP gun Abbot – FV 433 can be found in the alphabetical index under 'Abbot', and under '105 mm gun' in the self-propelled field gun section.